Common Property Resources and Human Rights

Politics of Water Struggles in India

Rose Mary George
Assistant Professor,
Department of Political Science,
Providence Women's College, Kozhikode, Kerala.

New Century Publications
New Delhi, India

NEW CENTURY PUBLICATIONS
4800/24, Bharat Ram Road,
Ansari Road, Daryaganj,
New Delhi – 110 002 (India)

Tel.: 011-2324 7798, 4358 7398, 6539 6605
Fax: 011-4101 7798
E-mail: indiatax@vsnl.com • info@newcenturypublications.com
www.newcenturypublications.com

Editorial office:
LG–7, Aakarshan Bhawan,
4754-57/23, Ansari Road, Daryaganj,
New Delhi – 110 002

Tel.: 011-4356 0919

First Published: **July 2012**

ISBN: **978-81-7708-320-0**

Published by New Century Publications and printed at Salasar Imaging Systems, New Delhi.

Designs: Patch Creative Unit, New Delhi.

PRINTED IN INDIA

In Memory of My Father

N.V. George (1954-2009)

About the Book

Recent wave of liberalization, privatization and globalization (LPG) of national economies has limited the policy options of a greater number of developing countries. The impact of LPG on public policy formulation is evident both at the macro and micro level. At the macro level, various national governments are no longer in a position to retain state regulation not only in the economic realm but also with respect to the social sectors. Macro level policies are aimed at increasing the stake of private players and the privatization drive is largely at the cost of state control. Micro level issues are sector- and case-specific.

LPG has impacted Common Property Resources (CPRs) in many ways. For example, there has been a fatal blow to the harmonious relationship between state regulation and community ownership regimes. The issue of water is a good case in point. The opening up of the state regime of CPRs to the free play of foreign and domestic capital has adversely affected the interests of marginal, vulnerable and socially disadvantaged groups of society. Privatization has resulted in the reckless exploitation of CPRs by foreign and domestic private corporations.

This work is an attempt to explore the multi-dimensional effects of globalization, liberalization and privatization on common property resources in the context of human rights.

About the Author

Dr. Rose Mary George is presently Assistant Professor, Department of Political Science, Providence Women's College, Kozhikode, Kerala. She did her Post-graduation in Political Science from the Department of Political Science, University of Kerala in 2004 and obtained her Ph.D. degree from the same university in 2010.

She has published a good number of research papers in reputed journals including *Indian Journal of Political Science; Newman and Society*, and *Journal of Management and Public Policy*. Besides, she has participated and presented papers at various state and national level conferences/seminars. She successfully completed UGC-sponsored Refresher Course in Political Science organized by the Academic Staff College, Jawaharlal Nehru University (JNU), New Delhi. She specializes in hydro-politics, and environmental studies.

FOREWORD

Although the process of globalization has started long back, an organized and structured form of globalization with focus on political economy, technology and communication is rather a new phenomenon. The political, social and cultural impacts of modern globalization are very deep and complex and it profoundly affects the lives of the marginalized sections of the society. As a response to the imperialist and commercial dimensions of globalization, the last two decades witnessed the rise of numerous non-state actors with wide-ranging ramifications. The decline of Westphalian notion of state sovereignty can be vividly noticed in the predicament of the contemporary nation-states of both developed and developing countries. Precisely for two reasons, the decline of the nation-state and the shift from welfare to neo-liberal agenda, the potential for the rise of new social movements and non-governmental organizations were opened up. It is natural that, when the conventional nation-state fails to perform its basic functions, the space will be filled by new forces and actors.

Undoubtedly, there is a close link between the march of 'imperialist-globalization' and the decline of Common Property Resources (CPRs). Consequently, this has led to the vulnerability of the poor in accessing the Common Property Resources. Several such incidents were reported mostly from Third World countries where the greed for profits by the Multi National Companies has resulted in damaging the eco-system and violating the basic rights of the people. As a response to this, local struggles have developed from unconventional organizations and non-political forces. We could also witness the increased involvement of human rights organizations and new social movements in highlighting the struggle where as the conventional organizations like the political parties and pressure groups failed to respond effectively. A new form of socio-political awareness and sensitivity has dawned at this juncture. It is heartening to see that some sections in the civil society including the 'new media' could seriously debate on this issue. Altogether the negative forces of globalization results in the deprivation of Common Property Resources. The grassroots struggles, although localized, can mobilize an international public opinion which the corporatist forces cannot easily ignore.

Dr. Rose Mary George took up the challenging task of studying the impact of Globalisation in affecting Common Property Resources with particular reference to the question of water rights. She developed a strong theoretical framework, by linking up globalization, Common Property Resources and the human right question. Agreeing with Sidney S. Tarrow, Rose Mary George succeeds in expanding the theory of *Political Opportunity Structure Thesis* in the specific context of rural India. At the same time, she critically reviews Garret Hardin's theory of *Tragedy of Commons.* She proves that unlike Hardin's argument that *Tragedy of Commons* is integral to open access and common property regimes, the real lacunae lies in the existence of ineffective regulatory mechanisms. She has also done an extensive survey of literature and discussed the role of World Bank and other financial agencies involved in water privatization in developed and developing countries. She addresses the issues of water privatization in India and the right to water under the Indian Constitution.

The case-study method constitutes the prominent research method for this work. The two case-studies conducted were the Plachimada water right struggle in Kerala and the agitation in Chhattisgarh over the question of privatizing the Sheonath river by a private company. Through field work, with the help of a structured questionnaire and through extensive interactions, she could collect enormous data regarding the multiple dimensions of the problems in the two study areas. The advent of Hindustan Coca-Cola Beverages Private Limited in extracting ground water in Plachimada, the environmental effects in the locality and the consequent water shortage problems are discussed. Through repeated visits she could sense the tempo of water right conflicts in the region. Similarly, the water right issue following the privatization of Sheonath river in Durg district of Chhattisgarh was also studied. She compares the sources of water availability prior to the project with that of the present situation. In short, the villagers lost their access and ownership to one of the most important water sources. Although government reinstated the water access, the privatization project continued affecting the lives of people.

She concludes that the Common Property Resource issue is a human right question. The framework of human right studies fits as an analytical tool for examining water right movements. The involvement of civil society in both the struggles has been examined in detail suggesting us to understand why non-party forces are getting involved in the conventional terrain of political parties. This trend is certainly linked to the changing role of the conventional state in the era of globalization. She has also presented few policy suggestions. Worth mentioning among these are the demand for reversing the public-private participation and the need for the upper hand of the public sector in public-private experiments. She also suggests that the government should adequately take care of the indigenous water management system before opening up CPRs for corporate business.

On the whole, the study is very relevant to the present scenario of the world. Public sensitivity to the issues concerning Common Property Resources on the eve of uncontrolled capitalism is very basic to human development. Local reactions against the invasion of globalisation forces are quite natural. But such movements need wider coverage at the level of international civil society. I am glad to introduce this work because it attempts to serve this basic function by linking up micro-studies with macro-problems. Similar studies should come out at this juncture and thereby enlarge the public sensitivity.

May 2012
Thiruvananthapuram

G. Gopa Kumar
Professor and Head
Department of Political Science
University of Kerala

Contents

Preface

"During the past four decades here in Quillagua, a town in the record books as the driest place on earth, residents have sometimes seen glimpses of raindrops above the foothills in the distance. They never reach the ground, evaporating like a mirage while still in the air. What the town did have was a river, feeding an oasis in the Atacama Desert. But mining companies have polluted and brought up so much of the water, residents say, that for months each year the river is little more than a trickle–and an unusable one at that.

Quillagua is among many small towns in Chile that are being swallowed up in the country's intensifying water wars. Nowhere is the system for buying and selling water more permissive than here in Chile, experts say, where water rights are private property, not a public resource, and can be traded like commodities with little government oversight or safeguards for the environment.

Private ownership is so concentrated in some areas that a single electricity company from Spain, Endesa, has bought up 80 percent of the water rights in a huge region in the South, causing uproar. In the north, agricultural producers are competing with mining companies to siphon off rivers and tap scarce water supplies, leaving towns like this one bone dry and withering" (*The New York Times,* March 15, 2009).

The Quillagua case is a good illustration of the intensifying water based conflicts across the world. In lion's share of cases it is the privatization of ground and surface water which has resulted in the emanation of water conflicts. The Indian context is unique in this regard as the state and the communities have a joint stake in the water management realm.

This work is an attempt to explore the multidimensional effects of globalization, liberalization and privatization (LPG) with respect to a relatively under researched domain within social sciences, Common Property Resources (CPRs). The liberalization and privatization of national economies, for the most part associated with the emergent globalization processes, has limited the policy options of a greater number of developing countries. The impact of liberalization, privatization and globalization (LPG) on public policy formulation is evident both at the macro and micro level. At the macro level various national governments are no longer in a position to retain state regulation not only in the economic realm but also with respect to the social sectors. For the most part, the macro level policies are aimed at increasing the stake of private players and the privatization drive is largely at the cost of state control. The micro level issues are sector and case specific ones. The worth considering issue is that the existing institutional-legal frame works at the micro level is insufficient to cope with the emergent policy shift. The transition from public to private regime is the hall mark of this policy shift and one can find a wide array of new/reformed socio-political processes in the developing world.

The emerging socio-political processes are extremely complex and diverse; but its interlinkage with the transition from public to private regime attracts a great deal of scholarly interest. This work is based on a comparative exploration of the policy shift in regard to Common Property Resources (CPRs). The impact of LPG on CPRs unfolded in three interrelated ways. Firstly, there has been a fatal blow to the harmonious relationship existed between the state regulation and community ownership regimes. It should be noted that regardless of the extensive penetration of state control into the grassroots, different modes of community ownership prevailed in most of the developing societies. The issue of water is a good case in point. The state has wielded regulatory power, especially in the context of clashes between different community ownership systems. The opening up of state regime of CPR to the free play of foreign and domestic capital, affected detrimentally on the existent CPR regime.

Secondly, privatization has resulted in the reckless

exploitation of CPRs by foreign and domestic private corporations. Unlike the more or less sustainable utilization of CPRs under the community ownership regime, privatization brought forth over exploitation of CPRs such as water in most developing societies. Given that short-term profit motive constitute the underline logic of the functioning of Private Corporations, CPRs were exploited without considering the intra and inter-generational equity considerations. Thirdly, the entry of private firms into CPR management has negative impacts on the universal access regime sustained by the state and community regulatory systems. It is widely observed that the privatization of CPRs took place mostly through excluding a larger section of the population from accessing Common Property Resources. Many of the privatization agreements with regard to CPRs became operational through creating exclusive zones wherein the local people have only limited or restricted access. Privatization basically involves the invocation of a market centric approach towards the utilization of Common Property Resources which invokes marketisation and thereby commodification. The individuals or groups depended on the CPRs for their livelihoods have now become consumers of the commodified variant of Common Property Resources.

The privatization of Common Property Resources in the wake of globalization prevented the natural right of the community's free access to and control over such resources, which ultimately has jeopardized their livelihood security. Water is generally regarded as a common property but now it has become a private commodity. As such its value is identified to its price and in globalizing period its value is determined by the fluctuations of demand and supply in the international markets, disrespecting the local need of water. This is a direct threat to the intrinsic value of water. The contemporary water management programmes in neo-liberal development tradition, come with projects of marketisation, commoditisation and privatization of water which deepen the crisis of livelihood security of the community. All these tend to monopolization of water by a few powerful companies. In the context of emerging scarcity of water world wide and particular to India the issue is more serious. As parallel to the increase in population water scarcity also increased which paved way for its marketisation. Now water is treated as a commodity in the international market. Moreover the water products like Mineral Water, Coca-Cola, Pepsi, etc. tightened the demand for water. It is easy for the companies to find out a market for their products but it is not easy for them to collect the raw material i.e., water, because in most of the states, the water resources are under the control of their respective governments.

This prompted the protagonists of marketisation of water to pressurize the politics and state for changing their policies in favour of market. Finally new type of power relations have emerged which protected the interest of market by negating the community's right to water. A reflection of this changing power relationship and pro-market conceptualization of water security can be seen in the National Water Policy, 2002 that seldom serves the intended purpose when the country is facing serious drought. The state governments are not an exception to this. They too fell into the traps of marketisation because of the lack of a coherent, stable and pro-people water policy. Given this background, it is intended to look into the policies that aimed at the privatization of Common Property Resources (CPRs), in particular surface and ground water, and the emerging grassroots based struggles to counter these policies. The work is predominantly based on two select cases—the Plachimada Water Right movement and the struggles against the privatization of Sheonath river. Marketisation of CPRs causes specific as well as general threats to the communities within a nation- state and worldwide. This has significance in the context of emerging local self-governing institutions in India. The case study of Plachimada issue, the role of local self-governing institutions and different contrasting local interests give a peculiar spectrum of power play in this regard.

The absence of well functioning local-self governing institutions in Chhattisgarh limited the scope of Sheonath struggle in a multitude of ways.

Globalization compressed the role of state as a facilitator of market, in the name of development and consequently state has lost its control over natural resources. Water now identifies as a commodity in the international level and national governments are amending their policies to favour this concept. In this context the most seriously threatened interest, appears to be that of politically weak, socially and economically backward sections, whose resource requirements are minimal, but whose survival is primarily dependent on the products of nature. This work analyses the water resource conflict between industrial monopolies and local people, the depth of alienation the people faced and the counter strategies developed by them in the form of water right struggle in the era of globalization. The study used insights from the human rights framework and social movement theory to analyze the nature and course of the water resource conflicts. Even though most of the water resource conflicts are isolated struggles and focused on short term livelihood needs, they address broader issues that fall within the human rights and social movement discourses.

Water right is a vital aspect of the very idea of human right. The emergence of human right as 'one of the most globalized political values of our times' is closely related to the ability of human right framework to give due consideration to those aspects of life which is critical to human flourishment. Water rights are not just an analytical abstraction as people all over the world depend upon water for their basic livelihood purposes. Unlike other human rights, water rights are often embedded in physical infrastructure and very often it is the physical infrastructure that determines the very nature of the water rights question. For instance the access, quality and quantity of water are closely related to the kind of physical infrastructure which an individual/group possesses in a given locality. Broadly speaking, there are two sets of rights that can be included within the water rights category. The first category, riparian rights, is water use rights based on ownership and possession of land adjacent to a body of water. Prior appropriation is the second category and it is based on historic water usage. Both categories of water rights are critical to the human well-being and hence it is well qualified to be termed as a human right.

Given the appropriateness to call water right struggles as human right movements, there is an imminent need to deploy the human right and social movement framework in the Plachimada and Sheonath cases. It is not appropriate to consider the two uprisings as mere responses against the appropriation of water sources by private players. They were just uprisings at the initial stage, but very soon attained the attributes of social movements. It is true that the scope of Plachimada social movement far exceeds when compared to Sheonath case, but one can locate lots of movement attributes in Chhattisgarh also. The political character of these two movements requires serious explanation. The sustenance of water right struggles in Kerala and Chhattisgarh happened mostly because of its simultaneous interfaces with the institutionalized and non-institutionalized political activity in the state. The support from established political parties and other civil-society organizations turns the water right struggles to a unique social movement experience. Henceforth, this work basically intends to invoke the human rights and social movement framework in the study of water right struggles in India.

Basically, the study is empirical in nature. Both primary and secondary sources are consulted. Primary sources include study reports, government records, official websites, data of the survey, etc. Interview method is an important source of primary data, which is conducted among the leaders of the struggle, political parties, social activists and local body members. Among the localities a survey is conducted with a structured questionnaire. Case-study method constitutes the prime mover of this work. This is relevant for focusing the contrasting and comparative issues raised in the work. The findings of the study are put into rigorous quantitative analysis which enabled the work to come out with concrete findings. The important limitation of this work is regarding the feasibility of comparing the Kerala and Chhattisgarh cases. Being a comparison of two cases with distinct socio-cultural embeddedness, there are limits for arriving at concrete results. It is a well-established fact that the two water right struggles inherit different movement cultures. There are also limitations in regard to the handling of fieldwork data. It is found difficult to deal with the qualitative data, as many of them were not conducive for quantitative statistical analysis.

I place on record my sincere gratitude to Dr. G. Gopa Kumar, Professor and Head, Department of Political Science, University of Kerala, for his scholarly guidance and constructive criticisms at all stages of the completion of this work.

Thanks are also due to Dr. M. Bhaskaran Nair, Dr. J. Prabhash, Dr. Shaji Varkey, all of the Department of Political Science, University of Kerala, for their valuable suggestions.

I appreciate with thanks the keen interest shown by Sri Lalit Surjan, Chief Editor, Deshbandhu, Raipur in the progress of my data collection.

With much respect, I acknowledge with deep appreciation the emotional support and care rendered by my beloved family members, especially my parents and sister. Finally, I extend my whole-hearted thanks to my husband Sajan Thomas for his constant support and encouragement.

June 2012 **Rose Mary George**

Kozhikode

Abbreviations/Acronyms

ADB	Asian Development Bank
AIBP	Accelerated Irrigation Benefit Programme
AISF	All India Students Federation
AIYF	All India Youth Federation
BBC	British Broadcasting Corporation
BOOT	Build, Own, Operate and Transfer
CGWB	Central Ground Water Board
CMM	Chhattisgarh Mukti Morcha
CPCB	Central Pollution Control Board
CPI	Communist Party of India
CPR	Common Property Resource
CRSM	Chhattisgarh Rajya Sangarsh Morcha
CSE	Center for Science and Environment
CSIDC	Chhattisgarh State Industries Development Corporation
CWRDM	Center for Water Resource Development and Management
DJB	Delhi Jal Board
EBRD	European Bank for Reconstruction and Development
EIB	European Investment Bank
FDI	Foreign Direct Investment
GATT	General Agreement on Tariffs and Trade
GATS	General Agreement on Trade in Services
GC	General Comment
GWP	Global Water Partnership
HCBPL	Hindustan Coca-Cola Beverages Private Limited
HEG	Hindustan Electro Graphite
IADB	Inter American Development Bank
ICIJ	International Council of Investigative Journalists
IFC	International Finance Corporation

IMF	International Monetary Fund
IIMI	International Irrigation Management Institute
INTACH	Indian National Trust for Arts and Cultural Heritage
IPR	Intellectual Property Rights
IRTC	Integrated Rural Technology Center
ISWD Act	Inter-State Water Disputes Act
KFW	German Development Bank
KGWB	Kerala Ground Water Board
KSPCB	Kerala State Pollution Control Board
KSSP	Kerala Sasthra Sahitya Parishad
LDC	Less Developed Countries
LPG	Liberalization, Privatization, Globalization
LSGD	Local Self-Government Department
MCM	Million Cubic Meters
MLD	Million Liters per Day
MNC	Multi National Corporation
MPAKVN	Madhya Pradesh Audyogig Kendra Vikas Nigam Limited
MWC	Manila Water Company
MWS	Manylad Water Services
NABARD	National Bank for Agriculture and Rural Development
NAFTA	North Atlantic Free Trade Area
NAPM	National Alliance of People's Movement
NATO	North Atlantic Treaty Organization
NDA	National Democratic Alliance
NGO	Non-Governmental Organization
NRDC	Natural Resource Defense Council
NSM	New Social Movement
NTADCL	New Tiruppur Area Development Corporation Limited
NTPC	National Thermal Power Corporation Limited
NWP	National Water Policy
NWRC	National Water Resource Council

OBC	Other Backward Caste
OECD	Organization for Economic Cooperation and Development
O&M	Operation and Management
PAC	Public Accounts Committee
PAP	Parambikulam Aliyar Project
PCB	Pollution Control Board
PIL	Public Interest Litigation
POS	Political Opportunity Structure
PUCL	People's Union for Civil Liberties
PWC	Price Waterhouse Cooper
RIDF	Rural Infrastructure Development Fund
RWL	Radius Water Limited
SAP	Structural Adjustment Program
SC	Scheduled Caste
SCMC	Supreme Court Monitoring Committee
SECL	South Eastern Coalfields Limited
SEZ	Special Economic Zone
SODECI	Societe de Distribution d'Eau Cote d'Ivoire
ST	Scheduled Tribe
TNC	Trans National Corporation
UN	United Nations
VAK	Vikas Adhyan Kendra
WB	World Bank
WTO	World Trade Organization
WUA	Water User Association
WWC	World Water Council

1

Globalization, Common Property Resources and Social Movements: A Theoretical Framework

The first chapter is aimed at presenting the theoretical framework of the work. The author's theoretical framework intends to explore the link between the privatization of Common Property Resources (CPRs) and social movements in the globalization context. The important attempt is to discuss the contemporary political and economic transformations wherein social movements with emphasis on environmental issues emerges and operates. The main thrust of this investigation concerns, the extent to which the privatization of CPRs is integral to the globalization processes and the policy limitations it encompasses.

1.1 Conceptualizing Globalization

This subsection is intended to elucidate the author's operational definition on Globalization. Globalization is often represented as a very current phenomenon, viewed from a number of disciplinary and institutional vantage points (Perkins and Shortland, 2006). Given that, globalization involves technological, political, economic and cultural dimensions, conceptualizing globalization processes is a complex exercise. Globalization is not just a casual process and it has critical effects on fluidity, multiple processes, contingency, resistance and contestation (Hopper, 2007). Theories of political economy and international relations are only limited tools to understand globalization. They provide a conceptual foundation, from which, begins the complex journey of explanation. Both theories cannot capture the nuances of the unfolding processes through which the role of communities, nations and the world undergoing multifaceted transformations (Dierks, 2001).

The increasingly integrated global political economy of recent years has emphasized the growing complexity of processes of governance, its multi-sited (from grassroots to global) and multi-actor (local, regional, international—institutional or otherwise) engagements. The turn towards globalization perspectives by state, as well as commercial and other political and economic entities, has been attempts to understand how to operate effectively in changed circumstances as about a recognition that the rigidly bounded frameworks of the past are problematic in circumstances where local—global connections need to be tracked through highly diverse linkages between grassroots, national, regional, international, political and economic processes (Youngs, 2003).

The complexity of globalization processes has resulted in the multiplicity of approaches and perspectives in regard to the exploration of contemporary global transformations.

The very idea of globalization is the object of controversy. Some of the more dramatic and simplistic versions of globalization thesis have been challenged by scholars and journalists who are sceptical about the actual extent of trans-nationalised economic activity and about the social and political effects which are frequently inputted to it. Common to these critics is a reluctance to embrace facile claims that the universal is negating the particular that globalized economic relations are supplanting more familiar social relations, cultural identities, and political forms and we have therefore entered a qualitatively new era of human social history (Rupert, 2000).

Broadly, globalization is regarded as having made for the shrinking, if not the death, of geographic distance. More, it manifests as it were the compression of both time and space in that events in one location can be visually and orally experienced, through the grace of modern technology, virtually instantly around the globe. More narrowly, economic globalization, which lies at the heart of the broader phenomenon of globalization, is now considered to be determinative of humanity's future, relentlessly propelling the different societies of the world to a common destination that of convergence in regard to income levels, social structure, and behaviour (Nayar, 2007).

Globalization might be understood in a number of ways. It can be seen purely as an economic project or the realization of one. This is for instance, the view held by Barnett and Cavanaugh, who speaks of globalization as the realization of global dreams by imperial corporations. For them, globalization is the planetarization of a global bazaar, with its concomitant K-Mart aesthetic realism, the global casino economy, the global labour market and the global shopping mall. Benjamin Barber shares some similarities with Barnett and Cavanaugh's approach.

In Barber's case, however globalization is merely the confrontation between MacWorld and Jihad which being ciphers of economic processes that register as cultural epiphenomenon, results in the evisceration of politics by economics (Mendieta, 2007). The following two common and competing conceptions of the global order can shed light on the complexity of globalization processes.

First, the notion that the present order 'somehow rises up spontaneously out of the interactions of radically heterogeneous global forces, as if this order were a harmonious concert orchestrated by the natural and neutral hand of the market', and second, that it is dictated by a 'single power and a single centre of rationality transcendent to global forces' which guides the historical development of order 'according to its conscious and all-seeing plan' (Harawira, 2005). There are lots of perspectives that fall in between the aforementioned competing conceptions.

Table 1.1 records the three dominant tendencies in globalization debate summarized by David Held (1999).

Table 1.1: Conceptualizing Globalization: Three Tendencies

	Hyperglobalists	Skeptics	Transforma-tionalists
What's new?	A global age	Trading blocs, weaker governance than in earlier periods	Historically unprecedented levels of global inter-connectedness
Dominant features	Global capitalism, global governance, global civil society	World less interdependent than in 1980s	'Thick' (intensive and extensive) globalization
Power of national governments	Declining or eroding	Reinforced or enhanced	Reconstituted, restructured
Driving forces of globalization	Capitalism and technology	States and markets	Combined forces of modernity
Pattern of stratification	Erosion of old hierarchies	Increased marginalization of south	New architecture of world order
Dominant motif	McDonalds, Madonna, etc.	National interests	Transformation of political community
Conceptualization of globalization	As a reordering of the framework of human action	As inter-nationalization and regionalization	As the reordering of interregional relations and action at a distance
Historical trajectory	Global civilization	Regional blocs/clash off civilizations	Indeterminate: global integration and fragmentation
Summary argument	The end of the nation-state	Internationalization depends on the acquiescence and support	Globalization transforming state power and world politics

The local presents a major challenge in theorizing globalization and culture. Because the current globalization process entails the further implement of a neo-colonial project, how different communities and peoples that constitute what we call the 'local' assume or reassume their positions and roles in confronting that process commands more attention. It is the local (largely represented by localities within the vast area formerly named the south, underdeveloped, developing, satellite or periphery) that compels a significant shift in our mode of theorizing. In other words, to understand local we must localize ourselves (Jameson and Miyoshi, 1998). Much of the critical literature on globalization follows a capitalist logic model that sees the logic of capital as producing new forms of economy, along with new technologies and forms of domination, and thus theorizes globalization as imposing a new form of domination (Calabrese and Burgelman, 1999).

The approach, through which Globalization is conceptualized, referred in this thesis has close allegiance with Tarrow's conceptualization in the article From Lumping to Splitting: Specifying Globalization and Resistance (2002). Tarrow disaggregated the globalization metaphor into two of its components: economic integration and internationalization. Economic integration refers to the loose combination of free-trade agreements, the internet and the integration of financial markets that is erasing borders and uniting the world into a single, lucrative, but brutally competitive market place. There is a strong version of the concept e.g. the thesis that all significant forms of economic activity today are governed by a neo-liberal international economic project.

The second component internationalization denotes the appropriation or construction of organizations, networks and institutions across national boundaries. Here Tarrow mentions about a strong and a weak variant: substitutive internationalization, which holds that international institutions grow up at the cost of the state; and supplementary internationalization, the extension of state and societal networks across boundaries (Tarrow, 2002). Such a holistic conceptualization of Globalization would be critical for the author's attempts to explore issues that were at the heart of contemporary global economic integration such as resource politics, grass root resistance and new social movements.

1.2 Resource Politics

There is a near consensus among the scholarly circles that globalization is a double-edged sword with positive and negative environmental impacts. As stated in the Organization for Economic Cooperation and Development (OECD) Environmental Outlook (2001) "globalization can improve the efficiency in natural resource use and management, but it can also pose threats to the health of world's natural ecosystems. The net effect of globalization depends on the pace and direction of economic growth, and the existence and effectiveness of institutions and policy frameworks to maximize the positive and minimize the negative environmental impacts". The general consensus in the academic circles that globalization is a two-sided coin makes it a controversial topic within the scholarly circles.

There are considerable number of scholars who argue that globalization destroys the environment by commodifying the natural resources and subordinating its management to economic policies. They mainly focused on the possibilities opened up by globalization in regard to the sustainable use of environment for socio-political progress. There is enough number of supporters for the argument in regard to market-based conservation of natural resources. It is argued that the expansion of worldwide knowledge transfer has improved development opportunities for countries, which are economically weak and depend heavily on natural resource extraction. Globalization, the argument goes, has enabled these countries to export the standards for the conservation of natural environment in response to the increasing global public opinion (Schellnhuber, 2001).

According to its critics globalization inevitably leads to the ruthless exploitation of Less Developed Countries (LDCs) by profit–driven Multi National Corporations (MNCs), to their subjection to external shocks, and to their marginalization, even as it damages the environment (Nayar, 2007). The environmental dimensions of globalization highlight the emergence of the conceptualization of the globe or a quality of globality. The term global, figures prominently in debates on climate change and stratospheric ozone depletion. Obvious in the high-profile actions and media coverage of Green Peace around the world, environmental questions are on the international political agenda. These apparently are new phenomena for politics that both require transnational agreement and limited sovereignty. These supposedly new forms of political action have been instrumental in bringing states to the negotiating table in Rio, Kyoto and elsewhere (Dalby, 2003). The critics of globalization advocates that economic globalization is harmful to the environment as it leads to commodity consumption, expanding resource use and increased disposal of polluting materials (Cavanagh and Mander, 2004). They add that the unhealthy levels of consumption have an increased impact on environment and natural resources (Krapivin and Varostsos, 2007).

No wonder, environment and natural resources have been emerged as two of the most important areas of globalization research. While most of these researches in this regard focus on its economic dimension, there is a wide gamut of literature that emphasize on the politics of environment and natural resources under a globalizing international order. Majority of this literature gave emphasis to issues such as the limits of unlimited economic growth and the sustainability question; the emergence of radical green politics; the pros and cons of public and private based management of natural resources; the feasibility of new variants of participatory conservation models, particularly the community based resource conservation models; and so on. The author would argue that the politics of natural resources forms the crux of these discussions. By politics of natural resources, the author meant the emergent patterns of political relations that focus on the access, control and utilization of environment and natural resources. This section intends to give a brief theoretical discussion of the politicization of environmental issues and natural resource conflicts that took place under the globalizing regime.

1.3 Key Issues of Resource Politics

This subsection is basically an attempt to delineate the key issues that comes under the resource politics category. The emphasis given to conflicts over natural resource's access, control, and management, has led to a situation in which the 'politics' of natural resources to the forefront of environment related discussions. A considerable section of these discussions give due weightage to the power relations and political processes that influence the dynamics of environmental changes that occurs at multiple scales with emphasis on local and regional settings (Gaile and Willmott, 2006). Across the world, one can find that ecological problems related to political problems and ecology movements in contemporary society are resultant of conflicts over vital natural resources (Shiva, 1991). Competition for resources has rapidly increased and conflicts among resource users have become a major phenomenon of politics (Smith, 1972). The importance of political dimension in environment and natural resource related issues emanates not from the decisive impact it have on the political processes of the locality/region but also due to linkage with fundamental political questions such as equality, justice and rights.

The question of equality had always been a widely debated issue with regard to environment and natural resources. The emerging area of environmental equality takes into account equal rights for all in the world to scarce natural opportunities. The temporality dimension makes environmental equality and equality of natural resources an indeed complex area of enquiry. According to the conception of intergenerational equality of resources, the future persons would have access to far few natural resources than present persons. Moreover, the accessible natural resources of future generation such as clean air and water would be of lower quality. The worsened natural resource base would give the future generation only relatively less equality of opportunity to the essential natural resources (Page, 2006). The proponents of intergenerational equality advocate that the current consumption of biospheric resources would not reduce the opportunity of future generations to enjoy the same level of consumption. A sustainable economy would institutionalize the principle that we inherit the world from our ancestors and borrow it from our offsprings, thereby requiring us to produce and consume environmental resources in less reckless ways, so that an equivalent level of environmental consumption would be available to those not yet born (Carens, 1993).

The question of justice has been addressed under the framework of environmental justice. Participants of Central and East European Workshop on Environmental Justice (Budapest, December 2003) defined environmental justice (and injustice) in the following way: A condition of environmental justice exists when environmental risks, hazards, investments, benefits are equally distributed with a lack of discrimination, whether direct or indirect, at any jurisdictional level; and when access to environmental investments, benefits, and natural resources are equally distributed; and when access to information, participation in decision making, and access to justice in environment-related matters are enjoyed by all. Since early 1990s, activists from the environmental justice movement have consistently criticized what they consider the mainstream environmental movement's racism, classism, and limited activist agenda, charges against which environmental organizations have responded in ways ranging from defiance to varying degrees of acceptance.

Discussions on rights and environment are mostly in lieu with human rights. The intersection between human rights and environment is a chaotic and contested terrain. For many international lawyers, it can best be mapped by clarifying new rights to the environment, such as rights to clean air and water, and a minimum standard of health. For environmental philosophers, the terrain is less about expanding than contracting human rights that is, clarifying and honouring ecosystem limits to individual human rights. The goal is to define, not rights, but responsibilities to the care of environment. Sometimes, these responsibilities are encapsulated in the rights of future generations to inherit a living, life-sustaining planet. For many, public interest advocates, the human rights-environment terrain which is about social justice. The allocation of environmental resources, like political and economic resources, is typically skewed towards the rich and the powerful. This is as true within a nation as it is at the global level. The poor and marginal suffer the brunt of environmental pollution and natural resource degradation. Indeed, they often suffer outright expropriation of land, forest, fisheries and other natural resources. Moreover, because the rights of the poor, to have a political voice receive the least protection, they are often least able to press for just compensation—or to just say no to unwanted development (Zarsky, 2002).

There is a large literature, in part scholarly, in part polemical, on the relation between women and the environment. The debate has tended to polarize between two approaches; a woman and environment and an Ecofeminist School. The first grew out of the WID (Women in Development) approach to project and planning interventions. It emphasized the importance of women in their role as environmental resource managers, their vulnerability to declines in resource availabilities and the need to develop environmental programmes directed at assisting women, essentially in parallel to and separately from, men's programmes. The Ecofeminist School has a different ideologically driven flavour. It derives from a philosophy of feminism grounded in women's affinity with the forces of nature, as opposed to men's urge to control and manipulate the natural world through application of the scientific method. It similarly advocates respect and support for women's effort to conserve the environment. It puts greater stress, however, on the active initiatives displayed by women in defence of environmental resources in various Third World settings (Joekes et al., 1994). The gender dimension is important to this study as access to water resources is highly a gender centric problem.

1.4 Liberalization and Environment

The Structural Adjustment Programs, which is an important part of Liberalization Privatization and Globalization (LPG), have a negative impact on the country's natural resources in many ways. It increased the export of natural resources on a large scale exceeding its imports for repaying the external debt in foreign exchange. Increased export shifted country's primary commodities such as agricultural and marine products, timber, mineral ores and manufacturing goods from natural resources into tradable sector rather than productive sector for local consumption. Secondly, there is a constant pressure on the farmers to increase production and export cash crops than that of food crops in order to earn foreign exchange for debt repayment. The craze towards overproduction will damage the environment through increased use of pesticides and insecticides, cutting down of forests and inequality in land ownership.

The Structural Adjustment Programs compels the government to amend its laws and policies towards reducing the government budget deficit by cutting expenditure rather than by raising revenues. The existing environmental laws and policies were amended in order to secure efficiency and increase international competitiveness in the industrial sector. To relax the existing environmental laws single door environmental clearance of projects, delicensing and automatic approval were introduced. Now industrial licensing has been abolished for almost all industries including fishing, cement, iron and biomass industries such as tea, textile, pepper, plywood, rubber, sugar, food processing, etc. irrespective of levels of investments that implies the indiscriminate use of resources (Nadkarni and Monga, 2001). In a sense, privatization is endowed with negative rather than positive impacts on the utilization of environmental resources.

Given that privatization has been a significant condition of the structural adjustment lending policies, there has been a significant level of privatization of large-scale and small-scale industries results in serious environmental hazards (Kirkpatrick and Lee, 1997). The structural adjustment polices also caused changes in the price of agricultural products, increase in agricultural input prices because of subsidy cuts and reduction in import duties, trade, industry and energy sector reforms which are likely to have significant environmental effects (Shiva, 1999).

Few policy changes from Indian states bear ample testimony to this fact. Even the comparatively developed states like Haryana, Punjab and Kerala announced certain policy changes in early 1990s that may hurt the environmental interests. [1] It is not only the industrial deregulation that affects environmental policymaking. Foreign Direct Investment (FDI) has emerged as the largest source of development finance and contemporarily there is a competitive lowering of environmental standards within the developing countries. Case studies shows that FDI often causes great environmental damage in developing countries, but the enforcement of general environmental standards are not improving in a greater pace.

The increased flows of FDI between national economies and the consequent presence of foreign investors in nearly all countries have led to concerns that these investors should get fair treatment from their host governments. Chapter 11 of the North Atlantic Free Trade Area (NAFTA) set out certain disciplines with penalty that must be respected by NAFTA governments for ensuring the security of foreign investors in the respective country. This includes: non-discrimination between domestic and foreign investors; prohibitions on certain types of performance requirements on investment, and prohibitions on direct and indirect expropriations, or measures tantamount to expropriation (Ekins, 2003).

In the wake of foreign investment, natural resources were seen as cost free means of fuelling industrial development in extensive rather than intensive ways of production. The gigantic influx of foreign investment has accelerated the exploitation of natural resources: oil in Soviet Union, Nigeria and Mexico; coal in India and China; wood in the Ivory Coast and Indonesia; and minerals in Zaire (Sachs, 1999). High levels of accumulated foreign debt, the scarcity in foreign capital flows, the depressed prices in the world's commodity markets and the competition among developing countries to attract foreign capital through multinationals at any cost has relegated the environment to a second place, as India's own recent liberalization move reflects (Nadkarni and Monga, 2001).

Post-liberalization period witnessed the relaxation of land ceiling acts in many of the Indian states. Since then there had been several instances of leasing agricultural lands (forest lands, in many cases) for industrial purposes. The tax holidays given to the industries in the north-eastern states are subsequently extended to all other backward regions, where the last vestiges of natural habitats and traditional cultures remain. The principle of 'eminent domain' is still applicable to state-takeover of people's land and resources, which are then transferred to global corporations. In India foreign companies can have 100 percent equity participation, but government will acquire the land, displace the people and deal with the law and order problems created by displacements. In the case of United States, federal, state and local governments are appropriating the property of citizens to hand over to large corporations (Shiva, 1999).

At present, many developing countries are promoting Special Economic Zones (SEZs) with the expectation that they will propel the industrialization process. In 2000, the Government of India replaced the old Export Processing Zones with SEZs several benefits such as tax incentives, standard plots at low rents with long lease period, single window clearance, free infrastructure facilities, exemptions from various restrictions, etc. to foster a conducive business environment to attract investment, in particular Foreign Direct Investment. As the policy is not a well-accepted one, dissenters expressed their concern over the displacement of farmers by land acquisition, loss of fertile agricultural land and huge revenue loss to the exchequer. Huge protest since its inception has been emerging against SEZs by civil society groups, political leaders, scholars, media, and those who lost their land (Agarwal, 2006). The Singur issue [2] in West Bengal is a good example in this regard.

1.5 International Trade System and Environment

One of the most important hallmarks of the prevailing international system is the abolition of protection measures, such as quotas and tariff imports. GATT (General Agreement on Tariffs and Trade) was devised at a time when environmental concern was low; but later it seems reasonable to have a fresh look at the trade-environment nexus in the context of growing environmental concern. From an environmental point of view, many of the GATT provisions impose constraints on environmental policy and it brought trade liberalization, trade rules and environmental policy into conflict. Some of the GATT provisions are (Ekins, 2003):

1. A country could not impose trade sanctions to protect its environment from foreign production, though a neighbouring country persistently polluted the air or water.
2. A country may not use trade policy to protect the environment outside its own jurisdiction.
3. Some environmental regulations imposing technical trade

barriers should be least inconsistent with GATT provisions.

4. Forbids the use of quantitative restrictions like quotas.
5. Subsidies by and large can be tolerated if they do not harm the export interests of other nations.
6. Environmental exceptions are considered only as part of general exceptions comes under Article 20 (Pearce, 1995).

At present, indigenous knowledge systems are fast becoming the private property of Trans National Corporations and they are usurping these systems to the domain of common knowledge through Intellectual Property Rights (IPR), which in essence promote intellectual piracy. In the present world, market economy, where knowledge represents money, those who own capital seek IPR to protect the traditional knowledge systems. The IPR regimes under Trade Related Intellectual Property Rights provides protection to the formal innovators and not to the informal indigenous innovators like, farmers, indigenous medical practitioners, forest dwellers, etc.

Bio-piracy is the expected result where the formal innovators like, scientist, plant breeders and technologists make minor modifications in the indigenous knowledge and then seek patents, thereby claiming the knowledge as their private property. Bio-piracy refers to the process through which the rights of indigenous cultures to their knowledge and resources are replaced by monopoly rights-leaves the donors poorer, as they are excluded from sharing the benefits of their own resources and knowledge (Shiva, 1999).

There are several ways in which the environment might suffer from trade liberalization, exactly free trade such as increasing economic activity, industrial and agricultural reorganization and increased specialization that may neglect the environment (Pearce, 1995). Liberalization of imports has also led to dangerous trends like the import of toxic wastes from industrialized countries (Singh, 2004). Toxic waste such as cyanide, mercury and arsenic is being shipped as recyclable waste but it often ends up in backyard smelting units because there is no such use and many of the importing units do not posses the technology and expertise to process the chemicals they are importing. [3] Under the new economic trade receipts of the World Trade Organization (WTO), transnational companies are seeking freedom to relocate the polluting industries to India drawn by the country's cheap raw materials, minimal labour costs, pliable bureaucracy, lax environmental standards and low processing and disposal cost for waste. Globalization is restructuring the control over resources that have accelerated and expanded environmental destruction and displaced millions of people from their homes and their sustenance base (Shiva, 1999). [4]

1.6 Common Property Resources

This subsection is an attempt to explore the discussion on Common Property Resources (CPRs) against the backdrop of the aforementioned discussion in regard to the politics of natural resources. The concept of Common Property Resources itself is traditional and comprehensive in its meaning and definition. As the term indicate these resources held as common to all and access to it has identified as a commonly shared public need. Hence it can be termed as a 'class of resource for which exclusion is difficult and joint use involves substractability.' It means that though exclusion of user is problematic, each user should subtract his use for the welfare of other users (Berkes, 1989).

Thus commons can be distinguished from both public goods and private goods, but having the features of both (Bromley, 1992). Common Property Resources refer to all such resources that are accessible to all and to which no individual has exclusive property rights. It primarily refers to the natural resources like water, wildlife, fish, forests, pastures, air, etc. But certain resources like radio spectrum, outer space, tourism, roads, intellectual property rights, patents, internet, etc. are also put under the category of CPRs in the name of 'New Commons' (Singh, 1994).

Jodha, defined CPRs as, "a resource that is accessible to the whole village, to which no individual has an exclusive right." According to Blaikie and Brookfield, it refers to a facility that is distinguished by individual use rather than individual possession, a number of users who constitute a collectivity and have an independent right to use a resource and to exclude others who are not members of that collectivity. CPRs have gained much academic attention particularly after the international conference of CPRs held in 1986, which gave thrust to the collective management of commons (D'Cruz and Raikar, 2006).

In CPR literature the terms Common Property Resources, Common Pool Resources and Commons are often used synonymously but have been controversial as it is based on two schools of thought opposing each other. There are three broad schools of thought deals with CPRs, particularly the institutional arrangements to avert the Tragedy of Commons. The traditional school of thought held that all natural resources are Commons and can be called as Common Property Resources that can be managed either as open access property, collective property and state property or as private property. Contemporary western view argues that there is no such things as Common Property Resource, there are only resources controlled and managed either as open access property, common property, state property or private property.

Thus CPRs are restricted to communally owned resources, i.e. those resources held and used collectively by an identifiable community within an institutional arrangement. There exists communal arrangement for the exclusion of non-owners and for allocation among co-owners. This property rights school argues that the problem of over exploitation and degradation of CPRs can be resolved only by creating and enforcing private property rights (Demsetz: 1967, Johnson: 1972, Smith: 1981; Cheung: 1970). Scholars like Daniel W. Bromley, Garret Hardin, Katar Singh, Gordon, Jodha, etc. held this position with the empirical evidence that in different settings these resources are controlled and managed differently. The third school believes in the 'assurance problem approach' based on voluntary compliance.

In recent years, an increasing number of scholars advocate that decentralized collective management of CPRs by their users could be an appropriate system for avoiding the Tragedy of Commons (Berkes: 1989, Wade: 1987, Jodha: 1986, Chopra, et. al. 1989). In practice every society has its own means and adaptations to deal with common pool resources and local level systems of resource management, which are based on the knowledge and experience of resource users themselves.

The first group of scholars used the terms to denote all natural resources while the second group of scholars used it for mentioning resources managed under collective property regime. Economists are not free to use the concept of Common Property Resources or Commons under conditions where no institutional arrangement provides managerial machinery. They reject the dictum that common property is everybody's property. As such, the potential resource users who are not members of a group of co-equal owners are excluded. The concept of common property in this non-traditional form is well established in formal institutions such as the Anglo-Saxon Common Law, German Land Law and the Roman Law where, common property refers to distribution of property rights in a resource regime with well-defined set of users and rights to use the resource, while all potential users not belonging to the group are excluded (Berkes, 1989).

Bromely severely criticized the traditional approach and according to him, the writers have failed to understand the concept of property. Most of the writers often treated that a particular natural resource would everywhere be controlled under a particular type of property regime. However, a considerable section among them failed to note that the world is replete with reasonably successful common property regimes. He summarized that the common property regimes exist and function very much like private and state property regimes for preserving the resource and to prevent anarchy (Bromley, 1992). Katar Singh, who holds a non-traditional notion have even distinguished between a Common Property Resource and a Common Pool Resource. He defined Common Pool Resource as those resources that are accessible to and jointly used by people living in a particular geographical location such as a village or a cluster of villages. These resources could be a private property, a state property, a common property or nobody's property. By this approach he clarifies that Common Property Resources constitute only a subset for a bigger set of Common Pool Resources (Singh, 1994).

1.7 CPRs: The Life Supporting Resource Systems

Since time immemorial, a large number of people particularly the rural poor all over the world depend to a large extent on the CPRs of land, water, forests, etc. for meeting the basic necessities of life. CPRs provide water for agricultural and other purposes, manure for cultivation, raw materials and common pastures for grazing and other social activities. The dependence on the CPRs has been substantial as it significantly contributed to the growth of village economies (Dhar, 2006). It is argued that the quantity, quality, degree and mode of utilization of natural resources determine, to a larger extent the level and pace of a nation's economic development. According to Bromley some 80 percent of the world's population depends on natural CPRs for their existence (Singh, 2004). [5]

A typical Indian village uses a number of common water sources like ponds and tanks, rivers and rivulets, water reservoirs, irrigation canals, water sheds, etc. for meeting their daily needs. The recent survey results of National Sample Survey Organization shows that 30 percent of the rural households use these resources for livestock rearing, 23 percent for irrigation and three percent for setting up household enterprises (Dhar, 2006). Jodha in his study conducted among seven states of India found that 84 percent to 100 percent of rural household's income comes from CPRs while the rich household's dependency on CPR is only 10 percent to 20 percent. Thus, CPRs sometimes becomes the only asset and main source of livelihood for the landless marginal farmers by providing resources for fuel and fodder for subsistence outside settled agriculture.

1.8 Common Property Management Regimes

The dramatic increase in population and industrialization led to a corresponding increase in the use of natural resources, which in effect resulted in its over exploitation and conflicts. The conflicts become acute when resources started facing scarcity either by decline, deterioration and natural calamities or by man made destruction. Discovery of new users for the CPRs, development and availability of new technologies for exploiting the CPRs, opening of new markets, etc. did promote the exploitation of natural resources. Each rational consumer places his self interest above the community interest and motivated to consume more and more till the resource is completely destroyed. Under these circumstances need for a coordinating agency became inevitable when the resource become scarce and demand for the resource increases in a reverse proportional way (Singh, 2004).

In the case of CPRs the co-ordination system appears in the form of property management regimes. A property regime is a set of institutional arrangements characterizing the relationship between co-users to one another with respect to the basic management of CPRs. The institutional mechanism defines the rights and duties of those who control the resource. Bromley defined a natural resource regime as 'an explicit (or implicit) structure of rights and duties characterizing the relationship of individuals to one another with respect to that particular resource'. The basic requirement of a property regime is an authority system like central, state or local government or resource development committees or user groups that can guarantee the rights of the users (Marothia, 2005).

Institutional arrangements establish people's relationships to resources as well as translating interest into claims and claims into property rights. Property regimes are critical institutions as they link societies to nature. They have the potential to coordinate human actions and natural systems in a complementary way with long-term sustainable objectives. These human artifacts are known as property right regimes having two components, 'property rights'- the bundles of entitlements defining rights and duties in the use of natural resources and 'property rules'- the rules under which those rights and duties are exercised (Hanna et al., 1996). According to Bromley, a "property is a benefit or income stream and a property right is a claim to a benefit stream that the state will agree to protect through the assignment of duty to others who may covet or somehow interface with the benefit stream" (Bromley, 1992).

Human societies have long faced the problems with CPR co-ordination and frequently have created social institutions that regulate them. Most of the CPR institutions are local and informal, community-based rather than government sponsored. The CPR system provides grassroots institutions for popular participation in development decision-making. They have certain critical roles in local communities as they provide the livelihood security. Common property regimes also provide mechanisms for conflict resolution with definite rules and regulations. CPR systems usually determine the mode of production by sharing their knowledge of the resource and its use rules as well as flexible work teams and principles; thus becoming integral part of local culture and civilization. These systems have the responsibility to conserve the resource through generations without degradation (Berkes, 1989).

Different institutions have evolved in the past in response to the changing local circumstances, to the need of resource preservation and the social and political changes. Redefinition of property rights is a natural consequence in each regime change or transformation. For instance, in post-colonial societies new legislations have been enacted which redefined the customary rights of village communities. The four-property management regimes emerged in the past are as follows:

1. Open Access Regime.
2. Communal or Collective Property Regime.
3. State Property Regime.
4. Private Property Regime.

This shows that a particular resource can be held under more than one regime or the four could coexist contemporaneously. This means that it is possible to manage CPRs partly as private property, partly as state or public property, and partly as common property. Which of these alternative regimes will be appropriate, where and under what conditions depends on the nature of society and political system. An explanation of these four management systems and the conditions under which they have been emerged to resolve CPR problems and the characteristics of their respective institutional arrangements are as follows:

1.8.1 Open Access Regime: In an open access regime the resource is accessible to all, and the use rights are neither exclusive nor transferable. In this system property rights are not well defined, user group is not identifiable, rules or conventions governing the use of resource not exist and exclusion of free riders seems to be difficult because resource use is not substractable (Singh, 1994). In open access regime common property is 'everybody's property' in the sense that it is 'owned by no one and belonging to everyone'. Commons were really open access in ancient societies characterized by anarchy. As said by Gordon an asset that is everyone's property is in fact no one's property; hence it is likely to be abused and overused. Garret Hardin later termed this overuse as *Tragedy of Commons* (Berkes, 1989). [6]

An open access regime is bound to have certain problems. The most prominent one arises from the unrestricted access due to the lack of ownership of the resource by any person. Moreover, open access results from the absence or breakdown of an authoritative system. Thus the system of open access is not sustainable in the middle of increased demand for commons. This paved way for new management techniques like collective property regime for excluding the non-users as well as for ensuring equality and sustainability (Singh, 1994).

1.8.2 Communal or Collective Property Regime: In a communal property regime ownership and user rights for the resource are controlled by an identifiable group and are not privately owned or managed by governments. In this system property rights were defined through convention rather than formal laws and there exists rules concerning who may use the resource, who are excluded from using it and how the resource should be used. Individuals have claim on collective good as members of recognized groups and they forms the work team for the ownership, control, maintenance and equal distribution of the property. Usually these management systems tend to be set at the village or sub-village level and share a common culture and knowledge of the local culture (Berkes, 1989).

Bromley characterizes the collective property regime as corporate group property because it represents private property for a group where exclusion of non-owners is possible. The corporate group may vary in nature, size and internal structure, but they are social units with definite membership and boundaries. Besides, a segment of the group property is amenable to private and individual use (Bromley, 1999). Under this self-management regime formal institutions are created for effective management, conflict resolution and to ensure resource justice. Generation and accumulation of power is evident in this system though state intervention was minimal.

Much of the literature on CPR management has demonstrated that self-governance is feasible to accommodate the postulated *Tragedy of Commons*. Elinor Ostrum is of the opinion that all CPR problems do not necessitate external intervention and mentions some of the collective management systems that protected the fragile commons for centuries (Singh, 1994). Vandana Shiva in her work, *Water Wars: Privatisation, Pollution and Profit* say that the Chobala Pond in Mundalana village is still communally maintained and serves the water needs of ten villages. Prior to the arrival of British in South India, committees managed water collectively through a system called 'Kudimaramath' means 'Self-Repair', which was based on self-management and not coercion.

Garret Hardin negates this thesis by arguing that CPRs under collective regime are really open access that is doomed to over exploitation and advocates for its privatization or nationalization. Anthropologists and Political Scientists criticized Hardin for his failure to recognize that geographically localized CPRs are communally managed to forestall the *Tragedy of Commons*. However, in the case of independent countries, governmental intervention and the establishment of state managed resource systems reduced the scope for communal arrangements. But in recent years the concept got a boost with the retreat of state in the context of globalization. For instance, the working of Water User Associations (WUAs) is a good illustration for the principles of collective property regime. In these projects the local communities or user's group and state—either central or local government—share the responsibility of managing water distribution networks through combining appropriate institutional skills of local resource users as well as technical, administrative and financial resources available from the state (Shiva, 1991). [7]

1.8.3 State Property Regime: In state property regime ownership, control and the responsibility for equal distribution rest in the hands of state. The government fully acquires a resource either by nationalization or intervening in the existing resource management system. The government then needs to develop the necessary administrative machinery for resource management. The state can lease them to groups or individuals who are thus given user rights over such resources for a specific period of time. People can use the resource but only at the forbearance of the state. Bromley is of the opinion that ownership resides with the citizenry at large, management and control resides with a class of bureaucrats, while the use resides with a subset of citizenry. Property rights are well defined in this system, user group is identifiable, rules and regulations governing the use of resource exist and exclusion of free riders with penalty seems to be lawful.

In India much of the forest nationalization process has started during the British rule. Forests were considered as common property until 1865 when the colonial British regime nationalized most of the good forests in the country. Legislation and necessary administrative structures were created in order to demarcate the offenders and to prosecute them. But this policy was diametrically opposing to the interest of indigenous local people that lead to conflicts and resistance movements which are not solved yet (Singh, 1994). Lack of transparency and unaccountability of bureaucracy are the main hindrances in the successful operation of nationalized projects. State action to regulate CPRs led to conflicts that may undermine user self-governance and may neglect the social capital of institutions, which have already developed at the local level. State action may also help to foster self-organization by providing independent technical advice and apt legislations (Bruns and Meizen-Dick, 2000).

1.8.4 Private Property Regime: In private property regime the claim rest on a specific party, an individual, a group or a firm who use the resource. In this system property is amenable to private appropriation only and user rights are highly exclusive and well defined in the sense that the right holder can exclude others from appropriating the property or benefits from it. Thus private property right is the legally and socially sanctioned ability of the holder to exclude others. Exclusion of free riders is easy because a user group is clearly identifiable. Even though rules, regulations and conventions are in existence, very few persons are bound to follow. Privatization can be accomplished either by partition or by putting the entire resource under the control of one single authority that could be an individual, a private firm, a cooperative, a voluntary agency or even a unit of government (Singh, 1994). [8]

Many property right scholars like Hardin, Smith, Welch, Cheung, Demsetz, etc. are of the view that the problems of free riding and *Tragedy of Commons* can be resolved only by creating and enforcing private property regimes. On the other hand it is argued that pure private ownership is often ineffective and inappropriate for resources where it is difficult to exclude natural monopolies and where utilization by one user has major influences on others (Bruns and Meizen-Dick, 2000). Vandana Shiva argues that John Locke's treatise on property effectively legitimized the theft of commons in Europe during the enclosure movements of the 17th century. Locke holds that property rights create only when idle natural resources were transformed from their spiritual form through the application of labour (Shiva, 1991).

1.9 Tragedy of Commons: The CPR Problem

If the users are unable to prevent the overexploitation of CPRs under changing circumstances, destructive competition and conflict among the users is bound to follow, which eventually results in complete degradation of the resource.

Garret Hardin, Ecologist, in 1968 characterized this eventuality as the *Tragedy of Commons.* By *Tragedy of Commons* he meant over exploitation of natural resources in the absence of institutional mechanisms to govern the management of CPRs (Singh, 1994). [9]

Hardin illustrates the logic of the *Tragedy of Commons* as follows:

Picture a pasture opens to all. It is to be expected that each herdsman will try to keep as many cattle as possible on the commons. Such an arrangement may work reasonably satisfactorily for centuries however, comes day of reckoning, as a rational being, each herdsman seeks to maximize his gain. Adding together the component partial utilities, the rational herdsman concludes that the only sensible course for him to pursue is to add another animal to his herd. And another...But, this is the conclusion reached by each and every rational herdsman sharing a commons. There in is the tragedy. Ruin is the destination towards which all men rush, each pursuing his own best interest in a society that believes in the freedom of the commons. Freedom in a commons brings ruin to all (Hardin, 1968).

In the course of his essay, Hardin develops the theme, drawing examples of latter day "commons" such as the atmosphere, oceans, rivers, fish stocks, national parks and even parking meters. A major theme running through out the essay is growth of human population, with the earth's resources being a general commons. The essay also addresses potential management solutions to common problems including: privatization, polluter pays and regulation. Keeping with his original analogy, Hardin categorizes these as effectively the enclosure of commons and notes a historical progression from the use of all resources as common (unregulated access to all) to systems in which commons are enclosed and subject to differing methods of regulated use (access prohibited or controlled).

Hardin argues against the reliance on conscience as a means of policing commons, suggesting that this favours selfish individuals over those more farsighted. In the context of avoiding over exploitation of commons, Hardin concludes by restating Hegel's maxim, 'Freedom is the recognition of necessity'. He suggests that freedom if interpreted narrowly as simply the freedom to do as one pleases completes the *Tragedy of Commons*. By recognizing resources as commons in the first place and by recognizing that, as such they require management, Hardin believes that "we can preserve and nurture other and more precious freedoms" (Crowe, 1969).

Hardin terms the CPR problem of *Tragedy of Commons* as 'no technical solution problems'. A technical solution may be defined as one, which requires a change only in the techniques of natural sciences, engineering and technology, demanding little or no changes in political or social systems. CPR problem require changes in human values, attitudes, behaviour and in the institutional foundation of the system. Since human values, attitudes and traditional institutions are difficult to change in the short-term, a long-term strategy is required to resolve the CPR problems.

Hardin's thesis of *Tragedy of Commons* has since become the dominant paradigm of the exploitation of CPRs resulting from their common ownership. His thesis served as a platform for numerous policy makers engaged in environmental legislation in many developed and developing countries. In essence Hardin advocates that resources should either be privatized or nationalized to ensure sustainable use and mentioned no possibility for collective management. He presumes the only alternative to the commons problems was what he called a private enterprise system on the one hand or socialism on the other (Singh, 1994).

Hardin makes an implicit assumption that CPRs under the collective management of a group is also open access in reality. These arguments are implicit in Thomas Hobbes's *Leviathan*. But Ophuls, (1973) and Ehrenfield (1972) argued for government control for protecting the public interest. Carruthers and Stoner (1981) argued that without public control, efficiency cannot be expected in the management of CPRs, while Robert J. Smith suggests that the only way to avoid the *Tragedy of Commons* is to create a system of private property rights (Ostrum, 1999).

1.10 Criticism to Tragedy of Commons

Like any other thesis it is not free from controversy. Some of this stems from disagreement about whether individual will always behave in the selfish fashion posited by Hardin.

Vandana Shiva makes a sharp criticism on Hardin's privatization arguments in her work, *Water Wars*. She says that his assumption about commons as unmanaged open access systems stem from the belief that management takes effect only in the hands of private individuals. But groups do manage themselves and commons are regulated rather well by communities. More over commons are not open-access resources as Hardin proposes; they in fact apply the concept of ownership, not on an individual basis, but at the level of the group. She summarizes that in Third World societies the principle of co-operation rather than competition among individuals still dominates and Hardin's thesis misses the critical point that under circumstances in which common lands even support the basic needs of the population a tragedy is inevitable – with or without competition (Shiva, 2002).

According to a major section of scholars the depletion of resources that have heretofore been associated with common property rights, may in fact be more a result of colonial or capitalistic policies or of industrialization and modernization. In this vein, R.W. Franke and B.H. Chasin attribute much of the tragedy in the management of CPRs in the Sahel to the loss of a traditional local bioethic with the transition to colonial production modes. The new bioethics of colonialism preached, unbridled personal accumulation, rather than self-sufficiency and restraint in the use of CPRs. When it comes to the fisheries sector, the *Tragedy of Commons* model has a cynical view of the mentality, character and personality of fishermen with respect to the explanation of how the tragedy develops. That view essentially assumes that as overall yields for a given level of effort dwindle, fishers inevitably develop a greedy 'take all you can and take it now' approach to the fisheries. As Mc Evoy appraised this point of view, "the farmers in Garret Hardin's *Tragedy of Commons* are fundamentally autonomous, self-serving, irresponsible creatures, as radically alienated from each other as they are from the grass, on which they feed their cows" (Goodwin, 1995). Despite all criticisms Hardin's

Tragedy of Commons continues to be one of the most important theoretical schemas that address the various dimensions of CPRs.

1.11 Social Movement Literature: An Appraisal

Social Movement scholarship is characterized with a wide array of perspectives and approaches. A section of scholars place movements as active agents in the deepening of world society and its norms. According to these scholars many of the international non-governmental organizations have a social movement character. Being active champions of central elements of world culture, they promote models of human rights, consumer rights, environmental regulation, social and economic development and human equality .and justice. They often cast themselves as oppositional grassroots movements, decrying gaps or failures in the implementation of world cultural principles in particular locales and demanding corrective action by states and other actors. Agents of social problems, they generate further structuration of rationalized systems (Guirdy et al., 2000). The aforementioned approach is best illustrative of the fact that social movements are typified with multiple tiers with complementary and conflictual interfaces.

The origins of social movement theory in the USA goes back to the attempts by the Chicago School to make sense of informal social action by understanding the rationality of the actors themselves (Purdue, 2007). Social movements are more than the aggregates of social actors based on properties in common. Collective action is embedded in a cultural context of meaning and reproduces it by this action (Eder, 1993). Social movements were initially theorized as mechanisms to cope with the stresses and strains in the society and as manifestations of social pathology by prominent sociologists of the first world. In contrast, social movements have later been perceived as vehicles of social transformation in Third World countries in the context of political liberation. Of late, they came to be recognized as instruments of social development (Oommen, 2004). The manner in which the movement processes has transformed, has also altered significantly.

The outcome of social movements has been the centre for such scholastic enquiries. It is widely acknowledged that a social movement's outcome may reflect its internal dynamics and resources, its external political environment or both. Analysts who have peered into the internal machinery of social movements link a movement's chances of success with its capacity to construct viable organizations, raise money to exploit the expertise of professional activist's recruit from existing groups, devise an effective repertoire of collective action for confronting political elites, pursue narrow goals, and articulate an ideology with widespread appeal. In contrast, social scientists who have concentrated on external factors claim that the success of social movements stems from opportunities created by political crises and unstable political alignments, and from the process by which state structures channel mobilization. The success of a social movement refers to a movement's attainment of tangible benefits that meet its goals, its formal acceptance by political elites, the legitimization of its goals and the transformation of individual group consciousness (Szymanski, 2003).

The communication approach to social movements offers a very different perspective. According to this approach the function fulfilled by social movements (being a special kind of collective actors) is to accelerate the communication of issues in society. Protest actors do not succeed or fail. They are part of a system that defines the contribution of protest–whether failing or not–to the reproduction of society. Social movements have been and are one of the constitutive elements of modern society: they guarantee the communication issues, a function that persists beyond their concrete existence as forms of mobilization or organization. This approach to social movements differs from the macro-sociological approaches dominating traditional social movement research. It no longer makes social movements simply additional or new carriers of social, political or cultural change. And it goes beyond the microanalysis of social movements that restricts the analysis of social movements to the analysis of forms and processes of collective mobilization (Eder, 1993). In this thesis the author intends to go beyond the traditional analysis of social movements to make a comparative analysis of the select movement cases from Plachimada and Sheonath.

There have been certain serious limitations in regard to the conceptualization of social movements. An obvious case in this regard is the neglect of the consequences of social movement in the whole literature. There is a clear dearth of scholarly studies that look into the various aspects of movement impact, on the potential consequences, in particular, on the conditions and circumstances that favour certain consequences as well as the processes leading movements to have an impact on the actual effects obtained by past as well as contemporary movements. The aforesaid limitation in the social movement scholarship owe particularly to the complex interface that the movement politics has with the normal institutionalized politics occurring through voting, lobbying, political parties, legislatures, courts and elected leaders. Social Movements are often perceived as challengers seeking to enter the institutionalized world of polity members who have routinized access to the levers of power. But social movements constitute an essential element of normal politics in modern societies and that there is only a fuzzy and permeable boundary between institutionalized and non-institutionalized politics. Moreover there are distinctly different behaviours at the extreme ends of the spectrum of institutional and non-institutional politics (Goldstone, 2003).

1.12 Characteristics of Social Movement

Giugni distinguish six movement characteristics. First social movement may address similar issues, themes and goals.

Different countries may see the rise of the same movements, such as peace, women's, and ecology movements. Also the demands, ideology and strategies of a particular movement in one country may reflect that of its counterparts in other countries. Second movements may display similar levels of mobilization that carry out similar number of protest actions or involve similar number of participants in those actions. For example, New Social Movements (NSMs) have mobilized to a roughly similar extent in Germany, Netherlands and Switzerland from 1975 to 1989 while in France their level of mobilization was much lower. However, this difference is less pronounced among the four countries as old movements were stronger in France than in the three other countries.

Third the strategies, tactics and forms of action may converge. Research on this crucial dimension has mostly focused on cross-national variations of action repertoires. More generally, though NSMs are usually more radical in certain countries (for example France) than in others, street demonstrations prevail everywhere. Fourth we may observe similar organizational structures, which refer to the level of resources and other organizational features (centralized/ ecentralized, formal/informal, integrated/isolated and so forth). For example, at the time of their emergence, the NSMs brought to fore non-hierarchical, participatory forms of organization, which Gerlach and Hine (1970) has called "segmented, polycentric, informal networks". Later, formalized and professional organizations emerged almost everywhere among NSMs.

Fifth movement cultural frames, ideas, and discourses may show similar patterns. Here, we refer to the ideological and symbolic contents of mobilization. The use of similar slogans are perhaps most typical. There are numerous examples: the Marxist-Leninist and Maoist slogans of the European student movements in the 1960s, 'the small-is-beautiful' slogan of the early ecology movement, the stress on sustainable development of the present-day global environmental movement, the nuclear-free-zone concept used by movements and so forth. Sixth, and perhaps most interesting, we may observe parallels in the timing of protest. This aspect is shared across countries both in the short and long term. Similar protest timing is illustrated by the rise of student protest in the late 1960s, mobilization against deployment of North Atlantic Treaty Organization (NATO) missiles in the early 1980s and the strong opposition to communist regimes in Eastern Europe at the end of the same decade. Protests against nuclear power plants which peaked in Germany, Italy, Switzerland and the United States between 1975 and 1977 are another parallel in mobilization timing (Giugni, 2002).

1.13 Social Movements: Old and New

At the outset there is a need to distinguish between old and new social movements. In the late 1960s the world was apparently undergoing deep, dramatic transformations–even a revolution, some thought. American civil rights and anti-war movements, the Mai 1968 revolt in France, student's protests in Germany, Britain, or Mexico, the orkerstudent coalitions of the 1969 hot autumn in Italy, the pro-democracy mobilizations in locations as diverse as Francoist Madrid and communist Prague, the growth of critical Catholicism from south America to Rome, the early signs of the women's and environmental movements that would shape the new politics of the 1970s: all these phenomena–and may more–suggested that deep changes were in the making. These processes have effects on the evolution and sustenance of social movements across the world.

Contemporarily, social movements have become permanent component of western democracies. It is no longer possible to describe protest politics, grassroots participation, and symbolic challenges as unconventional. Instead, references to a movement society seem increasingly plausible. Traditionally social movements had focused mainly on issues of labour and nations, since 1960s new social movements have emerged which cantered on concerns such as women's liberation, environmental protection, etc. these changes in the quantity and quality of protest prompted significant innovations in social scientist's approach to those questions. The principal theoretical models available at the time for the interpretation of social conflict–the Marxist model and the structural-functionalist model–both came to be regarded as largely inadequate (Porta and Diani, 2006). The new social movement framework has largely been emerged to fill this lacuna.

The reasons for the emergence of new social movement in the Third World are manifold. With the fall of second world, democracy came to be universally recognized both as a set of values and a system of institutions. The second wave of democratization (1943-62) was critical in regard to the implantation and consolidation of democratic institutions across the world (Avritzer, 2002). [10] In this democratic polity the hiatus between the people and the government is sought to be eliminated through building appropriate institutions, deployment of technology, dissemination of information and knowledge. But these institutions, instruments and inputs do not always deliver what they promise. This is the context in which New Social Movements believed to be common to the entire globe, are said to be emerging (Oommen, 2004).

NSMs such as the women's, student, peace, ecology, and anti-nuclear movements all emerged in the same time, approximately in the 1960s and grew to become the main extra institutional forces in the western world. Furthermore the goals of these movements are similar, although their size and influence may vary widely. Also, the targets of protest actions often coincide: nuclear power plants, air and water pollution, the army, nuclear weapons, and abortion rights are only some examples (Giugni, 2002). New social movements such as environmentalism, contemporary feminism or the anti-globalization movement appear to have very powerful capacities for self-education, and indeed find their members largely among the most highly educated; as movements, they make few if any demands on the formal educational institutions (Field, 2005).

The new social movement perspective holds that the collective search for identity is a central aspect of movement formation. Mobilization factors tend to focus on cultural and symbolic issues that are associated with sentiments of belonging to a differentiated social group where members can feel powerful; they are likely to have sub-cultural orientations that challenge the dominant system. New social movements are said to arise in defence of identity. They grow around relationships that are voluntarily conceived to empower members to name themselves. 'What individuals are claiming collectively is the right to realize their own identity, the possibility of disposing of their personal creativity, their affective life; and their biological and interpersonal existence' (Johnston et al., 1994).

The most important one in the category of new social movements is indigenous people's movement. Largely excluded and oppressed in their own societies, indigenous people have been able to find a new voice and new forum by joining together to take their shared grievances to the world community. Moreover goals of indigenous communities relate to those of other global social movements, particularly the environment and human rights movements (Synott, 2004). For many indigenous people, the greatest threat posed by globalization is the proliferation of multinational corporations, which exploit their resources. Indeed the plight of indigenous people from the Amazon in trying to protect their lands against exploitation from multinational corporations is well known. This problem is aggravated by state's unwillingness (and sometimes incapacity) to regulate multinational corporations, since they prioritize economic efficiency and foreign investment, which are neo-liberal economic ideals (Bargh, 2007). The author's case study of Plachimada is a clear example for the struggle between multinational corporations and indigenous people for natural resources.

1.14 Injustice and Mobilization

There is no simple relationship between injustice and mobilization. Social movement scholars have identified several factors affecting the rise of social movements. At the macro level, movements are considered more likely to occur when broad forces of social change (e.g. industrialization, war and cultural contact) upset existing power relations. Under these circumstances a faction of elites may break from the ruling consensus and sponsor challenging groups, or state policies may open political opportunities and facilitate challenges to the ruling group. At the organizational level, there is a broad agreement that mobilization is more likely when challenging groups have more resources at their disposal. Also studies have shown that the likelihood of mobilization increases as social networks among potential participants and social movement activists become denser (Johnston and Noakes, 2005). In this comparative study of Plachimada and Sheonath, the author explores the grassroots level political processes in regard to the emergence and participation in social movements.

A micro-level study of the grassroots political processes is critical in exploring the linkage between injustice and mobilization. As far as the environmental justice movements in India are concerned, the transformation of many grassroot-based movements needs serious academic scrutiny. There are many other examples of the people in India in various popular movements, collectively resisting projects that threaten their livelihood. The Chipko movement in Maharashtra saved the forests upon which much poor family's livelihood depended. In some other states, the *Van Panchayats* have been active in restraining the indiscriminate use of the forests and the *Pani Panchayats* have been established to manage water resources. The Save Narmada Protest led by Medha Patkar is also a good example of such resistance. All these movements indicate that the poor rural community is conscious of its own welfare and that the people are prepared to resist and counteract the power of vested interests. It seems in fact that destructive projects vis-à-vis both nature and people will be countered by these communities of resistance (Degaonkar and Gills, 2002).

At many times, the emergence or intensification of the struggle had not been an outcome of a direct threat upon the livelihood. There are instances in which the livelihood struggles get transformed into an ideological level where the grassroots groups lodge battle against the capitalist development schema. The grassroots group fighting in the Narmada struggle raised fundamental issues, elaborated the interconnections among them and wove them together into a comprehensive critique of the orthodox development standpoint. The livelihood issue raised by these groups was not allowed to remain at an intellectual level or a matter of theoretical discussion. The comprehensive critique and the concomitant demand for *paryayi vikas-neetee* (alternative development paradigm) formed a political agenda around which grassroots struggle in the Narmada valley was organized. Further the Narmada struggle and other similar struggles for environmental justice have now joined hands to evolve a nationwide campaign around this agenda. To this end, the group leading the Narmada struggle and the other major grassroots movements created the National Alliance of People's Movement (NAPM) (Wagle, 2002).

The Latin American case is critical in regard to the interface between political society and social movements. Under authoritarian regimes it is all too evident that this political society must itself be reconstituted by constitutional norms and electoral rules, which guarantee freedom of speech and association and provide for political representation and legislative procedure. There is no doubt that the re-emergence or deepening of political society varies widely between different regimes and within different processes of democratic transition. But there have been few concrete attempts to describe the difficult projection of social movements into political society, or to analyze the contribution of social movements to the many democratic transitions that have taken place in Latin America in recent years. Indeed there is a sharp division between the bulk of the social movement literature and the huge new literature on democratic transitions, and this has tended to produce an imbalanced and elite-centered view of the process of democratization (Foweraker, 1995). Similar to the case of Latin American societies, the interface between social movements and political society is highly significant in the Indian case also.

1.15 Institutionalized Politics and Social Movements

The interface of social movements with institutionalized politics is an important aspect to be looked into. Very often, the social movements, especially the left-wing ones, got incorporated into the existing political party framework. This has resulted in a situation in which the movement activities persisted within party structures and that incorporated social movements which exerted enduring influences on social policy. Movement integration into political parties in the past, very often, shaped the development and outcomes of social movements in succeeding periods (Hanagan, 1998). However, there are regional specific variations in the patterns of movement incorporation and its policy impacts. The case of Kerala Sasthra Sahitya Parishad (KSSP), which has a pro-left orientation and association, deserves special mention. The KSSP or Kerala Science Literature Association was established in 1962 by a group of science writers in Malayalam as their forum. Its objective was to popularize science among the people of Kerala in their mother tongue, Malayalam. In nearly four decades, it has grown into a massive people's science movement, with a membership of about 60,000. All of its members work on a voluntary basis. Unemployed educated youth and teachers are the main constituents of the KSSP.

Over these years, the KSSP has expanded its interests and activities. Now it is broadly involved in three types of activities: agitative, educative and constructive, in areas like environment, health, education, energy, development, literacy, and micro planning (Bhattacharya, 2004).

The transformation in the character of state also served as a potent factor in regard to relationship between institutionalized and non-institutionalized politics. Precisely because neo-liberal states no longer truly serve the interests of the majority, popular social forces have a much greater need to mobilize and organize in order to serve their own needs. They cannot rely on the state, or on political parties, as they may felt they could do in the past. The new global grass-roots movements of resistance are mainly organized and led from the south. In addition to the centrality of movements from the south in the new global resistance to neo-liberal globalization, their very composition and diversity reflects the effects of neo-liberalism around the world, such as on environment, women, farmers, indigenous people, children, migrants and many others (Gills, 2007).

1.16 Globalization and Resistance Movements

The emergence of anti-capitalistic/anti-globalization movement to oppose the neo-liberal domination of the world development agenda requires special mention. The anti-globalization movement is constituted by a diversity of social movements opposed to globalization, often operating at a local level in a semi-autonomous fashion linked loosely to a wider network. The anti-globalization movement differentiated itself from earlier anti-capitalistic movements by the specificity of its agenda. It is refreshingly engaged with real issues, rather than abstract political theory, albeit the anti-capitalistic/anti-globalization movement is not without its theorists (Powell, 2007). Resistance to globalization does not follow the traditional models of community organizing and social changes that are often built on highly centralize organization models; rather, the resistance to globalization is truly from grassroots. In fact the strength of the resistance to globalization right now lies in the fact that it is such diverse and widespread phenomenon. Even though the anti-globalization movement lacks central organization and lack of focus, its extensivity across the world made it a pertinent grass root formation (Peters 2006).

However, by then the anti-globalization movement was beginning to emerge, attacking the powers of finance capital and its primary institutions (the International Monetary Fund and the World Bank) became a mode of protest. With the state so clearly siding with the financiers and in any case performing as a prime agent in the politics of accumulation by possession, this movement looked to the institutions of civil society to transform the territorial logics of power on a variety of scales from intensely local to global (as in the case of environmental movement). The protest movements that surfaced through out the world were for the most part ruthlessly put down by state powers (Harvey, 2005). The manner in which the anti-globalization movements lodged their protests and the state response has interesting patterns.

The unfolding patterns of the anti-globalization movement also deserve due mention within the globalization research. Instead of targeting nation-states, the anti-globalization movement today tends to mobilize against corporations and multi-lateral organizations, and the agents of this resistance are NGOs and people's organizations which are either based and mobilized from the grassroots or at least, take their inspiration and gain their legitimacy from the grassroots. The processes through which ordinary people in the global South resist and manipulate the forces that are arrayed against and around them deserve special mention. As James Scott (1985) writes in the preface to his work *Weapons of the Weak* rather than focusing on grand scale, high-profile protests, rebellions and revolutions 'it seemed to be more important to understand what we might call everyday forms of peasant resistance—the prosaic but constant struggle between the peasantry and those who seek to extract labour, food, taxes, rents and interest from them'. Scott's main concern was about resistance in a rural context, draws on his two years living experience in a village in the Malaysian state of Kedah between 1978 and 1980. Everyday resistance, however, need not be restricted to the peasantry but extends to all walks of life and arenas of work (Rigg, 2007).

Anti-globalization movement across the world resorted to innovative strategies of protest. Many of these movements reject the established modes of protests and adopted more confrontational tactics. Some groups used non-hierarchical style of organizing, confronted the police and challenged the more institutionalized and passive nature of the 1980s movements. As a result of the shift in protest tactics, the state police developed more sophisticated modes of control that are neither purely repressive nor entirely negotiated. Rather, the current mode is an effective mixture of hard-and soft-line tactics, including the use of new non-lethal weapons as well as laws, codes, regulations and public relations strategies that attempt to control protest spaces directly and indirectly (Fernandez, 2008).

1.17 Opposition to Multinational Corporations

Contemporarily, the global economic order is characterized with multiplicity of political and economic actors characterized with constitutive power vis-à-vis the global institutional order. The emergence and critical role played by the multi-national corporations is one of the key attributes of contemporary period. By most estimates, production by multinational enterprises now accounts for over one-forth of the world's output and one-third of world trade. Moreover many scholars believe that the investments of multinationals commonly known as Foreign Direct Investment (FDI) have beneficial effects on economic growth, transferring technology and managerial expertise as well as providing capital. With contemporary global resource struggles pivoting along a north-south axis, economic power, formerly based in governments is increasingly concentrated in global Multi or Trans National Corporations (MNCs or TNCs respectively). These corporations are the key agents in the process of globalization (Crate, 2006).

Multinational companies are not connected with one country or territory, which facilitates the adaptability of multinational companies to events that might damage them. Thus, the possibility to transfer their personnel, their factories and services everywhere and to adapt themselves to events on world level, offers them some kind of superiority in point of manoeuvrability over the measures which could be taken against them. In the author's opinion, multinational companies may at any time avoid penalization through high taxation by merely changing nationality and thus safeguarding their excess profits (Elian, 1979). Notwithstanding the fact that MNCs impacted greatly on the economic side, the increased presence of multi-national corporations has ramifications on the social and political side.

The overarching influence of multi-national corporations in the international economic order is explored from various angles. State centric writings on the multinational corporation assert that the rise and success of the MNC in the modern world could have happened only within a favourable international political environment. They maintain that despite several theories of business economists, the MNC cannot be explained solely in terms of market forces and/or corporate strategies. While economic factors are obviously important for the emergence and success of MNCs they could not exist without a favourable international political environment created by a dominant power whose economic and security interest favour an open and liberal international economy (Gilpin and Gilpin, 2003). In the meanwhile, the relations between MNCs and state are highly determined by nation-state processes. Multi-national corporations require nation states, because the nation-state can meet needs that MNCs themselves cannot produce. These include defence of private property rights against political opponents; support for free circulation of factors of production, and integration of subordinate social classes into the social system. While nation-states wish to foster inward direct investment and to maximize local value-added production, multinational corporations seek the optimum global profit aggregate rather than profit maximization in individual countries (Holton, 1992).

Despite all the polemics against multinational corporations, there is little evidence to support the view that they have been very successful in replacing the nation-state as the primary actor in international politics. Where these business enterprises have influenced international political relations, they have done so like any interest groups by influencing the policies of their home governments. It is only true to argue that the state is now operating within an increasingly developed matrix of transnational interaction involving other states, inter-governmental institutions, MNCs and a whole range of cross-border groups and networks. While the evidence seems to support an increased concentration of economic power in MNCs, some argue that the impact of their business activity is exaggerated and that MNCs remain heavily nationally embedded and subject to regulation by national governments. There is also an argument that while MNCs have become important actors in the international arena, they are not stateless, footloose and preponderant over governments but rather are susceptible to pressure and persuasion from home state governments (Lynch, 2003).

1.18 Environmental Movements

The environmental movement is having growing impact on national and international politics, and there is little evidence to suggest that the movement's momentum will slow in the near future. A wide array of surveys indicates a sharp rise in public concern over environmental problems in western countries, which has contributed to the emergence of citizen's groups and ecological parties in those countries. Feeling intense pressure from various quarters, policymakers are enacting stringent regulations designed to abate pollution. While most countries initially confined their attention to specific environmental problems inside their borders, they are now focusing on transitional issues such as biodiversity, the depletion of the ozone layer, and global warming.

Given the traditional political and economic barriers inherent in international relations, a remarkable number of environmental agreements have been implemented (Kamieniecki, 1993). Consequently, whole nations are developing environmental strategies, with billions of dollars of commerce at stake. Multinational corporations, with revenues larger than many nation's have phalanxes of lawyers, engineers and environmental officers, all devoted to keeping the company out of trouble. Such developments are radically changing the conditions within which the environmental movement works.

According to Rootes (1999), environmental movements can be conceived as broad networks of people and organizations engaged in collective action in the pursuit of environmental benefits. Environmental movements are understood to be very diverse and complex, their organizational forms ranging from the highly organized and formally institutionalized to the radically informal, the spatial scope of their activities ranging from local to almost global, the nature of their concerns ranging single issues to the fully panoply of global environmental concerns (Rootes, 1999). The expansion of grassroots groups has been described as environmentalism's third wave. The defining characteristic of grassroots groups is their bottom-up, decentralized nature, as opposed to the centralized administration of the large mainstream membership groups. Grassroots group tend to be, but are not always, local or regional in focus; for example, there exists some national grassroots groups and group networks related to antitoxic activities. In addition, there are national groups that cannot be easily classified as either grassroots or mainstream.

While grassroots groups are diverse in their issue orientations, degree of professionalisation, size, and budgets, they share the hope of democratizing the policy process by shifting the focus of environmental policy to the local level (Helen M. et al., 1995). The presence of environmental groups at various levels will turn the understanding of movement dynamics a complicated exercise.

The global environmental movement has its origin in the United States of America. The commencement of this new social movement in the late 1960s is the cumulative effect of a whole host of interrelated factors; the most prominent among them is environmental consciousness that emerges out of increased occurrences of environment degradation. Earlier that decade, Rachel Carson's *Silent Spring* woke America to the dangers of pesticides. Smog was choking Los Angeles and other cities. And in 1969, pollution on the surface of Cleveland's Cuyahoga River burst into flames. That same year, Americans viewed the first photograph of planet Earth taken from outer space and realized how fragile and lonely our living planet truly is. Modern environmental organizations emerged in response to these newly visible consequences of industrialization.

The Sierra Club transformed itself from a quiet hiker's club to a lobbying powerhouse. Two years later, a group of young and idealistic attorneys determined to found the Natural Resources Defence Council (NRDC) to bring the full weight of scientific and legal expertise to bear on environmental policy. On 22 April 1970, twenty million Americans celebrated the first Earth Day. The modern environmental movement was born, and it shone like a candle in the dark night of race riots, political assassinations, and the Vietnam War (Shellenberger and Nordhuas, 2007).

However, in the case of developing countries of the South, one can find a different pattern. The emergence of environmental movement in Asia is an interesting case in this regard. By the early 1970s, one could detect a growing public concern in Asia over the inability of the state to address the environmental consequences of post-War population and economic growth. By the late 1970s, numerous non-governmental organizations emerge throughout east and Southeast Asia, often serving as a vehicle for grassroots communities to express their political dissent and socio-economic grievances. Since the 1980s increasing deterioration of the living and natural environment all over Asia has lead to a gradual emergence of environmental consciousness among the citizenry and the evolution of various types of environmental movement throughout the region.

In most cases, grassroots environmental resistance organizations in the region have emerged from a variety of oppositional political movements motivated by anti-colonial, national independence, Marxist, and feminist aspirations. Majority of these organizations started as groups to address common socioeconomic and religious concerns. Some discovering the inextricable linkages between and among poverty, domination by outsiders and environmental degradation have become ecologically and politically radicalized (Lee and So, 1999). During the post-independence period a greater part of the Asian countries has embarked on a state-led capitalist development schema with country specific variations. Big projects were the catchword of that phases and the most pertinent example in this regard is the Nehruvian view that 'dams are temples of modern India'. The environmental degradation and human displacement brought about by the big projects provided a fertile ground for the emergence of environmental movement in India.

Even though the environmental agenda emerged forcefully in the late 1970s and throughout the 1980s (Doyle, 2004) the environmental movement in the South has complex interconnections. In many countries, traditional, moral and religious motivations in the phase of increasing deterioration have helped to contribute to the increasing environment character of many popular movements. Religions "have been mutating into forms of inspiring (or reinforcing) ecological activism, both by articulating ideals that participants find compelling (and thus legitimations for resistance) and by providing concrete institutional resources for ecological struggles" (Lee and So, 1999). The Chipko Movement in North India is a critical case in this regard. The western scholars often undermine most of these complex interconnections, as their attempt was mostly to impose the western analytical frameworks to understand the environmental movement.

The gender dimension of the environmental struggles in India deserves special mention. The great vulnerability of poor women to the effects of enclosure and environmental degradation that was noted above is an additional factor explaining women's growing prominence in grassroots organizations. In many cases women are the guiding forces behind self-help organizations as they seek to rectify themselves the social and environmental problems that afflict them and their families. Livernash notes that 'women are organizing to cope with tasks such as providing water and fuel; growing crops; and generating income from food processing, handicrafts and similar activities'. The critical role of women in Chipko has already been noted and was related to the adverse impact on women of logging in the Himalayan foothills. Indeed 'sheer survival made women support the movement'. These examples illustrate that women are often playing a crucial role in the development of self-help and protest organizations in the Third World. This feminization of the grassroots movement illustrates the important point that grassroots organizations usually develop to assert local control over environmental resources but in doing so they may also aim to represent women's claims for social justice both inside and outside the local community (Bryant and Bailey, 1997).

1.19 Human Rights Question

The notion that all human beings share a basic level of equal moral worth in some significant respect is thoroughly a modern concept. Older natural rights theorists, such as English philosopher John Locke, tried to suggest that human or natural rights are non-visible properties of personhood. The older theorists relied on a metaphysical conception of human nature to ground their claims about natural rights to things of life and liberty. We have rights, they said, in the same way as we have a soul (Orend, 2002). Being a modern concept, human rights didn't have an agreed philosophical foundation from their existence. The existence of human rights has variously been criticized by utilitarians as non-sense, communitarians as fantasy, Marxists as bourgeois, and post modernists as relative. Human rights are non-sense to utilitarians since any notion of human rights might actually undermine the achievement of the greatest happiness of the greatest number of people in a given context. For Marx, human rights were simply legal protections for the further empowerment of propertied classes (Landman, 2006). Notwithstanding the philosophical disagreements, in the past fifty years, human rights have become one of the most globalized political values of our time (Wilson, 1997).

Human rights are not discovered by experience or observation; they are also not the conclusion of rational deduction from matters of fact. Human rights are a human creation that can be conceived, defined, reshaped, or abandoned as we choose (Campbell et al., 2003). There are two different approaches to human rights. According to the traditional view, human rights empower people in the fight against persecution and injustice. The second view sees human rights as power over people, expressed in exclusionary practices that deny the full participation of those who fail to support the interests of the dominant group (Evans, 1998). Social justice captures an important feature of the human rights framework as its emphasize on the moral imperative of eliminating glaring social inequality within societies and structurally embedded patterns of international support for these inequalities. The human right framework goes beyond a commitment to social justice and it supports other dimensions of a life, people value that are not focused entirely on reducing the suffering of the poor (Marks, 2004). The multifaceted focus of the human rights framework made it a congenial framework for the exploration of a wide gamut of issues pertaining to human flourishment.

The human rights impacts of globalization and globalization impacts on human rights are a major aspect to be looked into. Globalization is a package of transnational flows of people, production, investment, information, ideas and authority. Human rights are a set of claims and entitlements to human dignity, which the existing international regime assumes will be provided by the state. It is widely agreed that globalization have negative impacts on human rights as the greater flow of private capital will produce direct and indirect human rights violations. However, the emergence of an international regime for human rights, growing transnational social movement networks, increased consciousness and information politics have the potential to address both traditional and emerging forms of human rights violations (Brysk, 2002). Such a complex interconnection makes the human rights question a more complicated one.

1.20 Human Rights and Environmental Issues

The link between environmental protection and human rights was first explicitly recognized in 1972, in the Stockholm declaration, adopted by the UN Conference on the Human Environment. Principle 1 of this declaration proclaims:

"Man has the fundamental right to freedom, equality and adequate conditions of life, in an environment of a quality that permits a life of dignity and well-being and he bears a solemn responsibility to protect and improve the environment for present and future generations."

The relationship between the environment and human

rights is also stressed in the preamble to the Stockholm Declaration, which states that protection of the environment is 'essential to the enjoyment of basic human rights–even the right to life itself'. It is to be noted that these provisions do not directly recognize the right to a healthy environment as such. They rather amount to an indirect recognition of such a right, by establishing a link between well-recognized human rights such as the right to freedom and the right to life and the quality of the environment. Environmental quality is presented as a prerequisite for achieving adequate conditions of life (Dejeant-Pons, 2002). The ecological interpretation of human rights promoted rights as a mechanism to protect holistic environmental concerns, rather than as an argument used in support of economic growth at the expense of environmental considerations (Hancock, 2003).

The relationship between human rights and environmental protection is conceived in two main ways. First, environmental protection may cast as a means to the end of fulfilling human rights standards. Since degraded physical environments contribute directly to infringements of human rights to life, health and livelihood, acts leading to environmental degradation may also constitute an immediate violation of internally recognized human rights. Second, the legal protection of human rights is an effective means to achieve the ends of conservation and environmental protection. Thus the full realization of a broad spectrum of first and second generation rights would constitute a society and political order in which claims for environmental protection are more likely to be respected (Boyle and Anderson, 1998). The inter-linkage between environment and human rights is considered to be one of the growing areas of academic research.

The intensification of human-inflicted damage on the environment, exacerbated by globalization, has also helped to establish an interlinkage between environment and human rights. While, the west, as the original site of the industrial revolution, had long been the major source of pollution, by the mid-twentieth century emerging southern hemisphere and socialist industrializing states were contributing substantially to the problem. The combined and ever growing effect of world pollution and diminishing resources since World War II has no historic parallel, making the question of the right to a healthy environment, intensified in the International Covenant on Economic, Social and Cultural Rights a critical human rights issue (Ishay, 2004). The following section will look into issues pertaining to the relationship between human rights and multinational corporations.

1.21 Human Rights and Multinational Corporations

The relation between the role of Multi National Corporations (MNCs), development and human rights is complex. The so-called engine of development school maintains that MNCs directly promote economic and social rights and indirectly support civil and political rights. Unemployment rights and social security depend on the level of economic development. MNCs create jobs by bringing in new capital and technology and they also provide health care benefits. In contrast supporters of the Hymer Thesis argue that Third World MNCs create situations that lead to lower levels of human rights, especially violations of first-generation civil and political rights. Wealthy countries exploit poor nations and it is the organizational structure of MNCs that causes inequality among nations. There is a near consensus among the human rights scholars that MNCs have a direct as well as indirect relationship with the promotion and infringement of human rights (Walters, 2002).

Given that MNCs have a direct impact on the economic, political and social landscape of the countries in which they operate, their activities have considerable effects on individuals and human rights, both positively and negatively. The overarching influence veiled by MNCs pose limits to holding states solely accountable for human rights violations, asserts that corporations may have much or more power over individuals and governments. There are certain studies which argue that the presence of MNCs in Third World economies is beneficial, leading to increased life expectancy and reductions in illiteracy and infant mortality, along with increase in first and second-generation rights as a whole. Regardless of the evidence that corporate activities in the developing world improve human rights standards, it is still fair to say that MNCs often react to human right concerns slowly and callously (Claude, 2006). The inter-linkage between MNCs and human rights give strong rationale for viewing many of the grassroots level resistance movements against multinational corporations as human rights movements.

The institutionalization of the human rights regime provides a good background for looking at the unfolding inter-linkage between Common Property Resources and social movements. Globalization, particularly its foremost attribute, privatization offers new theoretical challenges in analyzing the issues pertaining to Common Property Resources, social movement and human rights. The privatization of CPRs and the social movement it triggers involve lots of theoretical queries and this chapter represents an attempt to delineate few of them. Social movements emerged as response to the privatization of CPRs cannot be just termed as a resistance movement, as the human rights question is also seriously involved. However, the human rights dimension related to the CPR regime change is different from the established human rights questions. Given that the privatization of CPRs is not solely intended to solve the management issue there are serious limitations for using the existing theoretical paradigms to most of the CPR related issues in developing countries. By using the case of water privatization, the attempts to fill many of the aforementioned theoretical lacunae exist with respect to Common Property Resources, Social Movement and Human Rights.

End Notes

1. Haryana has announced that all projects will be cleared through the State Pollution Control Board within fifteen days. Kerala

introduced the 'green channel' system to expedite industrial clearances. It may be noted that the Coca-Cola Company has entered the state in 1999 through green channel system. Punjab constituted a committee to ensure clearances within twenty-four hours of the submission of a proposal. Rajasthan exempted 155 small-scale industries from getting a No Objection Certificate from the Pollution Control Board and relaxed the inspection of Factories Act (Singh, 2004).

2. West Bengal government decided to acquire land in Singur for a car factory for Tata Motors has drawn much criticism from various sectors as it leads to widespread violence in 2008.
3. Though a committee was set-up to suggest conditions under which the import can be allowed, but still with liberalization, imports of such waste materials hold good chances. Greenpeace findings state that the amount of toxic waste from industrialized countries into developing countries has doubled the previous year. Imports from the United States, Australia, South Korea, Germany, Netherlands, France, Japan and United Kingdom account for about 67 percent of the total waste export to India.
4. Since 1985 Du Pont has been attempting to relocate a hazardous Nylon 6.6 manufacturing plant from the United States to the picturesque state of Goa. However the corporation was forced to give up its plans owing to sustained agitation by the villagers of the area where the factory was planned to be started.
5. Even today most of the India's rural poor depend, to a greater-extent for their livelihood on CPRs. Jodha, based on his sample survey estimated that between 84 to 100 percent of the poor households gathered food, fuel, fodder and fiber from the CPRs and in the dry rural districts the proportion of income among poor families based directly on CPRs is in the range 15 to 25 percent.
6. *Tragedy of Commons* is a thesis developed by Garret Hardin in 1968. His model makes two critical assumptions that CPRs are really open-access as well as resource users are individualistic and thus unable to cooperate towards the greater community interest.
7. In the *Kudimaramath* system a peasant paid 300 out of 1000 units of grain he or she earned to a public fund for its maintenance. By 1830 peasant payments raised up to 650 units, out of which 550 units went straight to the East India Company.

As a result the maintenance revenue had decreased and about 3, 00,000 water tanks built over centuries in Pre-British India were destroyed, affecting the agricultural productivity and earnings.

8. In India cases of privatization of land, water, forests and fisheries were reported. It happens through both legal and illegal means. Legal privatization has been effected under various land reforms and social welfare programs, but the illegal privatization is largely through encroachment.
9. *Tragedy of Commons* in India is evident from the continued and unabated degradation of CPRs. For example, CPRs like land are degraded due to water erosion, salinity, etc. Rivers and lakes are polluted by discharge of toxic effluents and sewerage. When rivers are dry, their banks and beds are encroaching by people. Groundwater is being depleted at a faster rate that exceeds the natural recharge in many arid and semi-arid regions. This is resulting in a progressively declining water table and hence increasing salinity ingress in coastal areas.
10. It is pertinent to note here that by the 1970s nearly one third of the world's thirty-two previously active democracies have reverted to some form of authoritarianism forming what has been called as the second reverse wave of democratization.

References

Agarwal, Aradhana (2006), 'Special Economic Zones: Revisiting the Policy Debate' in *Economic and Political Weekly*, 4 November 2006, Mumbai, pp. 4533- 4535.

Avritzer, Leonardo (2002), Democracy and the Public Space in Latin America, *Princeton University Press, New Jersey,* p. 23.

Bargh, Maria (2007), *Resistance: An Indigenous Response to Neo-liberalism*, Huia Publishers, Wellington, p. 160.

Beckwith, Karen (1997), 'Movement in Context: Women and Miner's Campaigns in Britain', in Edmondson, Ricca (ed), *The Political Context of Collective Action: Power, Argumentation and Democracy,* Routledge, London and New York.

Berkes, Fikrett (ed.) (1989), *Common Property Resources; Ecology and Community-Based Sustainable Development,* Belhaven Press, London, pp. 7-15.

Bhattacharya, Dwaipayan et al. (2004), *Interrogating Social Capital: The Indian Experience,* Sage Publications, New Delhi, p. 306.

Boyle, Alan E. and Anderson, Michael R. (1998), *Human Rights*

Approaches to Environmental Protection, Oxford University Press, New York, p. 3.

Bromley, Daniel W. (ed.) (1992), *Making the Commons at Work: Theory, Practice and Policy,* Institute for Contemporary Studies Press, San Francisco, p. 4.

Bromley, Daniel W. (1999), 'The Commons, Common Property and Environmental Policy', in Bromley, Daniel W. (ed.), *Sustaining Development: Environmental Resources in Developing Countries,* Edward Elgar, Cheltenham. pp. 2, 75-76.

Bruns, Bryan Randolph and Meizen-Dick, Ruth S. (ed.), (2000), *Negotiating Water Rights,* Vistaar Publications, New Delhi, pp. 33-34.

Bryant, Raymond L. & Bailey, Sinéad (1997), *Third World Political Ecology,* Routledge, London and New York, pp. 182- 183.

Brysk, Alison (2002), *Globalization and Human Rights,* University of California Press, Berkeley, p. 11.

Calabrese, Andrew and Burgelman, Jean-Claude (1999), *Communication, Citizenship and Social Policy: Rethinking the Limits of the Welfare State,* Rowman and Littlefield, Lanham, p. 246.

Campbell, Tom et al. (2003), *Protecting Human Rights: Instruments and Institutions*, Oxford University Press, New York, p. 25.

Carens, Joseph H. (1993), *Democracy and Possessive Individualism: The Intellectual Legacy of C.B. Macpherson,* SUNY Press, Albany, p. 129.

Carter, Neil (2007), The Politics of the Environment: Ideas, Activism, Policy, *Cambridge University Press,* Cambridge.

Cavanagh, John and Mander, Jerry (2004), *Alternatives to Economic Globalization: A Better World is Possible,* Berrett-Koehler Publishers, San Francisco.

Claude, Richard Pierre (2006), *Human Rights in the World Community,* University of Pennsylvania Press, Pennsylvania.

Crate, Susan Alexandra (2006), *Cows, Kin, and Globalization: An Ethnography of Sustainability,* Rowman Altamira, Lanham.

Dalby, Simon (2003), 'Globalization, Geography and Environmental Security', in Kofman, Eleonore and Youngs, Gillian (ed), *Globalization: Theory and Practice*, Continuum Publishers, London, pp. 36-37.

D'Cruz, Sharon and Raikar, Avinash V. (2006), 'Democratic Management of Common Property in Goa; From 'Gaonkarias' and 'Communidades' to Gram Sabhas', *Economic and Political Weekly*, 4 February 2006, Vol. XLI, No. 5, Mumbai, p. 439.

Degaonkar, Chaya and Gills, Dong-Sook S. (2002), 'The Economic Reform and Feminization of Labour in Agriculture: The Case of Rural Village Women in India', in Gills, Dong-Sook S. and Piper, Nicola, *Women and Work in Globalizing Asia,* Routledge, London and New York, p. 85.

Déjeant-Pons, Maguelonne and Pallemaerts, Marc (2002), *Human Rights and the Environment,* Council of Europe.

Dhar, Subroto (2006), *Tapping Local Resources to Increase Panchayat Incomes, Economic and Political Weekly,* 8 April 2006, Mumbai, pp. 1372-1375.

Dierks, Rosa Gomez (2001), Introduction to Globalization: Political and Economic Perspectives for the New Century, *Rowman and Littlefield,* Lanham, p. 27.

Doyle, Timothy (2004), *Environmental Movements in Minority and Majority Worlds: A Global Perspective,* Rutgers University Press, New Brunswick, pp. 2-5.

Eder, Klaus (1993), *The New Politics of Class: Social Movements and Cultural Dynamics in Advanced Societies,* Sage Publishers, p. 5.

Ekins, Paul (2003), 'After Seattle: What Next for Trade and Environment?', in Berkhout, France et al. (ed.), *Negotiating Environmental Changes; New Perspective from Social Science*, Edward Elgar, Cheltenham, UK, pp. 166-169.

Elian, George (1979), *The Principle of Sovereignty over Natural Resource,* Martinus Nijhoff Publishers, Netherlands, p. 146.

Evans, Tony (1998), *Human Rights Fifty Years on: A Reappraisal,* Manchester University Press, Manchester, p. 4.

Fernandez, Luis A. (2008), *Policing Dissent: Social Control and the Anti-globalization Movement,* Rutgers University Press, New Brunswick, p. 15.

Field, John (2005), *Social Capital and Lifelong Learning,* The Policy Press, University of Bristol, Bristol, p. 121.

Foweraker, Joe (1995), *Theorizing Social Movements,* Pluto Press, London, p. 7.

Gaile, Gary L. and Willmott, Cort J. (2006), *Geography in America at the Dawn of the 21st Century,* Oxford University Press, New York, p. 103.

Gilpin, Robert and Gilpin, Jean M. (2003), *Global Political*

Economy: Understanding the International Economic Order, Princeton University Press, Princeton, p. 288.

Gills, Dong-Sook S. (2007), 'The Political Economy of Globalization and Grassroots Movements', in Anthony G. McGrew and Nana K. Poku, *Globalization, Development and Human Society,* Polity Press, Cambridge, p. 198.

Giugni, Marco G. (2002), 'Explaining Cross-National Similarities among Social Movement', in Smith, Jackie and Johnston, Hank, *Globalization and Resistance: Transnational Dimensions of Social Movements,* Rowman and Littlefield, Lanham, pp. 14 - 15.

Goldstone, Jack A. (2003), 'Bridging Institutionalized and Non-institutionalized Politics', in Goldstone, Jack A., *States, Parties, and Social Movements,* Cambridge University Press, Cambridge, pp. 1-2.

Guidry, John A. et al. (2000), 'Globalizations and Social Movements', in Guidry, John A. et al, *Globalizations and Social Movements: Culture, Power, and the Transnational Public Sphere,* University of Michigan Press, Ann Arbor, p. 5.

Hanagan, Michael (1998), 'Social Movements: Incorporation, Disengagement, and Opportunities–A Long View', in Giugni, Marco et al, *From Contention to Democracy: Social Movements and their Potential for Change*, Rowman & Littlefield, Lanham, p. 3.

Hancock, Jan (2003), *Environmental Human Rights: Power, Ethis, and Law*, Ashgate Publishing, Surrey, p. 73.

Hanna, Susan S. et al. (ed.) (1996), *Rights to Nature; Ecological, Economic, Cultural and Political Principles of Institutions for the Environment*, Island Press, Washington D.C., pp. 9-35.

Harawira, Makere Stewart (2005), *The New Imperial Order: Indigenous Responses to Globalization,* Zed Books Limited, London, p. 8.

Hardin, Garret (1968), *The Tragedy of Commons*, *Science,* American Association for the Advancement of Science Publishers, Washington, 162 (1968), pp. 1243-1248.

Harvey, David (2005), *The New Imperialism,* Oxford University Press, New York, pp. 188-189.

Held, David et al. (1999), *Global Transformations: Politics, Economics and Culture,* Stanford University Press, California, p. 10.

Holton, Robert J. (1992), *Economy and Society,* Routledge, London and New York, p. 140.

Hopper, Paul (2007), *Understanding Cultural Globalization,* Polity Press, Cambridge.

Gills, Dong-Sook S. (2007), 'The Political Economy of Globalization and Grassroot Movements', in McGrew, Anthony G. and Poku, Nana K., *Globalization, Development and Human Security*, Polity Press, Cambridge, p. 9.

Ingram, Helen M. et al. (1995), 'Interest Groups and Environmental Policy', in Lester, James P., *Environmental Politics and Policy: Theories and Evidence,* Duke University Press, Durham, pp. 119 - 120.

Ishay, Micheline (2004), *The History of Human Rights: From Ancient Times to the Globalization Era,* University of California Press, Berkley, p. 264.

Jameson, Fredric and Miyoshi, Masao (1998), *The Cultures of Globalization,* Duke University Press, Durham, p. 374.

Jensen, Nathan Michael (2006), *Nation-states and the Multinational Corporation: A Political Economy of Foreign Direct Investment,* Princeton University Press, Princeton, New Jersey, p. 277.

Johnston, Hank et al. (1994), 'Identities, Grievances and New Social Movements', in Laraña, Enrique et al, *New Social Movements: From Ideology to Identity,* Temple University Press, Philadelphia, pp. 3-10.

Johnston, Hank and Noakes, John A. (2005), *Frames of Protest: Social Movements and the Framing Perspective*, Rowman and Littlefield, Lanham, p. 1.

Joekes, Susan et al. (1994), 'Gender, Environment and Population', in Ghai, Dharam, *Development and Environment: Sustaining People and Nature*, Blackwell publishers/UNRISD, Oxford, pp. 137-138.

Kamieniecki, Sheldon (1993), 'Emerging Forces in Global Environmental Politics', in Kamieniecki, Sheldon (ed.), *Environmental Politics in the International Arena: Movements, Parties, Organizations, and Policy,* SUNY Press, New York, pp. 2-3.

Kirkpatrick, Colin and Lee, Norman (1997), 'Market Liberalization and Environmental Assessment', in Wilson, Frank A., *Towards Sustainable Project Development*, Edward Eglar Publishers, Cheltenham, UK, Lyme, US, pp. 58-63.

Krapivin, Vladimir F. and Varotsos, Costas (2007), *Globalization and Sustainable Development: Environmental Agendas,* Praxis Publishing Limited, Chichester, p. 63.

Landman, Todd (2006), *Studying Human Rights,* Routledge, London and New York, p. 4.

Lee, Yok-shiu F. and So, Alvin Y. (ed.) (1999), *Asia's Environmental Movements: Comparative Perspectives,* M.E. Sharpe, Armonk NY, p. 5.

Lynch, Katherine L. (2003), *The Forces of Economic Globalization: Challenges to the Regime of International Commercial Arbitration,* Kluwer Law International, Netherlands, p. 44.

Marks, Stephen P. (2004), *The Right to Development: A Primer,* Sage, New Delhi, p. 1985.

Marothia, Dinesh K. (2005), *Institutional Reforms in Canal Irrigation System: Lessons from Chhattisgarh, Economic and Political Weekly,* 9 June 2005, Mumbai, pp. 3074 - 3077.

McAdam, Doug et al. (1996), 'Introduction: Opportunities, Mobilizing Structures and Framing Processes—Toward a Synthetic, Comparative Perspective on Social Movements', in McAdam, Doug, et al. (ed.), *Comparative Perspectives on Social Movements: Political Opportunities, Mobilizing Structures, and Cultural Framings,* Cambridge University Press, Cambridge.

McGoodwin, James R. (1995), *Crisis in the World's Fisheries: People, Problems, and Policies,* Stanford University Press, California, p. 94.

Mendieta, Eduardo (2007), *Global Fragments: Globalizations, Latinamericanisms, and Critical Theory,* SUNY Press, Albany, p. 113.

Nayar, Baldev Raj (2007), 'Globalization, Geopolitics and India', in Nayar, Baldev Raj (ed.), *Globalization and Politics in India,* Oxford University Press, New Delhi, p. 1-2.

OECD Environmental Outlook (2001), Organization for Economic Co-operation and Development, OECD Publishing, Paris, p. 47.

Oommen, T. K. (2004), *Nation, Civil Society and Social Movements: Essays in Political Sociology,* Sage Publishers, New Delhi, p. 18.

Orend, Brian (2002), *Human Rights: Concept and Context,* Broadview Press, Peterborough, p. 18.

Ostrum, Elinor (1999), *Governing the Commons; The Evolution of*

Institutions of Collective Action, Cambridge University Press, Cambridge, pp. 1-13.

Page, Edward A. (2006), *Climate Change, Justice and Future Generations*, Edward Elgar Publishing, Cheltenham, p. 59.

Pearce, David (1995), *Blueprint–4, Capturing Global Environmental Value*, Earthscan Publishers, London, pp. 80 - 81.

Perkins, Stephen J. and Shortland, Susan M. (2006), *Strategic International Human Resource Management: Choices and Consequences in Multinational People Management,* Kogan Page Publishers, London, p. 29.

Peters, Rebecca Todd (2006), *In Search of the Good Life: The Ethics of Globalization,* Continuum International Publishing Group, New York, p. 103.

Porta, Donatella Della & Diani, Mario (2006), *Social Movements: An Introduction,* Blackwell Publishing, Malden, USA, pp. 1-6.

Powell, Frederick W. (2007), *The Politics of Civil Society: Neoliberalism or Social Left?,* The Policy Press, University of Bristol, Bristol, p. 199.

Purdue, Derrick (2007), 'Dimensions of Civil Society', in Purdue, Derrick (ed.), *Civil Societies and Social Movements: Potentials and Problems,* Routledge, London and New York, p. 7.

Rigg, Jonathan (2007), *An Everyday Geography of the Global South*, Routledge, London and New York, p. 167.

Rootes, Christopher (1999), 'Environmental Movements: From the Local to the Global', in Rootes, Christopher, *Environmental Movements: Local, National, and Global,* Routledge, London and New York, p. 2.

Roush, G. Jon (1991), 'Introduction', in Donald Snow, *Voices from the Environmental Movement: Perspectives for a New Era,* Island Press, Washington D. C., p. 3.

Rupert, Mark (2000), *Ideologies of Globalization: Contending Visions of a New World Order,* Routledge, London and New York, p. 43.

Sachs, Wolfgang (1999), *Planet Dialectics: Explorations in Environment and Development,* Zed Books, London, pp. 129-138.

Schellnhuber, Hans-Joachim (2001), *World in Transition: Conservation and Sustainable use of the Biosphere,* Earthscan Publishers, London.

Shellenberger, Michael and Nordhaus, Ted (2007), *Break Through:*

From the Death of Environmentalism to the Politics of Possibility, Houghton Mifflin Company, New York, p. 21.

Shiva, Vandana (1991), *Ecology and the Politics of Survival: Conflicts over Natural Resources in India,* Sage Publications, New Delhi, pp. 24-26, 57.

Shiva, Vandana (1999), 'Ecological Balance in the Era of Globalization', in Nicholas Low, *Global Ethics and Environment,* Routledge, London and New York, p. 50-58.

Shiva, Vandana, (2002), *Water Wars; Privatization, Pollution and Profit,* India Research Press, New Delhi, pp. 26 - 27.

Singh, Katar (1994), *Managing Common Pool Resources: Principles and Case Studies,* Oxford University Press, New Delhi, pp. 4-61.

Singh, Bishwa Nath (2004), 'Economic Reforms and Environment: The Indian Evidence', in Singh, Jinithesh Kumar and Das, Debedra Kumar (ed.), *Environmental Economics and Development*, Deep and Deep Publications, New Delhi, pp. 77-80.

Smith, Robert Leo (1972), *The Ecology of Man: An Ecosystem Approach*, Harper and Row Publishers, University of Wisconsin- Madison, p. 413.

Synott, John P. (2004), *Global and International Studies: Transdisciplinary Perspectives,* Thomson Learning, Nelson, p. 149.

Szymanski, Ann-Marie E. (2003), *Pathways to Prohibition: Radicals, Moderates and Social Movement Outcomes,* Duke University Press, Durham, p. 6.

Tarrow, Sidney (2002), 'From Lumping to Splitting: Specifying Globalization and Resistance', in Smith, Jackie G. and Hank Johnston (ed.), *Globalization and Resistance: Transnational Dimensions of Social Movements,* Rowman and Littlefield, Lanham, p. 235.

Wagle, Subodh (2002), 'The Long March for Livelihoods: Struggle Against the Narmada Dam in India' in Byrne, John et al, *Environmental Justice: Discourses in International Political Economy*, Transaction Publishers, Edison, NJ, pp. 77- 78.

Walters, Gregory J. (2002), *Human Rights in an Information Age: A Philosophical Analysis,* University of Toronto Press, Toronto, pp. 96- 97.

Wilson, Richard A. (1997), *Human Rights, Culture and Context:*

Anthropological Perspectives, Pluto Press, London.

Youngs, Gillian (2003), International Relations as we Enter the Twenty-first Century, in Kofman, Eleonore and Youngs, Gillian (ed), *Globalization: Theory and Practice,* Continuum, London, pp. 7-8.

Zarsky, Lyuba (2002), 'Introduction: Conflicts, Ethics and Globalization', in Zarsky, Lyuba (ed.), *Human Rights and the Environment: Conflicts and Norms in a Globalizing World,* Earthscan Publishers, London, p. 1.

2

Globalization and Water Privatization: A Survey of Developed and Developing Countries

2.1 Introduction

Water is perceived in a number of ways by common people as well as scholars; as commons, as a commodity, as a basic right and as a sacred resource or divinity. Traditionally, water, perceived as a Common Property Resource means, 'a class of resource for which exclusion is difficult and joint use involves sub-stractability'. Water is one of the basic necessities, thus a fundamental human right without which life cannot sustain. In ancient Indian context water is considered as a sacred resource, an object that is divine and part of natural environment sustaining it and sustained by it (Iyer, 2003). Contemporary western view held water as a commodity to merchandise and not as a free natural good on the perception that if water is considered as a commodity, water market and prices would be established, as such sustainability would be taken care of, equitable distribution would be ensured and conflicts would automatically be resolved by market forces.

At present 120 crore of people spread across forty countries do not have access to safe water and 240 crore of people lack adequate sanitation services. Over the next twenty years, the world's population will increase from the present 6.4 billion to an estimated 7.2 billion whereas the average supply of water per person is expected to fall by one third. According to United Nations, by 2025 as many as 500 crore of people will face water shortage. Because global consumption of water is doubling every 20 years and it is expected that by 2025 the demand for freshwater will rise more than 50 percent of the present need. Water scarcity is estimated to cause annual global loss of 350 million tones of food production by 2025. Estimates suggest that at least five million deaths per year can be attributed to water born diseases.

In the case of India, the gap between the demand and supply of water is increasing rapidly. In 1951, the per capita availability of fresh water in India was 3,450 m^3 per year. In 1999 it was approximately 1,250 m^3 per capita year and will reduce to 760 m^3 by the year 2050 (Ballabh, 2009). Population growth, climate change, over use/misuse of water and pollution of the available water sources are the principal causes of the crisis. Thus in the international discourses on water resource management, water scarcity has taken as a starting point for policy agendas, since 1970s. Redressing this problem especially in rural areas of developing economies has at best focused on the issue of quantity; the quality aspects remain overlooked (Pascual, 2009).

The United Nations Conference on Human Environment held in Stockholm [1] in 1972 and the United Nations Water Conference held in Mardel Plata [2] in 1977 were identified as the first major steps towards this direction (Salman and Lank Ford, 2004) While the Stockholm and Mar del Plata conferences were primarily concerned with the task of providing clear drinking water and sanitation, the rest of the international conferences from Dublin Conference in 1992 to the Kyoto Forum 2003 were steps in developing the privatization agenda.

The agencies which promoted this agenda are three inter-related organizations—the World Water Council, the World Water Forum and the Global Water Partnership with strong representation of multi-national water companies and aid agencies with pronounced privatization bias. The Dublin Conference of 1992 was a significant move in evolving the privatization agenda. Principle 4 of the Dublin Statement proclaims that, "Water has an economic value in all its competing uses and should be recognized as an economic good". This conference recognized the past failures in realizing the economic value of water, which in their opinion ultimately lead to the wasteful practices (Singh, 2004).

2.2 Water Privatization

The advocacy of privatization in relation to water sector has its origin in the economic process of globalization and related dynamics of liberalization and privatization. The privatization agenda had found its way into several national policies across the globe since globalization. The state is surrounded by new actors like World Bank and Multi National Corporations to whom the decision-making power of the state is shifted. Market-oriented policies have developed by the state in order to cope with the Structural Adjustment Programmes (SAPs) as part of the neo-liberal economic policies. The state is trying to readjust to this new situation by commercializing the common properties, deregulating the industrial monopolies and privatizing the service sectors (Finger and Allouche, 2002).

Privatization of water involves destatisation of water, that is, to free it from the political-bureaucratic control of the state on the dictum that private is efficient, profitable, transparent, flexible, adaptable and innovative (Petrella, 2001). Water distribution services, traditionally by municipal governments in most countries are taken over by corporations either national or multinational. Unlike the earlier contract operators of civic authorities these are hugely powerful entities, with enormous financial backing of international financial agencies like World Bank, International Monetary Fund, Asian Development Bank, etc. As such the scale of operations has undergone an order of magnitude change; these MNCs are in a position to establish control over whole sections in the water sector.

In the last ten years there have been several new developments in the privatization of water. The emergence of bottled drinking water is an important facet of commoditization of water. While hydropower has been privatized for over ten years, privatization of irrigation is still to start in a full-fledged manner. On the other hand, privatization of water supply in cities and towns is very much a reality and several cases at various stages of development and implementation are really seen in different parts of the world. Through this privatization process, water is turned into a commodity, priced and sold in the market usually on the basis of ability to pay (Barlow and Clarke, 2003).

2.3 Models of Water Privatization

Since water is such a vital part of the economy and infrastructure, it is not surprising that there has been an enormous push for the privatization of water services. As a result in many parts of the world, the water sector has seen large-scale privatization. Water privatization means transferring water management services to private companies. The state can earmark a certain quantum of water from a specified source and ask the private party, who is then a contractor or licensee, to distribute it in a certain area. It may include ownership, control, collection, purification and distribution of water as well as treatment and disposal of wastewater and sewage services in an area. Traditionally, the local self-government institutions such as the panchayats, municipalities or corporations have provided these services with subsidies (Sampath, 2004). Privatization is possible in two ways, i.e., privatization of the existing water supply and sanitation services or privatization of the water distribution systems in a newly developed cities, townships, etc. It is felt that the former is difficult because the water tariff rates are very low and for achieving the full cost recovery plus profit the private companies have to increase the tariff which will evoke resistance among the consumers (Iyer, 2003).

There are several models of water privatization that are currently in trend in different parts of the world. Private firms can be brought into the operation and/or development of water services in different ways, which vary by their scope, extent of responsibilities and the contracting authority. Depending on the degree of privatization these models can be broadly categorized into:

1. **Service Contract**: In this kind of partial privatization the public authority retains overall responsibility for the operation and maintenance of the system and contracts out specific components like meter reading, billing and maintenance, for one to three years to a private company. Usually the private company refrains from investment attaching no financial risks to it and also no direct legal relationship with the consumer (e.g. Mexico City).
2. **Lease Contract:** As the name suggests, the civic authority leases out or appoints a private company for managing the facility. This is another way of service contract where the ownership remains in the public; private company is usually not responsible for new investments or expansion, e.g. Abidjan in the initial phases (Finger and Allouche, 2002).
3. **Management Contract**: In management contract, responsibility for operation and maintenance transfers to a private company for five or ten years with a definite fee pay by the government authority to the company. The company does not take the risks, as the public sector retains responsibility for investment and expansion. The public sector may also choose to keep control of billing and revenue collection (Holland, 2005).
4. **Build, Operate, Own and Transfer (BOOT):** In this popular model the infrastructure development of water treatment plant transfers to a private party under long-term contracts. The private operator is required to finance, construct, operate and maintain the facility for the specified period and then turned over to the municipality or the contract can be renewed. [3] The public authority assumes the related risks in water distribution while, the investor bills and retains user charges for the contract period. An example of BOOT model is Rasmara Scheme of Sheonath river in Chhattisgarh in India.

5. **Divestiture:** In this model, the government or public authority awards full ownership of a water source to a private party for a specific period under a renewable contract. The private sector firm is then expected to take the risks and recoup investments or profits. This model cedes tremendous power over water to private firms. A company or group of companies monopolizes ground water or surface water over an extensive area and they take water without any restriction. Competition is limited through the process of bids on divestiture.
6. **Joint Venture:** The local governments can share ownership with private stakeholders in a joint venture. In this system the company itself may either own the assets or be given a franchise by the local government either through a lease contract or through concession arrangements. The option is popular in Central and Eastern Europe (Finger and Allouche, 2002).
7. **Concession:** Concession is a long term contract in which the private company takes full charge of the system, takes responsibility for water delivery and is also responsible for the expansion, new investments, recovery of bills etc. (e.g. Buenos Aires).
8. **Public-Private Partnerships**: A typical P3 involves joint venture between a transnational water company and the local government in which former contracts to design, build and operate water treatment and supplies for a predetermined time period. As a popular model it implies public participation, democracy and accountability. In the decade that has gone by, over US$ 25 billion worth of investment has been made in P3s across the world, over 95 percent of this in developing countries alone (Sharma, 2003). [4]
9. **Consortium:** A consortium works by several companies and interested parties joining together to run a utility in water distribution. In this way, they do not compete with each other, e.g. Cochambaba in Bolivia (Holland, 2005).

10. **Privatization through Appropriation**: This model of privatization is not on the basis of a contract entered between a governmental authority and a private firm. Instead in this model an individual or a private company took control over a source of water through overexploitation and thereby violates the rights of others. The case of Plachimada in Kerala is an instance in this regard.
11. **Decentralization:** Decentralization as a concept is very close to privatization is in fact an underlying framework within which privatization should be located. It is the devolution of power and transfer of responsibility from the central government to sub-ordinate or quasi- government organizations or to the private sector. The World Bank distinguishes between four different forms of decentralization, i.e. political, administrative, fiscal, and market decentralization, the last being more or less equivalent to privatization.
12. **Deregulation:** Deregulation is another alternative suggested by World Bank to global water issues like privatization. It reduces the legal constraints on private participation in service provision or allows competition among private suppliers. In recent years privatization and deregulation have become more attractive alternatives to governments in developing countries (Finger and Allouche, 2002).

2.4 Role of World Bank in Water Privatization Until 1990

The World Bank puts greater priority when it comes to supplying people with water. The World Bank's role in helping member countries in the water sector is rooted in its very mission to finance infrastructure projects, which developing countries could not finance by themselves. It is the single largest source of funds for water projects in the world and thus plays a significant role in determining not only the number of water projects identified and financed but also in guiding the water policy making in developing countries. Indeed, the water sector comprises a significant portion of World Bank lending, accounting for about fifteen percent of the Bank's cumulative lending (Moore and Sklar, 1998). Within the World Bank, several organizational structures are involved constituting the water sector policies. The three most active ones are (1) the Water Supply and Sanitation Division–which is divided between a Rural Water and Sanitation Program and an Urban Water and Sanitation Program, (2) the Global Water Unit and (3) the Private Sector Development Division. All these organizational units combine to constitute the World Bank's multi-faceted approach to water (Finger and Allouche, 2002).

The World Bank has been an important actor in the global water sector as well as for many of the developing countries. Since 1950s, the World Bank invests substantially in different projects pertaining to irrigation, water supply, sanitation, flood control and hydropower (Moore and Sklar, 1998). Since its inception, water projects particularly large-scale dams, has been part of World Bank's portfolio of projects with an investment of 79 percent of Bank loans for construction of large dams.

The Mar Del Plata Action Plan, 1977 was a land mark in promoting increased investments in drinking water and sanitation sectors, greater role to donor agencies and reforms in water management practices at local, national and international levels. Thereby the 1980s were marked by a shift in focus towards a sharp increase in investments for improving access to clean drinking water supplies and sanitation. Together the declaration of United Nations International Decade on Water Supply and Sanitation (1981-1990) with objective to provide service to all and to extend safe, clean drinking water supplies and sanitation services to everyone by 1990 was a move towards this direction. As a result total global investment in the water sector was more than US$ 100 billion, with national governments contributing about 65 percent and international agencies, such as the World Bank, contributing the remaining one-third. [5]

2.5 World Bank and Water Sector Reforms Since 1990

Even though World Bank (WB) financed projects in the water sector have contributed to significant achievements, it has often encountered implementation, operational and social problems (Moore and Sklar, 1998). [6] Moreover, the global move towards an integrated approach to water management, the internal reforms within the Bank to formulate sectoral policies, plus the neo-liberal economic reforms, prompted the Bank to develop a Sustainable Water Resource Management Policy in 1993 in its Policy Paper. [7] Through this policy the Bank tries to ends up the critical water management issues with a serious simplification i.e. privatization rises as an answer to all environmental concerns. This new concept of global water vision regrouped the different World Bank water projects like, irrigation, sanitation, etc. into one single concept when dealing with the water sector (Finger and Allouche, 2002).

Without any doubt World Bank is one of the most important actors in the global water sector, be it in terms of financial aid or in terms of general policy-making. By the end of 1991, more than US$ 19 billion had been lent for irrigation and drainage, US$ 12 billion for water supply and sewerage, and about US$ 9 billion for hydropower projects, the total representing more than 15 percent of total Bank lending. The World Bank currently supervises eighty-six water and sanitation projects with loans totalling US$ 5.3 billion (Finger and Allouche, 2002).

2.6 Theoretical Rhetoric of World Bank Policies

The World Bank was established with an initial objective to finance infrastructure development in developing countries based on Keynesian economics whereby the nation-state should play a key role in development. However, this changed considerably after 1981 with a deep cultural transformation from Keynesian economics to neo-liberal economics that seeks to reduce the role of the state. The World Development Report, 1994 reflected these new priorities of World Bank infrastructure development that gave stress on technological innovations, decreasing role of state as well as larger role of private sector and the social and environmental concerns (Finger and Allouche, 2002).

2.6.1 Reduced Role of State in the Water Sector: By introducing a new approach to infrastructure development the Bank concluded that in developing countries the performance of government in infrastructure has been disappointing. In the water sector the delivery of services has been hampered by technical inefficiency and outright waste. In the management of water resources wrong political priorities and managerial inability appeared to be the major hindrances (Finger and Allouche, 2002). Thus the Bank proposes three compromising measures when it comes to water service provision, i.e. the wider application of commercial principles to service providers, the broader use of competition and the increased involvement of users. The Bank argued the private sector participation will reduce the financial burden on the state and will provide water to those people who presently have no access.

The Bank has incorporated all these considerations into the concept of Sustainable Water Resource Management while it is implementing the proposals through Structural Adjustment Program conditions (Finger and Allouche, 2002). Through its affiliate, the International Finance Corporation (IFC), the WB has dramatically accelerated water privatization in developing countries by making water supply and structural adjustment loans conditional on privatization. A review of its lending patterns in the water and sanitation sector shows that approximately 90 percent of the loans included requirements promoting water privatization (Singh, 2004). [8]

2.6.2 Concept of Sustainable Water Resource Management: Water Resource Management as a concept introduced in a 1993 World Bank Policy Paper that replaces the concept of Water Resources Development, which is judged to be unsustainable. The Bank's approach is based on two guiding principles–environmental and economical sustainability that requires the formulation of water resource management policies within the context of a comprehensive analytical framework. Such a framework will protect the aquatic ecosystem through the establishment of improved co-ordination among institutions, consistent regulations, coherent policies and targeted governmental actions. Economic sustainability in water management must be improved through water markets and pricing, greater reliance on decentralization, user participation, privatization and financial autonomy (Holland, 2005).

Other general elements of this policy include: national policy reforms and country specific strategies for water resource management, rehabilitation of existing water systems, extensive water conservation as well as protection of ground water sources and pollution control for industries, greater involvement of the private sector, Non Governmental Organizations (NGOs) and user groups, modernization in irrigation and hydropower, water-harvesting methods and watershed conservation practices, etc. (Moore and Skalr, 1998). Thus, the underlying assumption of water resource management is water should treat as an economic good.

2.6.3 Water as an Economic Good: The transformation of water from a Common Property Resource to an economic good is a precondition for privatizing water. In a theoretical level, the definition of water as an economic good appears to be quite simple in the words of John Briscoe, one of the World Bank's senior water advisers; he says, 'like any other good, water has an economic value to users, who are willing to pay for it. Like any other good consumers will use water so long as the benefits from use of an additional cubic meter exceed the costs so incurred' (Moore and Skalr, 1998). The Dublin Principle 4 reiterates this theoretical rhetoric by saying; 'water has an economic value in all its competing uses and should be recognized as an economic good'. Though the recipient countries have yet to accept that water is an economic good, the World Bank is forcing the argument on developing nation's governments through its water sector reforms.

2.7 Role of other Financial Agencies in the Water Sector

While the World Bank is promoting privatization of water through Structural Adjustment Programs and conditions the World Trade Organization (WTO) are instituting water privatization through free-trade rules embodied in General Agreement on Trade in Services (GATS). The GATS is intended to liberalize trade in services, including water and sanitation services (Holland, 2005). [9] It clearly favours trade in services by minimizing the capacity of governments to regulate the market forces by making the WTO provisions binding on governments and non-governmental bodies (Sharma, 2003). The European Union Commission used GATS as a way of creating new business opportunities for European water companies and has invited companies to discuss their objectives and obstacles in markets. The pro-privatization bias is also at the heart of EU's Water Initiative that boosted private sector involvement through subsidized Public-Private Partnerships (Holland, 2005). [10]

The WB is not alone in financing privatization adventures in water sector. The International Monetary Fund (IMF), the Asian Development Bank (ADB), the German Development Bank (KFW), the European Investment Bank (EIB) and the European Bank for Reconstruction and Development (EBRD) have joined the race. Like WB the IMF also imposed conditions of full cost recovery or privatization in 12 of its 40 loans granted in the year 2000. On 16 January 2001, ADB's Board of Directors approved a comprehensive water policy that recognizes water as a socially vital economic good. While the ADB has already initiated public-private partnerships in ten capital cities of Asia, the KFW has pumped in nearly US$ 400 million into 26 public-private partnership projects across Albania, Montenegro and Jordan (Holland, 2005).

2.8 Water Business

Water privatization indeed led to water business. The entire water sector, including wastewater treatment is a big business now, estimated to be worth US $200 billion. According to 1999 OECD summary of Environmental Business International Statistics, water utilities account for US$ 73.2 billion, baring agricultural and industrial output out of the total global environmental market of US$ 453 billion for goods and services (Sharma, 2003). After a decade of sweeping privatization, 460 million people around the world are now dependent on private water corporations for their supply. If the current trend prevails, the European water giants like Vivendi, Suez and Thames Water will control the global water market of the next decade. An investigation by International Council of Investigative Journalists (ICIJ) showed that six globally active water companies works very close with the WB over a period of 12 years have increased their business from about a dozen countries to about 58 at present (Singh, 2004). [11]

Private investment in the water sector thus provided an amicable climate for water business, in concrete terms, water marketisation, water markets and water pricing. Water marketisation is not synonymous with water privatization; the term refers rather to, 'a set of linked transformations related to establishment, private property rights, full-cost pricing of water, market mechanisms for the exchange of water-related goods and services, private actors in water supply services, international trade in water and the declining role of state'. The set of forces pushing water marketisation are the processes of structural adjustment, privatization, trade liberalization, neo-liberal economic reform and the corporate strategies of multinational firms (Conca, 2005).

2.9 Water Privatization in Developed and Developing Countries

The water industry was not subjected to heavy privatization such as the energy, telecommunication or pharmaceutical sectors until 1997. Privatized water was an exception in the European Union (excluding Spain) with France and Britain having majority of the population receiving water and sanitation services by national private operators. Within the other nations of Europe, privatization has been basically restricted to the Czech Republic, Hungary and to a more limited extent, Poland. However, the present trend in Europe and in the rest of the world is towards a privatization of water supply and sanitation services, so that major responsibility of the state is transferred to private stakeholders. A steady shift towards privatization has occurred mainly in the Asia/Pacific Basin and in Latin America, while recently African countries and North America have opened their water delivery services to private investors (Cesano and Gustafsson, 2000). Table 2.1 will clearly illustrate the proportion water privatization in Europe, America, Africa and Asia (Singh, 2004).

Table 2.1: Proportion of Water and Sanitation Services Privatized (1997 and 2010 projected)

Region	percent Privatized 1997	percent Privatized 2010	Value of privatized market (US$ billion)
Western Europe*	20	35	10
Central & East Europe	4	20	4
North America	5	15	9
Latin America	4	60	9
Africa	3	33	3
Asia	1	20	10

*Excluding France and UK

Source: Vivendi (1999).

2.10 Water Privatization in Developed Countries

Industrialized countries are of course confronted with very different problems compared to developing countries when it comes to water resource management as part of substantial public sector reforms. Like the World Bank and water TNCs in the South, in the North three organizations are promoting a standardized approach in water management following the Dublin principles. They are, the OECD (Organization for Economic Corporation and Development), the Council of Europe, and the European Union (Finger and Allouche, 2002).

Despite the overarching international policies and guidelines, the models used for managing water resources privately still differ considerably from country to country. For instance, France has a very weak regulatory structure compared to Britain, which moved in 1980s towards total privatization and as a result of some quite painful experiences, developed an interesting model of regulation. The regulatory system in Germany appears to be complicated and fragmented involving numerous actors. In US, big disparities exist between different states and where interstate co-operation within the larger federal structure is not always ensured. A closer look at the experiences of developed countries reveal the internal disparities and the degree of water privatization (Finger and Allouche, 2002).

2.10.1 Great Britain: In Britain, the Water Act of 1989 was enacted under Margaret Thatcher's Conservative government which led to privatization of water authorities as a follow-up to the EU's various environmental directives. The government argued for privatization on two counts: privatization would result in more efficient operation and private owners would fund the investments needed to meet tighter water quality standards and make up for past underinvestment. Before 1989, the water industry in England and Wales consisted of ten publicly owned water authorities and twenty-nine privately owned water supply companies. Initially the government privatized the ten previously public regional water and sewage companies in England and Wales through divestiture (sale of assets). As a first step to privatization, the government wrote off all the debts of the water authorities and sold to private companies with the entire infrastructure and the buildings for a twenty-five year contract.

The government split the water authorities, into two divisions. It transferred the main environmental regulatory responsibilities to the National Rivers Authority and converted the remaining water and sewage services into private companies to be sold on the stock exchange. The government also set up a new regulatory agency, Ofwat, which sets the maximum price that water companies can charge. The agency's primary duty is to ensure that the companies can finance themselves by earning a reasonable rate of return on capital. One of the major objectives in the new regulatory design was to avoid political interference in the regulatory process. As many as 2.7 million people became shareholders and made a tidy profit. Pre-profits of the privatized companies rose by 147 percent between 1990 and 1998. The companies raised the charges and gained US$ 28 billion between 1989 and 1998. Increasing numbers had their water supplies cuts off when they could not pay. As a result in Britain the 1998 Water Act stipulated that it is illegal to cut off water service (Holland, 2005).

Between 1973 and 1999 the workforce in several water distribution services was reduced from 80,000 people to 8,600 people. Water privatization in England and Wales always remain controversial. The Public Services International Research Unit, which is affiliated with trade unions and opposes privatization, conducted a study on water privatization in 2001. It is found that tariffs are increased by 46 percentage in real terms during the first nine years, operating profits have more than doubled in eight years, investments were reduced and public health was negatively affected through cut-offs for non-payment. But still renationalisation of water has no place in government's agenda.

2.10.2 United States of America: The United States has been identified as one of the largest water markets in the world. In U.S the contracting of O&M (Operation and Management) to a private company has been more common than the sale of utility assets to private parties. Major U.S. cities have not sold its water utility assets in recent decades although some smaller water utilities have done so. Those privatized water utilities have posed risks of rate hikes, negative economic impacts, inadequate customer service, and harm to natural resources.

In Hingham and Hull, Massachusetts-American, an American Water Works subsidiary, more than doubled water rates over a five-year period. In Huber Heights, Ohio American Water Works purchased Ohio Suburban Water, a small outfit that provided water for 40,000 customers. The city opposed the sale—concerned that the company would raise rates and extend service to areas beyond the city limits. After the contract the company increased its rates by 30 percent. In January 1999, the city of Atlanta, entered into a 20-year contract with United Water Resources Inc. to run its drinking water system. Later Atlanta terminated its contract with United Water because hundreds of residents had complained of brown water and poor service. United Water failed to repair a recurring leak that had been a problem for at least two years.

In US there are 52,509 community water systems. More than half of these are privately owned, which includes investor-owned and homeowner's associations as well as ancillary systems. These private systems are not regulated through any mechanism (Finger and Allouche, 2002). In California, water trading is becoming a very big business. In 1992, the US Congress passed a bill allowing farmers, for the first time in US history, to sell their water to cities. Then in 1997, a new system allowed inter-state sales of Colorado river water between Arizona, Nevada and California. In Sacramento Valley for the first time in the early 1990s, farmers in southern California bought water directly from farmers in northern

California, stored in the Water Bank and sold it when the price was right to sell. The results were disastrous: a small handful of sellers walked away with huge profits, while the water table dropped and the land sank in some places (Barlow and Clarke, 2003).

2.10.3 France: The French system of water management is based on the principle of delegated management in which the local authorities may either entrust the management of water services to a private company or take direct charge of it themselves. As per the water law of 1992, the state creates the general rules and regulations while the managerial supervision is the responsibility of the communes and their various bodies. The country is divided into six major water basins for a balanced management. Thus in France, the private sector took over the control of some 77 percent of the water market. Among this Vivendi, Lyonnaise des Eaux and Saur-Bouygues enjoys a monopolistic position at local authority level. Scarcity of water is an odd problem in France; the real problem exists with regard to pollution. Water is distributed through a system of delegated management in the case of some 85 percent of the population, while private companies already account for more than 35 percent of sanitation services and are tending rapidly to increase this proportion.

However, water management in France is increasingly geared mainly to the benefit of economic interests. Despite the state sets the general rules of regulation, in France the price of water has constantly increased in recent years. This has enabled the private companies to raise their profit levels significantly since the middle of the 1980s. Between 1990 and 1994, the average rise was 50 percent and in some towns the price tripled; in Paris the increase was 154 percent causing inequitable access to water (Petrella, 2001).

Since 1994 privatization of water spread rapidly, the water industry has become a sector with high rate of return. In 1990s the profits of Lyonnaise des eaux from its water distribution activities made up 60 percent of its total profits. If the price of water under private management is compared to that of public distribution system, the most expensive of the 40 towns with a population above 10,000 are those with a privatized management system. Besides the French water privatization system lacks transparency in awarding management concessions and the numerous corruption scandals were reported over the years. Even though the actual ownership of water remains in public hands under the French style in practice, the ownership has been swept away in real meaning of the word. In the French experience, water companies have gradually ejected politics from the decision-making process concerning norms, standards, prices, etc. (Petrella, 2001).

2.10.4 Germany: Germany has a long history as world leader in water management. The Ruhr Basin Water Association, the North Rhine/Westphalia are examples in this regard. Today the German water sector is one of the most developed in the world. Germany's water works have a lower failure rate in terms both quantity and quality than the European countries. Germany has a decentralized structure with approximately 20,000 autonomous municipalities, running 7000 water supply and 10,000 wastewater utilities in the form 'Stadtwerke'. They are municipal societies operated by the municipalities with independent bookkeeping. Among the 7000 local water supply and 10,000 local sewerage companies 200 utilities in wastewater management and 250 utilities in water supply are with private sector participation. These 450 utilities with private sector participation serve 40 percent of the population in Germany (Finger and Allouche, 2002).

Privatization of water is thus a relatively new phenomenon in Germany. The first BOOT (Build, Own, Operate and Transfer) contract was entered in the town of Algermissen in Lower Saxony in 1985. In 1992 the city of Rostock in the former East Germany decided to privatize its water and wastewater services in a combination of BOT and concession contracts. Thus the German system is closer to the French system with its much more decentralized model of water management. In Germany's federal structure each Land has its own Ministries plays a greater role in the formulation of water resource management policies (Finger and Allouche, 2002).

2.10.5 Canada: Canada's water resources are the most important one in the world, as it possesses 9 percent of the world's renewable water on the planet. The pressure on Canada to export its water is heavy since 1980s. In 1987 the government had proposed a law opposing large-scale exports of Canada's water through pipelines, although it did not oppose small-scale exports such as those through bottled water. But this law was rejected. In 1998 three cases against Canadian firms were filed, all concerning water trade rights. One of the cases was the Nova Group of Sault Sainte-Marie (Finger and Allouche, 2002).

In Canada within government bureaucracies and consulting circles, there is widespread recognition that privatization could help to solve the problems troubling water and wastewater systems. Numerous studies identified a tremendous range of potential benefits of privatization. Despite the studies endorsing the concept, privatization remains the exception to the rule in Ontario and, more generally, in Canada. Ontario has made several attempts towards privatization. In 1996, then Environment Minister announced his intention to privatize the Ontario Clean Water Agency. Although the Office of Privatization began a review of the agency in 1998, the proposal languished (Brubaker, 2001).

2.11 Water Privatization in Developing Countries

Public sector reform, deregulation, privatization and the *modus operandi* of TNCs are not fundamentally different in developed and developing countries. This section highlights how water privatization is different and related to each other in developing countries particularly, African, Asian, Central and Latin American, regions. For instance in Africa the lack of investment in the water sector caused low access to water and sanitation services. In the case of Asia, rapid industrialization and agriculture, population increase and urbanization raises the question of how concerns related to water management can be addressed through privatization. South and Central America are confronted with privatization and decentralization initiatives in the water sector (Brubaker, 2001). [12] The water sector reforms in developing countries can be owed to the significant role played by World Bank, IMF, ADB, etc. using privatization as a condition for granting loans. Most of the developing countries have handed over their water and sanitation services to private companies following a recommendation from the International Finance Corporation within the World Bank facing unequivocal problems.

2.11.1 Bolivia: Bolivia is one among the highly indebted countries subjected to water privatization as a condition for borrowing money from the World Bank and IMF. Since 1993 privatization has been a key component of Bolivia's neo-liberal economic policy. World Bank and IMF have pushed the Bolivian government to open up its public sector to private investors. The Bolivian government became forced to sell many of its public enterprises, including the national airline, electric utilities, the national train service and in 1999, Cochabamba's water system. Cochabamba is the third-largest city in Bolivia. In September 1999 the Bolivian government entered into a 40-year contract with Aguas del Tunari (a subsidiary of the consortium of London-based International Water Limited and San Francisco-based Bechtel Corporation) to run SEMAPA, Cochabamba's water system.

The contract was under a consortium consist of International Water, Abengoa—a Spanish engineering group, and several Bolivian construction companies. The government was not a signatory as it was entered between the regulatory body, La *Superintendencia* and the consortium that has granted exclusive control over water resources (Holland, 2005). Aguas del Tunari took over the water distribution system in October 1999 and was in full operation by the following January. Soon after its operation the water tariffs increased by 200-300 percent in many cases. As a reaction against the huge water prices, the public staged protests in Cochabamba in February 2000. Strikes, roadblocks and other forms of civil disobedience were used and the protesters were able even to shut the city down for four consecutive days. The protesters formed an organization called *La Coordinadora de Defensa del Agua y la Vida* (Coalition for the Defence of Water and Life) led by Oscar Olivera.

As the protests spread from Cochabamba throughout Bolivia, more than 50 people were detained. Dozens were injured. Six people were killed. Police broke into the homes of protest leaders. More than a dozen of them were arrested and sent to a remote prison in the Bolivian jungle. During the April protests, President Banzer placed Bolivia under martial law. The state of emergency, called for 90 days, allowed for the suspension of almost all civil rights, including the arrest and confinement of protesters without a warrant, restrictions on travel and political activity, and a curfew. The struggle culminated on 8 April when *La Coordinadora*, mobilized 1,00,000 people for a general strike in which a boy was killed. Finally, on April 10, President Banzer announced the termination of the water contract between Bolivian government and Aguas del Tunari and the operation of water supply was returned to the public water utility.

2.11.2 Argentina: The privatization of water and sanitation services in Argentina since 1990s was one of the world's largest privatization programs. The Argentinean government signed water and sanitation management with private sector in 28 percent of the country's municipalities covering 60 percent of the population. A large concession was signed in 1993 with a consortium led by the French firm Suez for the metropolitan area of Buenos Aires. The best-known case of private sector participation in the Argentinean water sector was this Buenos Aires contract, which revoked in 2006. Besides a consortium of mainly foreign companies, Aguas

Argentina operates the water and sewage services in Buenos Aires. When the government rescinded the concession in March 2006, it argued that Aguas Argentinas did not comply with obligations concerning expansion and quality.

As early as in 1995 Aguas del Aconquija, the French-owned company won the contract for water and sanitation services in the province of Tucuman. After its inception their bill jumped three times from 24 to 75 pesos for water that was dirty. The price rise was unaffordable for people who earn so little and they started the struggle. In this phase of people's protest, the company was finally forced to leave, although the contract was for thirty years. In Buenos Aires, a consortium Aguas Argentina operates water and sewage services under a contract between the municipality, the province and non-governmental organizations. Later the local community had to fight for water supply and they succeeded only after a long struggle (Holland, 2005).

2.11.3 Nicaragua: Water privatization in Nicaragua was first introduced in the cities of Matagalpa and Jinotega. Here former high-level bureaucrats own the new private water companies in national water utility ENACAL. The Inter American Development Bank (IADB) has promised an investment of 14 million dollars on the condition that the Nicaraguan Government contracts out the water systems in Leon and Chinandega to a multinational corporation at a time when the IMF is imposing severe Structural Adjustment Programs. While the IADB said that this privatization contract will expand access to water. After its implementation the water price increased by 30 percent for residential customers thus affecting majority of the population (Hall and Lobina, 2002).

This was in violation of existing laws requiring 30 day notice for price increase and requesting water tariff remained fixed for 5 years. The price hikes led to joint protest of trade unions, consumers associations, human rights and women's groups, which demonstrated peacefully and took legal action. The coalition of organizations claimed that the price increase violated the principle of public service and the right to access to a basic service. In response to the public outcry, the National Assembly of Nicaragua unanimously passed a bill in August 2002 to suspend the project. However under pressure from international financial institutions, the president promptly vetoed the bill (Sampath, 2004).

2.11.4 Indonesia: Since the end of 1960s, International Financial Institutions have been playing significant roles in the water sector in Indonesia. The role of World Bank has been even more significant in urban water treatment sector. For the past 28 years the World Bank has funded 29 water supply projects in Indonesian cities. World Bank has put in total of US$ 2,870.9 million in the water sector projects.

Since 1990s, private sectors have been involved in water management in Indonesia. For instance, BOO Bekasi in 1993, Batam Concession in 1996, and Jakarta Concession in 1997. Started from 1997 the role of central government has decreased in delivering drinking water to its people. Water privatization in Indonesia began in February 1998 with the award of two 25-year water concessions to serve the city of Jakarta (Santono, 2008). Suez and Thames Water are the leading water privatization companies in Jakarta. In 1998 in the eastern part of the city, Thames Water and a local partner (son of the former president Suharto) formed a consortium. Bidding procedure was absent in this case. When Suharto was replaced, Thames Water took over most of his son's shares.

Due to the impact of the 1997 East Asian financial crisis the contracts were renegotiated in 2001 and a Water Supply Regulatory Body (JWSRB) was established as an autonomous regulator in charge of supervising the concessions on behalf of the Governor of Jakarta and the Ministry of Public Works. In 2003, the UK ambassador asked the President to put pressure on Jakarta city to allow Thames Water to increase water prices by 20 percent. Otherwise the company would leave the country. According to a report, privatization in Jakarta had been rushed into, without establishing a regulatory framework.

The state administration also accepted the privatization proposal from Suez. In its annual report of 2003, Suez states that negotiations led to significant price increases in Jakarta. According to Jakarta Post the charges were increased by 40 percent (Holland, 2005).

2.11.5 Nigeria: Water has historically been a Common Property Resource in Niger, managed by the community. A strong sense of cultural tradition was present in Niger. Recently World Bank forced Niger to privatize its water sector. If privatization deal would be agreed the government was able to borrow money from the Bank. Yet the private company is not investing and refuses to take any risk. In place of private investment, the World Bank provides money because private lenders would charge high interest rate. Besides, the private operator is given contracts for extension of the network free of competition (Holland, 2005).

World Bank has forced the government to privatize water sector in order to borrow money from the Bank. The trade unions in the water companies at first opposed privatization, but agreed to it after a social contract was drawn up. The French company Veolia Water used this opportunity and entered a contract in which the employees own 10 percent of the company's shares. But this holding does not confer any power to the employees. But this holding does not confer any power to the workers. Subsequently the contract was broken and they are furious about the low wages. Two years after privatization there was still no regulatory authority to monitor the company (Holland, 2005).

2.11.6 Jordan: In Jordan, despite huge investment, it has problems with water supplies. The country's water and wastewater services are viewed as inefficient. The public water authority has financial deficiency to improve the water and sanitation systems. As a solution the country turned to private sector. In Jordan, in 1999 a consortium supported by World Bank largely run by Suez, called Lema Water, won the water and wastewater management contract on the conception that it will improve efficiency and will reduce the loss through economic billing. Lema was obliged to retain 50 percent of the employees for the first year of the contract. It had the right to reduce its payroll by 12.5 percent by the end of the contract. Charges for water were low till 1999 with state subsidies in water and sanitation services. Now in the absence of the state subsidies many ordinary households are unable to pay their bills. Ordinary households are able to pay except the poorest. The state not provides subsidies to the poor. If they do not pay, their water is cut off. Now Amman has the second highest charge in the Middle East and North Africa (Holland, 2005).

2.11.7 Ghana: The first attempt to privatize the water system in Ghana was in 1999. Ghana's Ministry of Housing and Works selected the Enron subsidiary, Azurix, over the two other bidders (Suez and Vivendi). When the deal started allegations were made against Azurix that it gave US$ 5 million to key politicians. Due to public protest the deal was withdrawn. The real beginning of water privatization in Ghana started even before the Azurix scandal. As a preparation towards privatization the government of Ghana formed the constitutional regulatory body—Public Utility Regulatory Commission (PURC)—in 1997 to ensure appropriate regulation. But the PURC has been subject to pressure from IMF and World Bank towards full cost recovery. But this private experiment was subjected to severe criticism. Women's groups, religious organizations, trade unions, public health workers, and environmental organizations raised their voice against water privatization. As opposition grew, the government began reassessing their positions (McDonald and Ruiters, 2005).

A World Bank development loan of US$ 110 million to Ghana was allowed for implementation of water privatization with an increase of 95 percent in water consumer fees. As full cost recovery is a prerequisite to privatization, the price of a bucket of water, which cost 400 Cedis earlier, costs 800 Cedis now. This seems to be unaffordable to majority of the population who earns less than a Cedis a day. Various groups have mounted an opposition against price increase, which is expected to increase further (Sampath, 2004).

2.11.8 Ivory Coast: Most water specialists refer to the Ivory Coast as a successful model for Sub-Saharan Africa when it comes to private participation in the water sector. In Ivory Coast, SAUR, following an international auction, became Abidjan's water supplier in the year 1959 and by 1974, SODECI (Societe de distribution d'eau Cote d'Ivoire) took the sole operation under a lease and concession contracts. Indeed by 1995 about 82 percent of Abidjan's population had access to adequate water supply facility in urban areas, compared with less than 30 percent in 1974. However, these figures seem underestimated if we add the informal sector. An average half of the population living in the urban periphery is not connected to the water piped system. The other half has access to safe water by purchasing it from street vendors, because of the lack of convenient standpipes, undistributed to the squatter areas (Holland, 2005).

2.11.9 Philippines: The decision to privatize Metro Manila's Water and Sewerage System (MWSS) was taken by the government, because of its failure to provide effective water distribution service and the desire to end government subsidies. Water privatization in Philippines so far seems to be limited to MWSS. Currently there are two companies, the Manila Water Company (MWC) and Manylad Water Services (MWS), which have been awarded 25-year concession contracts for the West and East zone of the MWSS. But the effective implementation of environmental policies and regulation seems to be absent, because in July 2000, Greenpeace reported that Metro Manilla's reservoir, contained toxic substances owing to the run-off of flood waters from a near dump site caused by heavy monsoon rains. However, Manylad had not taken stringent actions to prevent pollution of water (Holland, 2005). [13]

2.12 Issues of Water Privatization in India

With an average rainfall of 1,170 mm, and an annual exploitable groundwater potential of 26.3 million hectare-meters, India is one of the wettest countries in the world. Though the average rainfall is adequate, nearly three-quarters of the rain pours down in less than 120 days, from June to September. Besides, according to International Irrigation Management Institute (IIMI), the water table is falling almost everywhere in India and India is using its underground water resources at least twice as fast as they are being replenished. In the past decades, industrial and agricultural production has increased in India resulting in increased water consumption for these sectors at a rate of 4.2 percent per year. The Indian experience suggests that availability of an improved water source as defined by human development indices is no guarantee of regular, reliable supply. There are growing challenges: unsustainable exploitation of millennia-old deep aquifers to cater to growing populations; pollution of surface waters by untreated sewage, pesticides, fertilizers, and industrial chemicals; inefficient agricultural use; and the impact of climate change (Sampath, 2004).

As part of the global reforms in the water sector privatization has been sought in India as one of the solutions to address this looming crisis. As such the Indian government dutifully mentioned this in the National Water Policy of 2002. Article 13 calls for private sector participation in the planning, development and the management of water resource projects, on the ground that this may introduce innovative ideas, generate financial resources, introduce corporate management and improve service efficiency wherever possible'. Some of the states which decided to reform their traditional style of water management through the policy guidelines are, Tamil Nadu, New Delhi, Chhattisgarh and Kerala (Singh, 2004).

2.12.1 New Delhi: Degremont, a subsidiary of French water giant Suez–has been awarded a ₹ 2 billion contract under a 10-year BOT agreement with the Delhi Jal Board

(DJB) for a drinking water treatment plant in Sonia Vihar near New Delhi. The plant is expected to yield 635 million litres of drinking water a day when it is getting the raw water for free through pipelines from the Upper Ganga canal of the Tehri Dam Project in Uttar Pradesh. The DJB is not only providing Degremont with land and electricity but also providing a higher treatment cost compared to the charge it would get from the consumers when selling water. Since its inception, the Sonia Vihar plant has been plagued by allegations of corruption and irregularities in the allotment of contract to Degremont (Sampath, 2004). [14]

2.12.2 Chhattisgarh: In 1998 the Madhya Pradesh Audyogig Kendra Vikas Nigam Limited commissioned a project with Radius Water Limited to supply water to the Borai Industrial Growth Centre situated on the banks of Sheonath river. The project began its operation in 2000 i.e. after the formation of Chhattisgarh state, accordingly the contract was transferred to the Chhattisgarh State Industries Development Corporation (CSIDC). As part of the project, the company got absolute monopoly over a 22.6 km. stretch of the Sheonath river through a 22-year renewable contract.

The company built an integrated water supply system and set the water tariff at substantially lower rates than that charged by the neighbouring states of Madhya Pradesh and Maharashtra. The agreement assured Radius Water of payment for a minimum of four million litres of water per day by the state government, regardless of the amount of water used by the industries. But the agreed amount of water was not required to the industries and CSIDC loose ₹ 12.9 millions per year. Further more the company promptly prohibited the local people's access to it, causing resistance among them. Ultimately bowing to pressure from the people, government scrapped the ban and people's access to river was reinstated (Sampath, 2004).

2.12.3 Tamil Nadu: In Tiruppur, in 1995, the NTADCL (New Tiruppur Area Development Corporation Limited) issued a 30-year BOOT contract for a water supply project to a consortium including Mahindra and Mahindra, United International, North West Water, Larsen and Turbo and Bechtel. The consortium, United Utilities, would transfer water over a 55 km. long pipeline from the river Bhavani and supply 185 million litres of water per day to nearly 1,000 textile units and more than 1.6 million residents in Tiruppur and its surrounding area, while operation and maintenance fee will be recovered entirely from Tiruppur Municipality. Further the Tamil Nadu government has guaranteed profitability to the investors in the project by creating a hedge fund to pay the interest and operative expenses of the project in the event of a water shortage in the Bhavani river, with no stipulations on the amount of water withdrawal from the river for this project (Sampath, 2004). [15]

2.13 Water-based Industries

In the above mentioned countries, water distribution is privatized by the state governments through different projects. But there are lots of reported cases in which the privatization of water has been largely done through the appropriation method. All over the world the multi-national and national water-based industries have started their bottling plants which ultimately lead to water monopolization. It is a fact that in most of the places there are popular struggles against these operating units. Following the struggles some of the operating units are subjected to temporary/permanent closure.

For instance the Coca-Cola plant has a history of anti-trade union interventions in Pakistan. One of the important in this regard is the iron hand adopted by the company management vis-à-vis the trade union activities within the Coca-Cola bottling plant at Multan, Pakistan. The trade union was actually affiliated to the national federation of Food Beverages and Tobacco Workers which is an internationally recognized body. The company responded to the initiation of union activities through compulsory transfer of those employees who were part of the union, indiscriminate dismissal from the job, kidnapping the main trade union leaders and attempts to form parallel unions under company control. Recently, in order to escape from the legal complications the Coca-Cola company is now trying to restructure its organization so that employees would have the status of contractual labourers.

The Indian scenario is also similar to other developing countries where water-based industries are operating. Grassroot based protests is a common feature in most of the places in India where Coca-Cola has its bottling plants. There may be variations with regard to the intensity and nature of the struggle, but the common objective remains the same i.e. the closure of water-based industries and ban on water privatization. Even though the foremost problem created by Cocoa-Cola company is water depletion, one cannot undermine the water and soil pollution produced due to the company operations.

In 2003, the Central Pollution Control Board (CPCB) of India assessed the sludge at eight Coca-Cola bottling plants and found them all containing excessive levels of lead, cadmium or chromium. As a result, the CPCB ordered the Coca-Cola company in India to treat its waste at all its bottling plants as industrial hazardous waste and deal with it accordingly. In particular, the dumping of such hazardous waste violates the Hazardous Wastes (Management and Handling) Rules 1989 from the Ministry of Environment and Forests of India (Dhillon, 2010). The following are some instances in this regard.

2.13.1 Kerala: In Plachimada-an agricultural region in Perumatty Panchayath-water was over exploited by Coca-Cola's bottling plant. Plachimada is a rain shadow region of Chittur Taluk in Palakkad district, where the Coca-Cola company started production in 2000. For producing soft drinks daily they had extracted four to six lakh litres of water per day, causing groundwater depletion. Since its establishment the waste treatment plant of the company was not functioning well which resulted in the pollution of water bodies in Plachimada. The people began their struggle in 2002 and achieved their goal with temporary closure of the factory in 2003 (VAK, 2004). Still the legal battle and people's struggle is going on for the permanent closure of the factory.

After Coca-Cola, another soft drink major Pepsi has come on the radar of the government in Kerala which has alleged that its plant in Puthusseri Panchayath of Palakkad district was extracting excess ground water and discharging effluents and solid wastes with pollutants. The plant at Puthussery was found to have been depleting the water table in the locality over the years. Consequently, the Puthusseri Panchayath has cancelled its license in 2003. But the company challenged the cancellation order in Court on the ground that the Panchayath is not empowered to cancel the license of a company working in an industrial area which got consent as per the Single Window Clearance Act 1999. Accordingly, the Division Bench of High Court judged against the Panchayath. Further the panchayath was also not permitted to move appeal by the state government.

Taking a serious note of the alleged exploitation of groundwater by Pepsi, the Water Resource Department constituted a panel headed by State Water Resource Minister N.K. Premachandran. The report, tabled in the Assembly, however, did not ask for the closure of the plant, which provides employment to 3,500 people. The plant situated over 53 acres, uses nearly 48.5 percent of the ground water, according to the report. Thus the committee recommended imposition of curbs on extraction of water by the Pepsi plant. Their key suggestion was to reduce the water extraction by Pepsi at 2,34,000 litres per day from the current average of 700,000 litres a day. On the issue whether the plant was causing water pollution, the report said that the possibility could not be ruled out, but requires detailed study. The committee also argued that the industrial units using groundwater as the main raw material should be generally discouraged. The report comes at a time when a high-level panel is finalizing its report on socio-economic damage allegedly caused by the Coca Cola plant at Plachimada, which has been declared a drought-hit area.

2.13.2 Rajasthan: The Kaladera region in Rajasthan is a water-stress area and the government declared the area's groundwater resources as over-exploited in 1998. The Coca-Cola company built a new bottling plant in 2000 in a region that is dependent on groundwater. Over the years, an agitation has been building up against this bottling plant. With the intense anti-Coca-Cola sentiment in this area, about thirty villages and a number of organizations have mobilized under the banner of *Jan Sangharsh Samiti* (People's Committee for Struggle) and each elected a convener for the *village Samiti.* Farmers from these villages hold that Coca-Cola is primarily responsible for declining ground water levels in the region and the resultant harm to local agriculture.

According to the report of the study conducted by scientists from the Central Ground Water Board, Western Region and the Rajasthan Pollution Control Board among others, the Coca-Cola plant extracted 1, 37,694 cubic meters of water in 2002-03, and 1, 74,301 cubic meters in just nine months to December 2003. Nearly fifty villages which fall in Chomu and Amer taluks have been affected, including Kaladera, Anop Pura, Kanarpura, Bai Ka Bans, Sabalpura and Dhinoi. With the water table falling approximately six meters every year farmers are digging bore wells as deep as 45 meters.

The Central Groundwater Board in 2009 confirmed that between 2007 and 2008, groundwater levels in Kaladera plummeted six meters in a 5 sq. km. radius around the gigantic plant. The plant is accused of bringing disaster to the 20,000 villagers in Kaladdera who has seen their crops wither and their livelihoods shrink. With insufficient water, they cannot grow the fodder they need for their cattle, compelling them to buy fodder from the market and keep fewer cows and buffaloes. The Energy and Resources Institute (TERI) conducted a study and found that the plant was a significant contributor to the water shortages in Kaladera and should stop using groundwater because of the damage it was doing. But the Kaladera farmer's protests to close the plant have failed. In a region mostly dependent on groundwater, the plant has brought disaster for 10,000 families in a five-kilometre radius of the plant (Adve, 2004).

2.13.3 Uttar Pradesh: Similar to Kaledara, Coca-Cola's bottling plant is working in Mehdiganj, Varanasi. The plant is indiscriminately dumping the industrial hazardous waste, across the plant premises, in complete violation of the laws regarding handling and disposal of industrial hazardous waste in India. The Effluent Treatment Plant is non-operational, and the wastewater spreads into surrounding agricultural fields and a canal that feeds into the river Ganges. Protest by the local community in association with elected representatives, government officials, people's movement groups, non-governmental organizations and international groups is mounting in Varanasi demanding the closure of the unit. The bottling plant in Sinhachawar Ballia is a Coca-Cola franchisee operated by the Brindavan Bottlers Limited. The community accused the bottling plant causing pollution and also illegally occupied the land held by the village assembly. A visit by community members to the factory premises in May 2007 found the bottling plant indiscriminately dumping its hazardous waste inside and outside the factory premises (Dhillon, 2010).

2.13.4 Maharashtra: Villagers around the Coca-Cola plant in Wada taluk in Thane district are thirsty for water. Many blame Coca-Cola plant for grabbing water at the expense of villagers. At present villagers are forced to travel long distances in search of water which has dried up in their area as a result of Coca-Cola's operations. Villagers are questioning the subsidized water, land and tax breaks that Coca-Cola receives from the state. Coca-Cola sources, however said the state irrigation department had allowed the company to tap water from Vaitarna river. It has built a pipeline to transport water from a river to its plant. But for the past years the river has been practically dry during summer seasons. The company is now getting its supply of water with tankers five kilometres away from the plant. The company pays only ₹ 378 per 10,000 litres. Now the plant is encountering strong opposition from villagers as well as the pro-communist All-India Democratic Women's Association, because it has reportedly deprived water to thousands of people (Srivastava, 2010).

2.13.5 Tamil Nadu: In Tamil Nadu South India Bottling Company Private Limited (SIBCL), a Coca-Cola franchisee started a soft-drinks unit in Gangaikondan village of Tirunelveli district. The elected members of local governments have extended their support to the company in the name of job expansion. The Tamil Nadu Pollution Control Board (TNPCB) on 3 March 2005 granted consent for running the unit while the company had applied to the board only on 28 February 2005. The bottling plant is said to be drawing around 6 lakh litres of water a day paying one paise per litter which caused ground water depletion. Many local residents, political parties and environmentalists are now opposing the water-intensive plant because water from Tamiraparani river cannot fully meet even drinking water and agricultural needs of local communities. But the Tamil Nadu government is reluctant to oust Coca-Cola from their land though the local people protested and resorted to various forms of agitation, seeking cancellation of the license given to SIBCL. Grassroot struggles are also going against the Coca-Cola plant at Padamaathur in Sivagagnga district of Tamil Nadu (Jayaraman, 2005).

2.14 Genesis of Right to Water

In the traditional societies water has been treated as a natural right—a right arising out of human nature, historic conditions, basic needs and notions of justice. Thus, water rights as natural right do not originated with the state; they evolved out of a given ecological context of human existence. As natural rights, water rights are usufructuary rights i.e., water can be used as a resource that sustains life, but not owned (Shiva, 2002). Water rights as formal rights originated with the state, out of a given social context where water scarcity and violation of water rights became usual. Customary laws and regulations were adequate, in ancient societies for providing water, but in the legalistic societies of today formal law has more importance in preventing violation of water rights. Besides climate change and increasing population has aggravated the already existing conditions of water scarcity in the country challenging its equitable distribution. Hence it became necessary to talk about the Right to Water (Iyer, 2003).

Recognition of the serious problem of water scarcity and attempts to address them started in the 1970s from the international community. In 1972 the United Nations Conference on Human Environment held in Stockholm identified water as one of the natural resources that needs to be safe guarded. Five years later in 1977, the United Nations Water Conference held at Mar del Plata in Argentina issued a Mar del Plata Action Plan, which was designed to address the problem of water resources. The Action Plan consists of a number of recommendations and resolutions, pertaining to the crucial issues in water sector. The recommendations includes assessment of water resources, water use and efficiency, policy, planning and management, etc. and the resolutions addressed areas such as community water supply, research and development, river commissions, international co-operation, etc. An important outcome of the Conference was the agreement to proclaim the period 1981 to 1990 as the 'International Drinking Water Supply and Sanitation Decade' during which governments would assume a commitment to improve the drinking water supply and sanitation sectors (Salman and Lankford, 2004). [16]

Mar del Plata Conference was a milestone in originating the debate on right to water, provided the basis for further discussion even continuing today. Resolution II of this Conference declared the content of right to water for the first time, i.e. "all people whatever their stage of development and their social and economic conditions, have the right to have access to water in quantities and of a quality equal to their basic needs". While the Stockholm and Mar del Plata conferences were primarily concerned with the task of identifying water as a basic human right the rest of the international conferences from Dublin Conference in 1992 to the Kyoto Forum 2003 were steps in developing the concept of water as a social and economic good. Principle 4 of the Dublin Statement clarifies that "it is vital to recognize first the basic right of all human beings to have access to clean water and sanitation at an affordable price". It confirmed the right to water at an affordable price and not free of charge (Salman and Lankford, 2004). [17]

In 1996 the world community witnessed the establishment of World Water Council (WWC) and Global Water Partnership (GWP) having strong representation of multinational water companies and aid agencies to act as a think tank on water resource matters. In the following years three world water forums were held in different parts of the world under the auspices of these bodies. The Marrakech Declaration issued in the First World Water Forum held in Marrakech, Morocco, 1997 did not go as far as Mar del Plata, Dublin or Rio with regard to Right to Water.

The second World Water Forum held in Hague, Netherlands in 2000, recognized that the 'access to safe and sufficient water and sanitation are basic human needs'. The Kyoto World Water Forum, 2003 merely stated that - "We will enhance poor people's access to safe drinking water and sanitation" (Salman and Lankford, 2004). [18] The World Water Forums also adopted the principle of Integrated Water Resource Management which reiterates the principle that water should be treated as an economic, social and environmental good. It advices that water should be managed at the lowest appropriate level–decentralization and stakeholder participation are important (Ahmed, 2008).

The importance of declaring water as a basic human need and a fundamental right was further highlighted in the United Nations General Assembly in its resolution on Right to Development. This resolution reaffirmed that in the realization of the right to development, the rights to food and clean drinking water are fundamental human rights and their promotion constitutes a moral imperative for the national governments and the international community. Moreover reducing by half the proportion of people without sustainable access to safe drinking water forms one of the prime goals in the UN Millennium Declaration 2000. In December 2000 the General Assembly proclaimed the year 2003 as the 'International Year of Fresh Water' and another resolution adopted in December 2003 declared the decade 2005-2015 as 'International Decade for Action, Water for Life' (Salman and Lankford, 2004).

On a large scale, the UN Committee on Economic, Social and Cultural Rights in November 2002 adopted its General Comment on the Right to Water. The Committee underlines in its General Comment (G.C.) that while, 'the human right to water is indispensable for leading a life in human dignity and that it is a prerequisite for the realization of other human rights'. The G.C. was a remarkable achievement and path breaking legal development. The main declarations of G.C. are; water should be treated as a social and cultural good and not primarily as an economic good; the factors that apply in all circumstances in enjoying right to water are, availability, quality and accessibility; right to water includes freedoms and entitlements to drinking water, water for household and agricultural purposes and sanitation; the relationship of the right to water with the human right to life and human dignity is obvious (Kothari, 2004).

The G.C. again calls for states to "accept comprehensive and integrated strategies and programs to ensure that there is sufficient and safe water for present and future generations, to distribute without any discrimination". The committee urges states to pay particular attention to the relevance of water resources and entitlements for women. By giving these messages to states, G.C. emphasized the negative role of the state in preventing water right violation and positive role of the state to implement measures for the realization of right to water. It explicitly stated that, "Water should never be used as an instrument of political and economic pressure" (Kothari, 2004).

2.15 Violation of Right to Water

Rising demand of water for household, agricultural and industrial, purposes plus the deteriorating environment lead to water scarcity. This paved way for water conflicts and water right violations. Though we have formal water rights, water right violation and struggles against it were reported globally. Water right violation can be seen from minor overuse in household level up to large level industrial exploitation. Water right can be violated by the entities like individual, groups, companies, etc. When state is inefficient to regulate this entities state itself becomes a violator of water rights. Besides the failure to have a just national policy and failure to legislate and enforce relevant laws are also under the purview of water right violation by the state.

The UN General Comment on Right to Water identified the range of violations, which the states are prone to. The G.C distinguishes the inabilities rising from the unwillingness of the state to comply with obligation towards ensuring water rights. It states that, "a state which is unwilling to use the maximum of its available resources for the realization of right to water is in violation of its obligations under the Covenant" (Kothari, 2004). The G.C identifies some of the possible violations by the state includes, exclusion from water services; discriminatory or unaffordable prices of water; pollution and diminution of water resources affecting human health; failure to protect water distribution systems; the failure to take measures to reduce the inequitable distribution of water; failure to adjust mechanisms for emergency relief, etc.

2.16 Water and the Indian Constitution

In the Indian Constitution a confusion regarding whether water is a state subject or national subject has still not come to an end. According to Entry 17 of the State List, water is a state subject, subject to Entry 56 of the Union List. The legislative competence of a state under Entry 17 must be exercised in such a manner as not to prejudice the interest of other states and creates a water dispute within the meaning of Article 262. Thus the relevant positions in the Constitution are Entry 17 in the State List, Entry 56 in the Union List and Article 262. The arguments often made is that under the Indian Constitution water is a state subject, and the centre must refrain from encroaching into this area; the other agrees that water is a state subject but the centre needs to play an important role in regard to this precious resource, and in order to facilitate this, water should be transferred to the Concurrent List (Iyer, 2003). [19]

The hold of the state governments under Entry 17 of the State List remains unfettered only because Parliament has not made much use of the powers vested in it by Entry 56 of the Union List. So, water is potentially as much a central subject and a state subject, particularly most of the country's rivers are inter-state. The role of the centre regarding water is reinforced by the provisions of Entry 20 in the Concurrent List, namely economic and social planning, by virtue of which major and medium irrigation, hydro power, flood control and multipurpose projects have been subjected to the requirement of central clearance for inclusion in the National Plan. Apart from the above-mentioned Entries provisions related to water in the Constitution can be seen in the lists of subjects to be devolved to *panchayats* and *nagarpalikas* under 11th and 12th Schedule of the Constitution. The list of subjects include *inter alias*, drinking water, water management, watershed development and sanitation (Iyer, 2003).

2.17 Constitutional Position of Groundwater

The importance of groundwater in our national life is evident: around 50 percent of irrigated agriculture is based on groundwater, and 85 percent of rural drinking water comes from groundwater. There is no specific reference to groundwater *per se* in the Constitution, though we could of course assume that 'water' includes groundwater. The two basic entries relating to water–Entry 17 in the State List and Entry 56 of the Union List, are primarily concerned about river waters. Further article 262 and the Inter-State Water Disputes Act 1956 (ISWD Act) passed by Parliament under that article are about river water disputes and they have refrained from taking an overall view of water resources covering both surface water and groundwater. But it has generally been assumed that the reference to water in the Constitution includes groundwater. On that understanding, groundwater seems to be a state subject falling within the purview of Entry 17 in the State List; having no relevance with Entry 56 in the Union List (Iyer, 2003). [20]

There is a great asymmetry between groundwater and surface water in ordinary laws. As far as surface water is concerned, the law recognizes only use-rights and not ownership or proprietary rights over flowing water. In the case of groundwater, under Indian law, the ownership of land carries it with the ownership of the groundwater under it, subject to regulation and control by the state. Under this Easement Right it has been said that 'groundwater is attached like a chattel, to land property' and that 'there is no limitation on how much groundwater a particular land owner may draw' (Iyer, 2003).

2.18 National Water Policies

The water sector was managed exclusively on an ad-hoc basis till 1987 when the first ever National Water Policy

(NWP) came into existence. The NWP, 1987, emerged from the need of a national consensus recognizing the importance of water and the federal structure of the country plus the need to move towards issues of resource policy than that of discrete projects. Over the years it become reference document relating to diverse issues of water although the original objective of the policy was to get all the states to subscribing to a minimal set of general propositions. The NWP 1987 was a short document containing the following propositions: water is a scarce and precious natural resource; groundwater exploitation should be regulated; in water allocation the first priority should be for drinking water; there should be a close integration of water use and land use policies, etc (Iyer, 2003). [21] The policy had some useful aspects, but it totally neglected the constitutional issues, presumably because of divergence of view among the participants and reluctance by some states to visit contentious issues. It did not consider water as a scarce and valuable natural resource (Ray, 2008).

By the late 1990s there was a general recognition that it was necessary to review the NWP 1987 as per the suggestion of the National Commission for Integrated Water Resource Development Plan. The government prepared a fresh draft water policy in 1998 and in the meeting of the National Water Resources Council (NWRC) held on 1st April 2002 the amendment proposed to the National Water Policy, 1987 were approved, and a new NWP, 2002 came into being. Several changes have been made in the 1987 text of the NWP: additions, amendments rewordings, rearrangement of matter and so on. Some of the changes are, realizing the importance and scarcity attached to fresh water, treated as an essential environment for sustaining all life forms, watershed management, preservation of forest, popular participation in projects, need of getting optimal productivity per unit of water, etc. In the Policy first priority has been given to the drinking water and second priority to agriculture and non-agricultural industries come almost on the bottom of the priority list (Iyer,

2003).

2.19 Right to Water as a Fundamental Right in India

Right to water as a fundamental right was not added to the Constitution originally. Thus water rights existed in the Indian Constitution as riparian rights under Article 262. This provision was created in order to resolve the conflicts between states regarding inter-state river waters. This article clearly defines the rights of each state over inter-state rivers and constituted an institutional mechanism for its efficient implementation (Iyer, 2003). Later the identification of water more as a fundamental right than a riparian right felt as an urgent necessity due to the increasing demand and scarcity of fresh drinking water.

Judiciary has rightly intervened in times when conflicts surmounted the provisions related to right to water. In such a context the Supreme Court ruled that clean drinking water is a fundamental right of all citizens, in Surana Oils/Derivatives (India) Limited case. The Court said that Article 21 of the Constitution guarantee right to life and it also includes the 'Right to Clean Drinking Water'. The court also quoted the 1977 resolution of the UN Water Conference that pledges access to clean drinking water for everybody, to which India is signatory (Singh, 2004). Further the apex Court gives some explanations about ecology and its protection through M.C. Mehta case and other cases. [22]

Any disturbances of the basic environment elements, namely, air, water and soil, which are necessary for life would be hazardous to life within the meaning of Article 21 of the Constitution." In the leading M.C. Mehta Vs. Union of India the court directed the government to set up an authority at the central level to deal with indiscriminate extraction of ground water. In Narmada Bachavo Andolan vs. Union of India, Justice Kripal observed: "water is the basic need for the survival of human beings and is part of the right to life and human rights as enshrined in Article 21 of the Constitution of

India and can be secured only by providing source of water where there is none."

2.20 Water Laws in India

The question of ownership of water in India has been debated more and understood less. An in-depth study of the Indian context affirms that it is a sort of jurisprudential understanding that underlies the earlier legislation in India, such as The Limitation Acts (1859-71), The Northern India Canal and Drainage Act, 1873, The Bengal Irrigation Act, 1876, and also the Specific Relief Act, I of 1877. These acts asserted the right of the state to use and control water and gave less preference to its ownership questions. The notion of 'riparian rights' over water resources came to be recognized by the Indian Easements Act, 1882. The main principle of the notion is that a riparian owner has a natural right to use water of a stream which flows through his land. However the Act was subject to the government's power to regulate in public interest, the collection, retention and distribution of water from rivers and streams flowing in natural channels. But this does not make the state the absolute owner of water (Upadhyay, 2009).

In India the lack of clear and well defined laws leaves too much room for arbitrary, short-sighted and opaque decision making. In such a situation powerful interests and political expediency made considerable influences over the decision making process. Though government approval is necessary to impound, divert or extract water from rivers or even local streams, the situation gets worsened when the state is dually responsible for allocation and actual exploitation of water. For instance, The Indian Easement Act is subject to more recent regulations like that it should not affect the neighbours use, state allows individuals to exploit ground water in commands. Another contested premise of water law is the debate between the concepts of 'eminent domain' and 'pubic trust'. Eminent domain give thrust on the right of the state to appropriate private property for a public use, usually on the payment of compensation to the owner. The public trust doctrine requires states to hold on to public resources as trustees and prohibits them from transferring it or converting it into private or commercial use. But the supremacy and significance of these doctrines are still being debated (Vaidyanathan and Jairaj, 2009).

Likewise fouling of water is punishable under the Indian Penal Code, which has been in force since 1873. The Water (Prevention and Control of Pollution) Act of 1974 is regarded as the first legal measure for water pollution control. It provided for the establishment of an institutional mechanism at the centre and in each state comprising a board at each place. The Environment Act of 1986 is an umbrella act covering all aspects not covered by the Water Act. This act empowers the central government to take measures to protect the environment (Tyagi, 2009). The pollution control laws and institutions have not been able to prevent the growing pollution and contamination of water sources. There are problems of fluoride and arsenic content in groundwater in some places, in India. Water pollution is in fact a great threat to water security (Iyer, 2007).

Regarding ground water legislation we don't have a concrete and comprehensive ground water law to regulate it's over use. Judiciary in many circumstances has intervened effectively where ground water is exploited. The Court emphasized Public Trust Doctrine in many judgments and prevented monopolization of water for the sake of people. Further the Precautionary Principle enacted by Rio de Janeiro Conference held in June, 2005 was approved the higher judiciary as part of our national jurisprudence, in many cases against industrial pollution.

The Supreme Court in Kesoram/State of Bengal case ruled that, "deep underground water belongs to the state in the sense that the doctrines of Public Trust extends there too. Holder of a land may have only a right to user and cannot take any action or do any harm as a result where the rights of others are affected." Besides despite the doubts expressed by ministry of water resources, the Supreme Court mooted the establishment of a regulatory authority that resulted into the formation of Central Ground Water Authority (CGWA) in 1997. But it is not yet a very effective or fully operational body and its constitutional position is also in confusion like that of CGWB. Because according to Entry 17 in the State List, ground water seems to be a state subject and this autonomous organization cannot derive authority from this provision (Iyer, 2003).

The attempt to introduce actual ground water legislation at the state level has by and large failed. For the first time in 1970, the central government circulated a Model Bill to state governments, but the response of the states was poor. The CGWB made some initiatives to set up state level regulatory bodies but only few states have passed the legislation. As per this order, Tamil Nadu and Uttar Pradesh enacted such laws and created ground water authorities. Kerala has enacted the law in 2002 namely, The Kerala Ground water (Control and Regulation) Act 2002; as per this act the entire power to control ground water use is vested in the Ground water Authority. But this Authority is created very recently and not developed in its full swing yet.

End Notes

1. Principle 2 of the Stockholm Declaration on Human Environment states that, "the natural resources of the earth including the air, water, land, flora and fauna and especially representative samples of natural ecosystem must be safeguarded for the benefit of the present and future generations through careful planning or management, as appropriate".
2. The Mar del Plata Conference issued a Mar del Plata Action Plan that was designed to address the problem of water resources. The Action Plan consists of a number of recommendations and resolutions, pertaining to the crucial issues in water sector. The recommendations include assessment of water resources, water use and efficiency, pollution control, regional and international cooperation.

3. This model is prevalent in developing countries and examples of BOOT include Tiruppur project in Tamil Nadu and the experience of Cochambamba in Bolivia.
4. Currently public-private collaborations in water services receive millions of aid dollars. In India alone there are thirty such collaborations in water services.
5. Approximately US$ 9.7 billion was for support of combined rural and urban water supply and sanitation projects. More than US$ 17 billion of the loans and credits were for irrigation and hydropower projects, with large dam-related loans accounting for about US$ 12 billion. Rehabilitation and operations and maintenance projects amounted to about 18 percent. Alternatives such as small-scale irrigation, watershed development and water conservation projects amounted to only US$ 815 million.
6. Its Operations Evaluation Department (OED) found that Water supply and irrigation projects have been performing poorly for the years. For the twenty-one irrigation projects approved between 1961 and 1978, agricultural production actually declined after project completion in 43 percent of these projects, and 70 percent of projects had a lower economic rate of return than estimated at completion. Water efficiency was lower than anticipated in 60 percent of the projects. Another OED report showed that for 129 water supplies and sewerage projects reviewed, more than half suffered from cost overruns, almost all had economic rates of return below 10 percent and 64 percent had excessive levels of lost.
7. This paper served as guideline for the World Bank in developing a new policy grounded in a general theory of water resource management at the local, national and international levels.
8. For instance of the 276 loans that the WB granted for water projects between 1990 and 2004, 84 called directly for privatization, the majority during the last seven years. In 2000, 91 percent of loans included water privatization clauses; in 2004, 100 percent of loans included such clauses. It has been directly involved in promoting and shaping privatization processes in Buenos Aires, Manila and many other cities around the world. Further more, the Bank has acted as adviser in many countries and has supported private companies by offering loans.
9. Trade in services is a rapidly expanding market across the world. Each country in the WTO lists the services it is willing to open

up to other countries. They may be business services, tourism, transport, energy, and environmental or other services. Under the agreement any country can demand of another, that services in the public sector should also be opened to other actors, namely private companies, if that country has already engaged the private sector within a particular service. Foreign and domestic companies should be able to compete on equal terms.

10. The EU Commission wants seventy-two countries to open their water supplies to foreign interests. Among these countries are Bangladesh, Bolivia, Botswana, Brazil, Egypt, Honduras, Panama, Paraguay, and Tunisia.
11. The world's top two private sector water companies, Vivendi with a turnover of US$ 17.1 billion and Suez with a turnover of US$ 5.1 billion, both French, control 70 percent of all private water services between them. The third largest is Thames water, now part of German utilities conglomerates of RWE (a German energy company).
12. In some parts of Africa developments go in the opposite direction. Increasingly companies have begun to withdraw contracts in countries south of the Sahara.
13. According to world Resource Institute, Philippines, compared to other Asian countries have a relatively high rate of access to safe drinking water and sanitation.
14. A Delhi based NGO Research Foundation for Science; Technology and Environment has accused the Delhi Jal board of wasteful practices. The Delhi Jal Board, which does not rule out an increase in water prices for the residents of New Delhi, has not made public any of the project documents.
15. The New Tiruppur Area development Corporation Ltd. (NTADCL) was set up by the state government in 1995 to execute ₹ 13 billion water supply project, with financial support from USAID and the World Bank.
16. The United Nations General Assembly did not refer in Resolution 32/158 (adopting the report of United Nations Water Conference) for the recommendation to declare the decade of 1981-1990 as the International Drinking Water Supply and Sanitation Decade. However this matter was addressed by the General Assembly in a later resolution in 1980. Resolution 35/18, adopted by the General Assembly on November 10, 1980 at the 55th Plenary Meeting, after referring to the Mar del Plata

Action Plan, proclaimed "the period 1981-1990 as the International Drinking Water Supply and Sanitation Decade."

17. However, the Dublin Principles did not explain the concept of 'affordability', nor do they suggest means through which its content and meaning could be determined.
18. The WWC is supposed to act as a think tank on water resource matters, while the GWP is established as a working partnership among all entities involved in water to support countries in integrated water resource management.
19. Entry 17 in the State List run as follows: 'Water, that is to say, water supplies, irrigation and canals, drainage and embankments, water storage and waterpower subject to the provisions of Entry 56 of List I'. While Entry 56 in the Union List, runs like this: 'Regulation and development of inter-state rivers and river valleys to the extent to which such regulation and development under the control of the Union are declared by Parliament by law to expedient in the public interest'.
20. The National Commission for Integrated Water Resources development Plan, in its report of September 1999, puts the utilizable component at 396 BCM.
21. The NWP 1987 was subjected to severe criticism, that neither was it formulated without the participation of people nor did it allocate any role to the communities involved in practicing traditional water conservation. The only role sort for non-governmental organization was in educating farmers in efficient water use management.
22. "The resources like air, sea, water and the forests have such a great importance to the people as a whole, that it would be totally unjustified to make them a subject of private ownership. The concept 'environment' bears a very close relationship to the 'Public Trust Doctrine'. The doctrine enjoys upon the resources for the enjoyment of the general public, rather to permit their use for private ownership or commercial purposes."

References

Adve Nagraj (2004), 'Rising Struggles, Falling Water: Anti-Coca-Cola Agitation Picks up in Kaladera, Rajasthan', available at http//www.indiaresource.com, accessed on 8/7/2010.

Ahmed, Sara (2008), 'Gender and Integrate Water Resource Management in South Asia: The Challenge of Community-managed Alternatives' in Lahiri-dutt, Kuntala and Wasson Robert J. (ed.), *Water First: Issues and Challenges for Nations and Communities in South Asia*, Sage Publications, New Delhi, pp. 185-186.

Ballabh, Vishwa (2009), *Governance of Water: Institutional Alternatives and Political Economy,* Sage Publications, New Delhi, p. 4.

Barlow, Maude and Clarke, Tony (2003), *Blue Gold; The Fight to Stop Corporate Theft of Water,* Left Word Books, New Delhi, pp. 88-89.

Brubaker, Elizabeth (2001), *The Promise of Privatization,* Prepared for The Walkerton Inquiry, Energy Probe Research Foundation, 225 Brunswick Avenue, Ontario.

Conca, Ken (2005), *Governing Water: Contentious Transnational Politics and Global Institution Building,* The MIT Press, Cambridge, pp. 215-218.

Cesano, Daniele and Gustafsson (2000), Jan-Erik 'Impact of Economic Globalization on Water Resources; A Source of Technical, Social and Environmental Challenges for the Next Decade', in *Water Policy 2 (2000) 213-227*, Division of Land and water Resources, Royal Institute of Technology, KTH, 100 44, Stockholm, Sweden.

Dhillon, Amrit (2010), 'Coca-Cola Suspected of Sucking the Land Dry', available at, http//www.indiaresource.org, accessed on 10/7/10.

Finger, Matthias and Allouche, Geremy (2002), *Water Privatization, Transnational Corporations and the Re-regulation of the Water Industry,* Spon Press, London and New York, pp. 81-82.

Hall, David and Lobina, Emanuele (2002), *Water Privatisation in Latin America*, Public Services International Research Unit, University of Greenwich, Park Row.

Holland, Ann-Christin Sjolander (2005), *The Water Business, Corporations Versus People,* Zed Books, London and New York, pp. 81-82.

Iyer, Ramaswamy R. (2003), *Water, Perspectives, Issues and Concerns*, Sage, New Delhi, pp. 77-81.

Iyer, Ramaswamy R. (2007), *Towards Water Wisdom: Limits, Justice, Harmony*, Sage Publishers, New Delhi, p. 27.

Jayaraman, Nityanad (2005), 'Water Wars and Bottle Battles', available at indiaresource.org, accessed on 27/8/10.

KGWCRA (2002), *The Kerala Ground Water (Control and Regulation Act) 2002*, The Law Department, Government of Kerala, Secretariat, Thiruvananthapuram.

Kothari, Miloon 2004), 'Making Water a Human Right', *Combat Law*, June-July 2004, Mumbai, pp. 10-11.

Manthan Adhyayan Kendra (2002), *Document on Water Privatization in India*, Badwani (M.P.), pp. 4-5.

Moore, Deborah and Sklar, Leonard (1998), 'Reforming the World Bank's Lending for Water: The Process and Outcome of Developing a Water Resource Management Policy' in Jonathan A. Fox and L. David Brown (ed.), *The Struggle for Accountability, The World Bank, NGOs, and Grassroots Movements,* The MIT Press, Cambridge, p. 345.

McDonald, David Alexander and Ruiters, Greg (2005), *The Age of Commodity: Water Privatization in Southern Africa,* Earthscan, London.

M. C. Mehta vs. Kamal Nath, AIR 2000 SC 1997.

M. C. Mehta vs. Union of India (1997) 11 SCC 312.

Narmada Bachao Andolan vs. Union of India, AIR (2000) 10 SCC 664.

Pascual, Unai et al. (2009), *Water, Agriculture and Sustainable Well-being,* Oxford University Press, New York, p. 7.

Petrella, Ricardo (2001), *The Water Manifesto: Arguments for a World Water Contract*, Zed Books, London and New York, p. 15.

Ray, Binayak (2008), *Water: The Looming Crisis in India,* Lexington Books (A division of Rowman and Littlefield), Lanham, pp. 28-31.

Salman and Lank Ford (2004), *The Human Right to Water*, World Bank, Washington D. C., p. 7.

Sampath, Anitha et. al. (2004), *Water Privatization and Implications in India*, Association for India's Development, University Station A 6220, SOC#108.Austin, TX, USA, available at, http//www.studentsorgs.utexas.edu, accessed on 14/5/07.

Hamong Santono (2008), *Water Privatization in Indonesia and the Chance of PuPs as Alternatives*, available at, http://www.tni.org/water-docs/adbsantono.pdf, accessed on 16/608.

Sharma, Sudhirendar (2003), 'Water Markets Exclude the Poor', in Smithu Kothari et al. (ed.), *The Value of Nature*, Rainbow,

Noida, pp. 143-144.

Singh, Raajen (2004), 'Water for All, Is Privatization the Only Solution'? *Combat Law*, June-July 2004, Mumbai.

Singh, Arun Kumar (2004), *Privatization of Rivers in India,* Vikas Adhyan Kendra, Mumbai, p. 62.

Srivastava, Amit (2010), 'Community Files Police Report Accusing Coca-Cola of Water Theft and Pollution', available at, http://www.indiaresource.org, accessed on 8/710.

Tyagi, Partosh C. (2009), 'Water Pollution and Contamination', Iyer, Ramaswamy R. (ed.), *Water and Laws in India,* Sage Publishers, pp. 335-340.

Upadhyay, Videh (2009), 'The Ownership of Water in Indian Laws', in Iyer, Ramaswamy R. (ed.), *Water and Laws in India,* Sage Publishers, pp. 135-139.

Vaidyanathan A.and Jairaj, Bharath (2009), *Legal aspects of Water, Resource Management in* Iyer, Ramaswamy R. (ed.), *Water and Laws in India,* Sage Publishers, pp. 4-10.

VAK (2004): Report, Coca-Cola: Quit Plachimada: Quit India: The Story of Anti-Coca-Cola Struggle at Plachimada in Kerala, Vikas Adhyan Kendra, Mumbai.

Websites

http://rru.worldbank.org/documents/publicpolicyjournal/115vdbrg.pdf., accessed on 20/8/07.

http://en.wikipedia.org/wiki/Water_privatization_in_England, accessed on 13/10/07.

http://www.serconline.org/waterPrivatization/fact.html, accessed on 8/9/07.

http://www.citizen.org/documents/Bolivia_(PDF).PDF, accesses on 28/10/07.

http://en.wikipedia.org/wiki/Water_privatization_in_Argentina, accessed on 30/1/07.

3

Private Monopolies in Ground Water Exploitation: A Case Study of Plachimada Issue in Kerala

The state of Kerala lies in the southwest corner of Indian peninsular between 8°18' and 12°84' North latitude.

The state is bounded by Western Ghats in the East, the Arabian Sea in the West, Tamil Nadu in the South and Karnataka in the North. The state has been divided into 14 districts spread over 63 Taluks and 1452 Revenue Villages. Kerala occupies a total land space of 1.18 percent and the western coastal belt facing the Arabian Sea constitutes 10 percent of the total coastal line in India. Following a cross disciplinary interest in the paradoxical relationship between social and economic development, this south western Indian province has come out as a model for the developing societies across the world. The exceptional correlation of these two development outcomes in Kerala continued to attract scholarly attention, notwithstanding the precedence of social development by the human development framework since late 1980s. Kerala paradox in this new development framework is all about high figures in the statistical indicators of human development despite continuing patterns of low per capita income. The position of Kerala in the Human Development Index is even comparable to the societies in Europe and North America, thanks to high figures of life expectancy at birth, school enrolment ratio and adult literacy rate (Sajan, 2008).

3.1 Water Scenario in Kerala

From the point of view of water resources Kerala is having both abundance and scarcity. The average annual rainfall of the state is 3000 mm, the bulk of which is received during the

Southwest monsoon (June to September).

Kerala has got 41 west-flowing and 3 east-flowing rivers originating from the Western Ghats. The total annual yield of all these rivers together is 78.041 Million Cubic Meters (MCM). Taking an all India perspective the rivers of Kerala are not so significant; even the largest of them cannot find a place among the major Indian rivers. The elevational difference between high and low land in Kerala leads to a quick discharge of river water into the Lakshsdweep sea in the monsoon itself. The state has not been able to utilize the river water sources to a major extent. In the state 67.29 percent of the surface water area is constituted by brackish water lakes, backwaters and estuaries.

Ground water has been the mainstay for meeting the domestic needs of more than 80 percent of rural and 50 percent of urban population in Kerala. But the ground water potential is very low as compared to that of many other states in the country. The estimated ground water balance is $5590Mm^3$. Dug wells are the major source of ground water extraction in Kerala. The open well density in Kerala is perhaps the highest in the country–200 wells per sq. km. in the coastal region, 150 wells per sq. km in the midland and 70 wells per sq. km. in the high land. The ground water withdrawal is estimated as $980Mm^3$ and the effective recharge as 8134 sq Mm^3.The ground water level receding drastically during the summer season and drying up of wells is a common feature in many parts of Kerala. Recently, problems of decline in water table, contamination of ground water, seawater intrusion etc. are also being reported at many places.

3.2 Water Policy of Kerala

The Water Policy, 2007, states that the ownership of water resides with the state as a publicly owned resource with entitlement for individuals, communities and service providers to use water without owning it. The policy says that it is necessary to redesign the present institutional arrangements in order to guide and regulate water use and achieve better stakeholder participation. Thereby sustainability of water resources can be ensured with the participation of stakeholders and Local Self-government Institutions.

Though the state receives an average rainfall of 3000 mm the water scenario in Kerala is not much better. Ground water level has declined drastically and pollution levels in the water bodies and drinking water sources have gone up at an alarming rate. The Policy made a priority list for allocating water among various categories of users. Such a prioritization should base on the integrity of ecosystem and will also take into consideration the physical, environmental and social background of the state. The list is in the following order: domestic use, agricultural use, power generation, agro-based industrial use, industrial and commercial use, all other uses. The policy document also states about water use entitlement, management of existing water resource projects, water resource planning, etc. (Water Policy, 2007).

3.3 The Plachimada Case

Plachimada, a village situated at Chittur Taluk of Palakkad district in the South Indian state of Kerala is a small agricultural region. Plachimada belongs to Perumatty Grama Panchayat that was formed in 1948 with three villages, Perumatty, Moolathara and Vandithavalam. At present the Panchayat is divided into 15 wards in 60.79 sq. km that shares its borders with Tamil Nadu on the eastern side and Pattanchery Panchayat on the western side. Perumatty Panchayat with a total population of 29,500 is part of Chittur Block Panchayat and Pattanchery District Panchayat. Socially and economically Perumatty Panchayat lags behind other panchayats in Palakkad district.

The Tenth Five Year Plan (2002-2007) Development Report of Perumatty Panchayat says that lack of market for agricultural products and unemployment adversely affected the economy of the panchayat. It pointed out that industries working in the panchayat did not reduce the huge unemployment problem and their contribution towards development is meagre. Diary farming is also affected due to the high input rates. Construction work has also affected due to economic crisis that contributes more to the unemployment scale and thereby increases the number of Below Poverty Line families.

Public participation in Grama Sabha, Kudumbasree, project implementation, etc. is less in Perumatty Panchayat compared to other regions in the district. Better educational facilities are of an urgent necessity as it comes under the Chittur Taluk, one of the less literate area in Kerala. Access to better health infrastructure has not been materialized so far leading to the outbreak of many contagious diseases. Infrastructure facilities in the tribal colonies are also poor that worsens the condition. One of the major problems aroused recently in the panchayat is scarcity of drinking water due to climate change and other problems. The drinking water projects of the Kerala Water Authority are not functioning well, because the panchayat is not able to meet the expenses related to its maintenance including wages to the labourers. It is in this context that there witnessed the arrival of Hindustan Coca-Cola Beverages Private Limited in Plachimada in the name of development through employment expansion.

3.4 Socio-economic Profile of Plachimada

The socio-cultural composition of the people in Plachimada is a blend of Tamil Nadu and Kerala traits, as majority of them migrated from Tamil Nadu in search of livelihood means and settled here few decades ago. Majority of the population in the village belongs to the socio-economic backward classes consist of Eravalar, Malasar and Vilvedans. The other communities present here are Ezhavas, Goundans, Muthaliyars, Chettis and Muslims. The educational and health status of the people remains abysmally low. Only 5 percent of the population has attained the secondary and higher secondary education. Women, tribes and Other Backward Caste communities form majority of the illiterates.

Predominantly people in Plachimada are farmers and agricultural labourers. Paddy, coconut, groundnut, vegetables, horse gram, maize, mango, flowers, sugar cane and banana are the major crops, of which coconut dominates. The farmers have an average land holding of 1.5 to 10 acres. The agricultural labourers and other daily wage-labourers, mostly from the Scheduled Tribe community possess one to ten cents. Besides agriculture and wage labouring, another category of people is self-employed in trade, business or small enterprises. Though Plachimada is located near the Kanchikode Industrial area, very few people depends in industrial labour for their livelihood (VAK, 2004).

3.5 Important Water Sources in Plachimada

Plachimada is located in a rain shadow region of Chittur Taluk. Plachimada situates just 5 km away from Tamil Nadu border and 30 km. east of Palakkad town. Though the region gets little rainfall, conditions for ground water recharge are better here because of the gently undulating nature of the terrain. Plachimada received an average rainfall of 1413 mm in between 1994-2004; whereas the normal annual rainfall of Kerala is 3,107 mm (national average is 1,197 mm). This shows that the entire region has to depend upon ground water and canal water for domestic as well as agricultural purposes. Table 3.1 depicts the average annual rainfall received in Chitturpuzha Rain Gauge Station in Palakkad District (CWRDM, 2005).

In 2004, the Central Ground Water Board (CGWB) assessed the annual available ground water resource in Chittur Block and Plachimada water shed on the basis of ground water estimation methodology—1997 guidelines approved by the Ministry of Water Resources.

In Chittur Block the availability is 66.7 Million Cubic Meters and the total demand is 62.5 MCM, while in

Plachimada watershed, the availability is 3.67 MCM and the demand is 3.42 MCM.

Table 3.1: Annual Rainfall as Recorded in Chitturpuzha Rain Gauge Station in Palakkad District

Year	Rainfall–Annual Period (June-May) (in mm)
1994-1995	2135
1995-1996	1449
1996-1997	1430
1997-1998	1493
1998-1999	1759
1999-2000	1344
2000-2001	1185
2001-2002	1281
2002-2003	1031
2003-2004	1021
Mean Rainfall	1413

Source: CWRDM Report, 2005, p. 19.

However, Centre for Science and Environment (CSE) estimated the annual ground water yield is in between 16.6 and 33.2 MCM. In 2004 Centre for Water Resource Development and Management (CWRDM) reported the annual recharge as 66.7 MCM and the demand for domestic sector as 16.8 MCM and irrigation demand is that of 45.7 gives a surplus water of 4.2 MCM (Paul, 2005). Table 3.2 depicts these facts.

Traditionally ponds, wells and tanks are the main water sources in Plachimada. Since 1974, the entire paddy cultivation in Plachimada depends on the canal water of Chitturpuzha Irrigation Project popularly known as Parambikulam Aliyar Project (PAP). Apart from this, three surface water reservoirs—Meenkara, Kambalathara and Vengalakkayam—provides water for irrigation in the region. The river Chitturpuzha runs about 2 km. from here and the irrigation canal from Meenkara dam also surrounds Plachimada. By 1980s, rural electrification paved way to electric motors and thereby came large number of bore-wells and dug-wells for irrigation purposes. This transformation from canal irrigation to lift irrigation gave way to destruction of traditional tanks and ponds as well as the introduction of water-intensive cropping patterns, especially coconut (Paul, 2005).

Table 3.2: Estimates of Demand and Supply of Ground Water in Chittur Block

Items	CWRDM	CGWB	CSE
Total available recharge	66.7	66.7	16.6 to 33.2
Demand for domestic sector	16.8	-	9.25
Irrigation demand	45.7	-	54.86
Surplus for commercial sector	4.2	-	-47.51 to -30.91
Total Demand	62.5	62.5	64.11

Sources: CWRDM, CGWB, CSE Reports.

These transformations in the water use pattern pushed Plachimada into acute water scarcity by the end of 1990s. Several households experienced water insecurity and lost their self-reliance in access to water. The users deepened the wells as the water level depleted and some of them have dug two or three wells to meet their irrigation purposes. Very rich farmers are now using high power centrifugal tube-wells to extract deep underground water. Water supply through the canals stops during summer and the region face acute water scarcity during this period. Water requirements of the three tribal colonies in Plachimada—Vijayanagar Colony, Plachimada Colony and Rajivnagar Colony - are met by ground water. The 200 tribal families in Plachimada have only 16 wells for their domestic water needs. Through out the year availability of safe drinking water is an issue before them. This situation gets aggravated with the entry of Coca-Cola Company in 2000.

3.6 Advent of Hindustan Coca-Cola Beverages Private Limited

Hindustan Coca-Cola Beverages Private Limited (HCBPL) is a subsidiary of Coca-Cola Company in Atlanta, USA. Coca-Cola Company was expelled from India in late 1970s when the Foreign Exchange Regulation Act of 1973 was effected. But in the wake of liberalization the post-1991 economic reforms paved way for the re-entry of Coca-Cola into India. In 1997 the Cabinet Committee of Foreign Investments granted approval to set up two subsidiaries as holding companies and down stream ventures. Later in February 2000, the two holding companies and four downstream subsidiaries were united into a single company called Hindustan Coca-Cola Beverages Private Limited (Wrammer, 2004). The arrival of HCBPL in Kerala in 1999 was at the specific request of the then Left Democratic Front government in the name of development through employment opportunities. On October 8, 1999 HCBPL applied to Perumatty Panchayat for a license to start its bottling plant in Plachimada.

The company got license on January 27, 2000 with 11 conditions [1] from the District Medical Officer when the company submitted the consent letters from Pollution Control Board, Fire Department Divisional Officer, Factories and Boiler's Inspector, Ministry of Agricultural/Food Processing Industry and Chief Electrical Inspector. The company got license from June 3, 2000 for producing Coca-Cola, Thums Up, Sprite, Fanta, Kinley Soda, Limca and Maaza by using water from one open well with a motor of capacity 2600 HP. As per the permission of Kerala State Pollution Control Board the company can produce 5,61,000 litres of soft drinks per day. The license was granted up to March 31, 2003 and the panchayat collected a license fee of ₹ 30,500. HCBPL is located at 10°35’30’ North latitude and 76°46’15’ East longitudes. Location map is shown in the following figure. The factory is situated along the Palakkad-Meenakshipuram-Pollachi road and just three kilometre north of the Meenkara reservoir and about hundred meters west of the Kambalathara and Vengalakkayam storage reservoirs. Chitturpuzha itself is two kilometres north of the plant site and Moolanthodu main canal passes about 10 meters north of the factory compound (VAK, 2004).

The daily water demand of the of the plant is met by drawing ground water from six bore wells and one open well with water meters. As such the company does not bring water from outside. But during summer the plant brought water from outside in tanker lorries. The plant does not draw electricity from the common grid because it has the captive electricity generator set (INTACH, 2004). It is reported that the plant does not have a registration number as the conversion order from Land Utilization Board was not sanctioned as per the Kerala Land Utilization Act 1967. The plant started its production in March 2000 in its 35.64-acre (14 hectare) land in Plachimada with 130 permanent workers and 250-300 contract labourers (VAK, 2004).

The production process of soft drinks is rather simple. High-grade sugar procured from sugar mill is subjected to Hot Carbon Treatment for preparing purified sugar syrup. Carbon dioxide, sugar syrup, treated water and soft drink concentrate manufactured in Pune is then blended to form the final product. The glass bottles returned from the market are thoroughly cleaned at high temperature using sophisticated bottle washers and cleaning agents. The bottles are then transformed to the filter area and then the beverage is filled by using high speed automated filling machine (KSPCB, 2003). As against the Panchayat stipulation the company extracted ground water from six bore wells and two open wells.

The amount of water used by the plant is still involved in controversy. The exact volume of soft drinks produced by the firm is not published. It is said that the production of one bottle of coke requires nearly four litres of water. HCBPL claims that it extracts four to six lakh litres of water everyday. The plant got the license for producing 5,61,000 litres of soft-drinks daily, means the company requires around 22 lakh litres of water per day. R.N. Athavale, an Emeritus scientist claimed that the company operates at 60 percent of its capacity. At 60 percent production level it would require around 13 lakh litres per day. The Central Ground Water Board estimated an average use of 5.1 lakh litres everyday, while CWRDM reported that the company used around 5 lakh litres in a day (Paul, 2005).

During the production process solid and liquid waste were generated from the factory. Purification of ground water, soft drink preparation, cleaning of bottles, disposal of spoilt beverage and other processing activities generated a large amount of waste. Plastic, paper, metallic and other forms of waste were also generated after the production and distribution (INTACH, 2004). The waste generated during the water purifying process is collected in a light collared sludge form. The sludge contains dirt, clay and other suspended matter, undesirable organic matters, microbial matters, heavy metals and other compounds.

The liquid waste generated during the process is directed to an effluent treatment plant. In the treatment plant the effluent is directed through bar screens for removal of large objects and then passed through a chamber for removal of oil and grease. The effluent is then collected in a collection pit and then to an equalization tank. In the next step the organic matter is removed from the effluent and then subject to secondary clarifier, chlorine dosing. The treated effluent partially goes for gardening, crate washing, floor cleaning and to toilets and fire tanks (KSPCB, 2003).

The continually sprayed wastewater on the garden was percolated down and reached the water table, causing pollution of the well water. Besides the continuous heavy withdrawal of ground water may adversely affected the water table. Thus salinity and hardness of ground water have also increased drastically because minerals from the deeper soil layers could be moving to the upper layers and contaminating the water. In addition to this, the dark collared sludge generated from the effluent treatment plant was stacked in plastic bags and transported to farmers as manure. It got spread around through irrigation canals over a large area contaminating the soil and water (INTACH, 2004).

3.7 Local Level Impacts of HCBPL

Since 2000 water availability in the open wells and bore wells has drastically fallen. People reported that they could pump water for irrigation continuously for twenty-four hours before the arrival of Coca-cola plant but when the plant has started operation within four hours of pumping, their wells go dry. As a result agriculture was affected badly. Water from most of the wells tasted bitterly and became unpotable. Water from some of the wells on boiling and subsequent cooling developed an intense milky colour and within few hours a white precipitate was formed. Tribal women who used this water reported that rice and dhal do not get cooked but became hard and going bad quickly (INTACH, 2004).

The continuous use of polluted water for a long period caused much health hazardous among the people. Many diseases like abnormal hair falling, burning of eye, stomach disorders, pains in limbs, etc. have started. Women labourers employed to spray wastewater on the garden inside the factory compound reported deep dark pigmentation on their palms, forearms and feet as well as infection in wounds. People who bath in the water reported skin reactions. Subsequently, a medical camp was conducted in November 2003. They found the most prominent symptom among the people as anaemia.

At present the colony people are collecting drinking water from two kilometres away. For other purposes they are depending on the water supply of the panchayat through pipelines and tanker lorries started in 2003. Farmers started bringing water from the next villages in vehicles. But the poor people in colonies have no other options (VAK, 2004). The survey results of Vikas Adhyan Kendra (VAK) showed a sharp decrease in the agricultural production since the company started its function. Paddy cultivation and production of coconut and vegetables were also affected. The irrigation system managed by the farmers was also damaged due to the depletion of ground water. The VAK presents an alarming finding that the use of contaminated water by the pregnant women caused reduction in birth weight.

By 2002 April the people from the tribal colonies organized under the leadership of Mayilamma, a 55 year old lady from Vijayanagar colony. C.K. Janu, leader of Adivasi Gothra Mahasabha, inaugurated the struggle on 22nd April. They formed a *Coca-Cola Virudha Samara Samithi* (Anti-Coca-Cola Agitation Council) and within one year it got support from many environmental and human rights organizations worldwide. The Perumatty Panchayath initially played a passive role in resolving the water insecurity problem. When political pressure mounted high, the panchayath committee was forced to take an active role in tackling the water problem. After a yearlong agitation the Perumatty Panchayat cancelled the license of HCBPL in 15th May 2003 (VAK, 2004).

3.8 Results of Scientific Studies on Environmental Issues in Plachimada

When the struggle received national and international attention within one year many governmental and non-governmental agencies were rushed into Plachimada for further investigation. The first of this kind was the test conducted by Integrated Rural Technology Centre (IRTC), an independent organization in June 2002. IRTC collected water samples from different wells and conducted a number of tests. The result showed high levels of hardness, salinity, alkalinity, chlorides and sulphates (IRTC, 2002). One of the test results is shown in Table 3.3.

During July 2003, BBC (British Broadcasting Corporation) radio 4's Face the Facts presenter John Waite visited the plant on coming to know that the sludge from this plant was being used as manure in the nearby farming fields. As part of the probe he collected the samples to study and sent to UK for examination in the University of Exeter. The tests revealed the material was useless as a fertilizer and it contained a number of toxic wastes, including cadmium and lead (BBC, 2003).

Table 3.3: Water Quality Analysis Report-IRTC

S.N	Parameter	Unit	Limit	Test result
1.	Odour	-	Unobjectionable	Unobjectionable
2.	Taste	-	Agreeable	-
3.	Turbidity	NTU	10	11.2
4.	Total dissolved solids	Mg/l	500	1100
5.	Ph	-	6.5-8.5	6.7
6.	Temperature	Co	-	28
7.	Conductivity	Us/cm	-	180
8.	Dissolved oxygen	Mg/l	4-8	4.2
9.	Total hardness	Mg/l	300	1110
10.	Calcium hardness	Mg/l	75	450
11.	Magnesium hardness	Mg/l	30	660
12.	Chlorides	Mg/l	250	519.4
13.	Salinity	Ppt	-	949.2
14.	Alkalinity	Mg/l	100	1390
15.	Sulfide	Mg/l	0.4	3.2
16.	MPN count	-	Nil	34

Source: IRTC Report, p. 1, dated 29/6/2002.

Meantime, Centre for Science and Environment reported that there are high levels of pesticide contents in samples of Coca-Cola sold in various parts of the country. Later on August 22, Lok Sabha formed a Joint Parliamentary

Committee (JPC) under the chairmanship of Sharad Pawar to enquire into the issue of standards for soft drinks and other beverages. The JPC asked Central Pollution Control Board (CPCB), Kerala State Pollution Control Board (KSPCB) and the Supreme Court Monitory Committee (SCMC) to look into the issue. The SCMC conducted a visit on August 14, 2004 and formed a local environmental protection committee for further monitoring. Moreover it criticized the illegal dumping of toxic wastes around the company and asked HCBPL to provide safe drinking water to the nearby local people (Paul, 2005).

But Kerala Ground Water Board (KGWB) in its January 2003 report stated, "as such we cannot observe that pollution, if any in this area is due to M/s Coca-Cola factory discharge." The KSPCB in its September 2003 report recommended that the waste generated from the factory is not advisable for applying on land for agriculture as manure. The company should handle the solid waste following the procedures and safeguards prescribed by the Hazardous Waste (Management and Handling) Rules, 1989 amended in 2003. According to a joint survey conducted in 2004 by the Central Ground Water Board and the State Ground Water Department, there has been a spurt in ground water extraction in Kerala during the last decade. They have classified five blocks as *overexploited*, 15 as *critical* and 30 as *semi-critical*. The five blocks are, Athiyannur in Thiruvananthapuram district, Kozhikode in Kozhikode district, Kasargode in Kasargode district, Chittur in Palakkad district and Kodunganllor in Thrissur district. In *critical-areas* and *over-exploited* areas there should be intensive monitoring and evaluation and future ground water development be linked with water conservation measures and micro level studies (KSPCB, 2003). [2]

The Kerala High Court in 2003 directed the CWRDM to conduct a scientific investigation into the allegation that the works of Hindustan Coca-Cola Beverages Private Limited has resulted in shortage and scarcity of drinking water in neighbouring areas. The duration of the project was for one year, commenced from 2nd week of January 2004. Based on CGWB's estimate, according to which the annual ground water resource in Chittur Taluk is 66.7 MCM and the total demand is 62.5 MCM leaves a surplus of 4.2 MCM, CWRDM found that the extraction of 5 lakh litres except during weak monsoons a day by HCBPL would not affect adversely the water availability in the block. Their micro level analysis also claims that the annual yield of ground water at Plachimada watershed at 3.67 MCM and its demand at 3.42 MCM that leaves a surplus of 0.25 MCM. But as per the estimate of CSE the annual water yield is in between 16.6 and 32.2 MCM, and thus the surplus is negative. Negating these findings CWRDM argues that commercial extraction of ground water would not worsen the water insecurity at Plachimada (CWRDM, 2005).

3.9 Other Reports

Yuvajanavedi, a youth organization published a report in November 2002 based on a study conducted by them in Plachimada. In this report they argued that the fluoride and chloride content as well as the electrical conductivity is high in the water samples collected from the areas where the Coca-Cola and Pepsi factory is situated. The organization appointed a commission to study the problem in the area headed by Dr. A. Achyuthan. The commission enquired about the environmental impact assessment done by the company. But the company did not produce any reports on before the commission. Indian National Trust for Arts and Cultural Heritage (INTACH), a Thiruvananthapuram based NGO conducted an investigation in the area and found that the continuous heavy withdrawal of ground water in the plant site has adversely affected the water table. Besides, the partially processed waste water from the plant is continually sprayed on the garden being raised within the factory compound is percolated down and reached the water table which caused ground water contamination (INTACH, 2004).

In 2003, Vikas Adhyan Kendra, a voluntary organization in Mumbai conducted a study in Plachimada and concluded that the working of the plant caused the denial of right to water and livelihood. Several uncommon diseases were started because of the polluted ground water. *Jananeethi*, a registered charitable society in Kerala conducted a study by testing a number of samples from public and private wells near the factory and found that the chloride and magnesium levels as well as the hardness are high. *Kerala Sastra Sahitya Parishad* (KSSP) produced a report on the water utilization of the factory and found that if the company used about 2 lakh litres of water per day that may affect the aquifer as a whole and the ground water availability in future.

3.10 Findings of the Field Survey in Plachimada

This section discusses the findings of field survey conducted by the author at Plachimada in 2005. The objective of the field survey was to understand the socio-economic profile of Plachimada, to understand the water availability and utilization pattern that prevailed in Plachimada up to 2000, to explore the changes that took place in water availability and its utilization pattern since the working of company and finally to find out the impacts of water pollution and depletion among the people. The survey was conducted in three phases during 2005. The first phase, the pilot study, was conducted for three weeks from 1st to 21st February, 2005. On this occasion the field and its surrounding areas, including the Kanchikode industrial area and the places near to Tamil Nadu like Meenakshipuram and Vandithavalam were familiarized. The research site–the people, the struggle, the nature of water, the factory, etc. were well observed.

The second phase of field visit commenced on the third anniversary of Anti-Coca-Cola struggle i.e., on 22nd April 2005 and over by 30 days. During this period a sample survey was conducted with the help of an open-ended questionnaire. By the end of this study, the research area, the number and category of households, etc. were selected through simple random sampling. The third visit started on 10th September 2005. In this phase the final survey was conducted with a closed questionnaire. The way of agitation and reaction of the people towards this issue were made clear through non-participant observation. Interview with political party leaders and leaders of the struggle were also conducted. In addition primary data related to the sanction and cancellation of license, working of the company, various study results, scientific reports, development report of the panchayat, etc. were also collected. Later, the empirical data were statistically analyzed, while other kinds of primary data were put into qualitative analysis.

3.11 Demographic Pattern in the Study Area

The field survey conducted throughout Plachimada area affirmed the fact that it is a socio-economic back ward region. Caste-class difference is openly visible in this area with the absence of a considerable number of middle class because of socio-cultural, geographical and temporal variations. Unlike other parts of Kerala all the upper class people belongs to upper caste and traditionally they are land lords. The population also showed reluctance to occupational mobility. The estimated population of the study area in Plachimada comes to 1195. The total number of households in the study area is 239 and the average household size is five. Out of the 239 households in the study area a survey among 100 families were conducted.

In Plachimada women folk constitute majority of the survey respondents. The decision to include more women participants were taken during the sampling process itself. Because, like the environmental movements all over India, Plachimada struggle is also popular for its increased women participation and leadership. It is clear that a considerable number of the celebrities of Plachimada struggle were also women. In most of the marches, picketing and other struggle related activities women constituted a major chunk of population. The gender wise distribution of the population had later been proved to be critical to the water rights based struggle in Plachimada.

The age-wise distribution is also pivotal for the Plachimada movement. This is particularly because of the fact that the 36-50 age group in particular women, make up a greater part of the group that participated in the water rights struggle. The fact that nearly all of these struggle participants are housewives add new dimensions to the Plachimada struggle. Given the emergent socio-political context of gendered access to water across the world, the Plachimada struggle is a clear illustration to the unfolding global patterns of gender wise inequality. Notwithstanding the fact that lion's share of these housewives have trespassed their child bearing functions, access to water has found to be important to their well-being in a multitude of ways. The most important one in this regard is the responsibility of housewives to collect entire water for all family members.

Unlike most of the residential areas in Kerala, Scheduled Castes and Scheduled Tribes constitute the numerical majority within the study area. The prominent tribal groups in Plachimada are Eravalar, Malasar and Vilvedars. As discussed in the earlier section of this chapter the aforementioned tribal groups have not been tribes in the strict sense of the term. Unlike the forest dependent tribes in other parts of Kerala, the tribal groups in Plachimada are products of labour driven migration from Tamil Nadu. The very fact that Scheduled Tribes with Tamil origins came to the forefront of a Kerala based movement is an under-discussed issue within the Plachimada movement. Regardless of the fact that the Tamil tribes in Plachimada form a classic example of 'double victimization', their participation in the struggle has turned to be an interesting case of grassroots mobilization. Double victimization is a reality because both the Tamil minorities and Tribal groups are often marginalized and victimized by the mainstream Kerala society. It is pertinent to note here that except Muslims, Ezhavas and a greater part of the Scheduled Castes, the non-tribal groups, the Chettis and Goundan in the study area are of Tamil origin. Now the discussion here goes to the caste-wise composition of the study area.

From Table 3.4, it is clear that among the 100 households 2 families constitute petty businessmen, 15 constitute the farmers and the remaining 83 constitute agriculture and other daily wage labourers. It is a fact that a greater part of the sample population is agricultural and daily wage labourers. While a considerable number of the agricultural wage labourers work in paddy and coconut fields, the remaining section is indulged in mango, maize, banana and vegetable cultivation. The female wage labourers in Plachimada are also used to go as agricultural wage labourers.

Table 3.4: Caste-wise Distribution of Occupation

Occupation	Scheduled Tribes (ST)	Scheduled Castes (SC)	Other Backward Class (OBC)	Forward Castes (FC)	%age
Agricultural and other daily wage labourers	77	6	-	-	83
Farmers	-	-	5	10	15
Petty businessmen	-	-	2	-	2

It is worthwhile to note here that lion's share of these agricultural wage labourers are working in the farm lands owned by Chetti and Goundan, two of the most important land owing caste groups in Plachimada. Among the non-agricultural wage labourers, the substantial segments are involved in toddy tapping, construction industry, and various household related labour activities. The remaining Other Backward Class population is involved in petty business and trade.

The wage patterns have crucial bearing to the political economy of the region. As compared to wages of male labourers, the female wage labourers are getting only ₹ 45-60 per day. It should be noted that the wage levels in Plachimada and adjoining area are relatively lower when compared to other parts of Kerala. The low wage patterns of the region have later proved to be a key determinant in the social legitimacy of the company. But the company had given little preference to the natives of Plachimada in regard to the employment in the water bottling plant. Given that few natives of Plachimada got employment in the bottling plant with a relative high wage level in comparison with the existing wage patterns, the company has been able to proceed without considerable local protest at the initial stage.

The caste wise monthly income patterns of Plachimada are in stark contrast to the general income statistics of Kerala. In the general Kerala case, the presence of a numerically considerable middle class often bridges the rich-poor disparity of the given region. However, the absence of a significant middle class population has turned the study area as one of the highly unequal regions within Kerala. The survey results illustrate that the ₹ 800-1600 income range (i.e. the Scheduled Tribe population) constitute the majority group in the study area. The very fact that none of the ST households found a place in the ₹ 2401-5000 and above ₹ 5000 category points to the disparity-ridden scenario in Plachimada. Being the land owning community of the region, the forward castes have access to different income sources and thus lead a higher standard of living. Table 3.5 shows the socio-political implications of the land holding patterns in the study area.

Before going into the land holding patterns in Plachimada, there is a need to mention few aspects of the demographic landscape of the study area. Most of the scheduled castes and scheduled tribes are living in *Lakshamveedu colonies* (under the one-lakh housing scheme of yester years) nearly for the last three decades. Being living in a clustered manner with 4-10 cents of lands, these colony people are devoid of exclusive water sources. The Lakshamveedu colony households are only endowed with few public wells to meet their water requirements. In contrast to the four to ten cent landholders in the above-mentioned colonies, holders of more than ten cents of land in study area have access to different water sources which, would ranges from two to three individual wells [3] per households to surface water sources such as, ponds, streams, etc. The very fact that the greater part of the struggle participants belong to the four to ten cents category can shed light on the water-based inequality regime exists within the study area.

Table 3.5: Land Holdings across Population

Land holdings	ST	SC	OBC	FC	Percentage
4-10 cents	77	2	-	-	79
11 cents-2 acres	-	4	4	-	8
2-10 acres	-	-	3	8	11
10 acres and above	-	-	-	2	2

Any discussion on the demographic pattern of the population in Plachimada study area will not be complete without a proper discussion on the educational background. The educational background has also later become a crucial factor for the progress of the water right movement in Plachimada. Not withstanding the fact that whole of the study area comes within the literacy wise forward Kerala state, the Plachimada people, shows very little educational mobility. It is well understood that nearly seventy-eight respondents from the study area were either illiterate or school dropouts at the primary level. Out of these respondents nearly twenty are full-fledged illiterates.

The survey also bears ample testimony to the fact that very few people, regardless of their caste background, have been able to reach up to the upper primary and secondary school level. When it comes to the water rights movement, it is an interesting fact that nearly all of the leaders with grassroots origin have attained little formal education. Considering the fact that the Plachimada movement has later been elevated to a global scale, the relatively backward educational statistics of the study region requires serious elaboration. This will elaborate while discussing the movement nature, but it is worthwhile to mention here that it is the middle players who acted as an intermediary between the victimized local population and the propagators of a global resistance movement.

3.12 Water Availability in the Study Area until 2000

Given that the functioning of Coca-Cola bottled plant since 2000 had impacted upon the water availability in Plachimada, the author had collected information regarding the availability of pure drinking water and rainwater till 2000 and from 1995 onwards respectively. There are three tribal colonies in Plachimada–the Plachimada colony, Vijayanagar colony and Rajivnagar colony. Plachimada colony consists of 105 families and they have only two bore wells and four open wells for collecting potable drinking water. Likewise, in Vijayanagar colony there is six open wells and one bore well for its fifty-three households. The forty-nine families in Rajivnagar colony depends on two bore wells and one large open well for drinking water. With these estimates it is clear that high-level inequality in access to water exists in between the farmers and tribal people in the water distribution system of Plachimada.

According to the survey results greater share of the people (88 respondents) opined that pure water was available till 2000. It is worth mentioning that the most affected population of the company activities, the scheduled tribes, was of the opinion that there had been uninterrupted supply of drinking water till 2000. Other respondents also shared similar opinion. Even though the availability of rainwater does not have any direct correlation with the functioning of the company it seems that the scarcity of rainwater during the last couple of years have already affected the availability of water in Plachimada. A significant number of the respondents in the study area were of the opinion that there is a sharp reduction in rainwater availability during the last one decade. This is best illustrated from the responses of the scheduled tribe population that is, the last five to ten years was very significant in regard to the reduction in rainfall and thereby the ground water availability. It is in this context, the Hindustan Coca-Cola Beverages Private Limited arrived with its bottling plant and it intensified the water scarcity.

3.13 Sources of Water

In order to look into the sources of water till 2000, the author made a three-fold classification of the water sources in Plachimada. They are drinking water sources, water sources for household purposes and water sources for agriculture. At the outset it should make clear that these three categories are not the resultant of a clear-cut classification as there are numerous instances of overlap between the three. Henceforth, this classification is just for the analytical convenience. The aforementioned overlaps between the three categories have ramifications in regard to the access and utilization of water and will discuss the same in due course.

Table 3.6 on water sources has close allegiance to the discussion we already have in the landholdings section. From the study it is clear that except a microscopic minority, lion's share of the scheduled tribe population in Plachimada depends on public wells and bore wells, which are few in number. These figures have close correlation with existing landholding pattern in the region. Own wells are only the prerogative of a small number of Scheduled Castes/Scheduled Tribes (SC/STs) and the different landholding households hailing from the forward communities. It is proved that water rights are closely interconnected with land rights.

Table 3.6: Major Water Sources in the Study Area

Sources	ST	SC	OBC	FC	%age
Own wells and ponds	8	3	5	10	26
Public wells and bore wells	69	3	2	-	74

Moreover the canal water constitutes the most important household water source in the study region. It is found that seventy percentage of SC/ST population depends on canal water for their household water needs. The huge disparity exists between the canal water users and those who rely on wells and ponds gives a clear picture of the importance of public water source in the study area. Regardless of the fact that there are few public wells in the study region a greater part of the Plachimada households go for canal water to meet their household water requirements such as, bathing, washing and selected kitchen purposes. The caste wise differences in regard to the utilization of canal water also deserve special mention. From the survey it is understood that very few non-scheduled tribe households depend upon the canal water. The survey on household's water sources reiterates the already established point that water rights in Plachimada are inextricably intertwined with the access to land resources.

Any discussion of the water utilization scenario in Plachimada will not be complete without a mention to the agricultural water sources in the study region. Even though access to agricultural land is severely limited in Plachimada, food and cash crop agriculture has crucial bearing upon the region's political economy. Only Other Backward Classes and forward castes are endowed with own wells and ponds in the study area. Except paddy cultivation, which is largely based on canal and rainwater, all other agricultural water needs were met through own wells and ponds until 2000.

3.14 Water Availability since the Advent of HCBPL

The survey among the house holds in Plachimada regarding the impact of HCBPL reinstated most of the established facts and shed light to others. People reported that HCBPL conducted a satellite study before applying for license which revealed the ground water potential in Plachimada. Besides the company was satisfied with this area on the misconception that the tribes would not recognize and resist if a problem comes. These people was made to believe that there comes a theatre and the voice of resistance was absent during the construction.

It is alleged that the company operations in Plachimada caused much depletion and pollution of ground water. But some of the results obtained from the field explorations had not been in close terms with the existent scientific and popular literature on the water question in Plachimada. A greater part of the fieldwork reports on Plachimada analyzed the issue from the depletion point of view. By depletion point of view, the author referred to those studies, which looked into the Plachimada issue from the water depletion scenario since the functioning of the company. These studies give over emphasis to the fall in the water table ever since the company operations. However the data collected by the author did not rule out the depletion point of view, rather it prompts us to consider the issue from the pollution point of view (Table 3.7).

Table 3.7: Water Depletion

Response	ST	SC	OBC	FC	%age
Highly depleted	2	-	2	4	8
Depleted	18	3	2	5	28
Not depleted	57	3	3	1	64

The comments of the respondents in the study area, especially farmers who rely on alternate sources of ground water, such as ponds, wells, etc. points to the depletion of ground water in the region. It is well understood that the lower caste majority, who depends largely on wells to meet the water requirements, would not feel depletion as a major problem. Majority of the respondents observed that it is difficult to make a direct correlation between the company's operations and the depletion of ground water (Table 3.8).

Table 3.8: Water Pollution

Response	ST	SC	OBC	FC	%age
Polluted	75	6	7	8	96
Not polluted	2	-	-	2	4

Rather the greater share of the respondents opined that there have been considerable levels of water pollution since 2000. They have mentioned about different types water pollution which are explained below. It is worthwhile to note here that the respondents, cutting across caste barriers point out the extensiveness of water pollution in their locality. Henceforth it is better to consider the not polluted respondent category as an outlier in regard to the water pollution scenario in Plachimada. According to Mayilamma, who was the local leader of Plachimada struggle, one cannot find a single unpolluted well in Plachimada and nearby areas. She added that the change in taste and colour of the water has negatively affected the day to day household needs. [4] The survey on the nature of water pollution shed light on the diversity of patterns prevalent in regard to the contamination of the local water sources. The most significant point is that a major chunk of the respondents revealed that they have experienced nearly all types of water pollution (colour change, bitter taste, precipitation after boiling, not good for cooking, etc.), since the functioning of the Coca-Cola Company. The fact that a larger number of the scheduled tribe population raised the point of total contamination bears ample testimony to the vicious state of water pollution in Plachimada (Table 3.9).

The drastic decline in the dependence on ground water sources compelled the people to search for other options such as tanker lorry supply, from next village and sometimes even far away from 2 kilometre. The increased dependence upon tanker lorry supply in a region bestowed with ground water sources offer a good case for the detrimental impacts of bottling plants on the regional water sources. The emerging practice of relying upon adjoining villages for the water needs is going to be a big problem in the future.

Table 3.9: Current Water Sources

Source	ST	SC	OBC	FC	%age
Tanker lorry supply	41	2	3	4	50
Public taps	16	1	3	-	20
Wells (2 km. away)	20	2	1	-	23
From next village	-	1	-	6	7

3.15 Impact on the Local Population

The following section will show the impact of HCBPL on the Plachimada population. The author has analyzed the survey results in such a way that the multi-faceted impacts of the company activity in Plachimada could be properly discussed in the work (Table 3.10).

Table 3.10: Negative Impacts on the Intake of Water

Reduced the intake of water for	ST	SC	OBC	FC	%age
Drinking	66	-	-	2	68
Household	11	6	6	-	23
Agricultural	-	-	1	8	9

The functioning of Coca-Cola factory in Plachimada has made detrimental impacts on the intake of water. However these impacts have varied patterns across the different caste groups in the study region. Except a few, majority of the respondents mentioned about reduction in the intake of water during the last five years. But the concerns of the Plachimada people were closely related to the nature and extent of water utilization all through the last five years. Depending on the water utilization purposes (drinking, household, agricultural, etc.), nearly all of the respondents pointed out the reduced intake of water. While the forward caste farmers mentioned about a sharp reduction in the water intake for agricultural water use, the scheduled tribe population interlinked the whole water shortage problem to that of the basic drinking purpose.

Though the functioning of the company has detrimentally impacted upon the water table and quality, people began to dig new wells. But the initiatives to dug new wells and deepen the existing ones mostly come from the forward castes. While seven out of ten forward caste household deepened the existing wells, the same has done only by three Scheduled Tribe households. Sometimes the upper caste people purchase water from the next village. They never depended on the tanker lorry supply or public taps or their women never went to collect water. This is pointing to the fact that the forward caste had been in a position to find alternatives to their exhausted water sources (Table 3.11).

Table 3.11: Health Problems among the Local People

Health problems	ST	SC	OBC	FC	%age
Stomach pain	6	2	3	2	13
Stomach pain, anaemia, joint pain and skin reactions	67	4	2	-	73
Abortion	4	-	-	-	4
No problem	-	-	2	8	10

Regarding the health impact two issues are important. The first one is the simultaneous occurrence of various diseases—stomach pain, anaemia, joint pain and skin reactions—among the population in the study area. Moreover, the author had documented limited instances of abortions. Given that the lower caste population largely depended on the polluted water for long time, they were the worst hit category in regard to the aforementioned diseases. The caste bias of the diseases was largely attributable to the fact that the higher caste population had limitedly relied upon the polluted water for drinking and other household purposes as they had alternatives. Therefore few of them did not report any health problem.

A greater number of the respondents in the study area opined that their subsistence economy was seriously affected by the functioning of Coca-Cola Company in the region. The people of Plachimada had mentioned about a wide array of related problems; but larger part of their concerns was related to the negative impact on the economy. To begin with, it is relevant to explain the concerns from the agricultural side. Being a region with water-intensive cropping pattern (mostly paddy and coconut), reduction in the water table would be detrimental to the cultivation pattern in a multitude of ways. Most of the paddy and coconut farmers find it difficult to continue with their existent modes of cultivation. Another considerable group had pointed out the negative impacts on the crop yield. Following the failure to find additional water sources, several farmers are now thinking about disposing their existing land and migrating to the adjacent villages.

In fact, for the farmers in Plachimada the problem was more of a double jeopardy. They were also suffering from the crop destruction, which is all-pervasive in Kerala due to ill-time rains, uncontrolled pests, etc. During the survey, the author found that few farmers in Plachimada tried alternative crops to cope up with the emergent issues of water scarcity. Moreover, the consequent reduction in the demand for agricultural labour had ripples in the economy of agricultural labourers. The poor job prospects in Plachimada compelled many of them to migrate to regions where employment opportunities are more.

3.16 Water Conflicts

From the survey it became clear that cutting across caste lines none of the respondents have mentioned about the occurrences of water conflicts till 2000. Barring few isolated and petty issues, there had not been any considerable conflict over the access of water in Plachimada. However, with the advent of Coca-Cola Company the entire chain of events got a u-turn. Water based conflicts have become an indispensable part in the daily routine of many sections in Plachimada. This is especially true in the case of ST population. Regardless of the fact that these water conflicts affected nearly all inhabitants in the study area by one way or another, those with alternative water sources managed it without much catastrophe. The aforesaid diversity of pattern is best manifested in the response of the OBC and FC population who were less affected by the water scarcity in Plachimada.

The high proportion of Scheduled Tribe population in the water conflicts gives clear indication that the Plachimada movement is fore headed by the worst hit population. The fact that the most important rationale for the struggle was both to get water and to close the factory is illustrative of the correlation between the functioning of Coca-Cola bottling plant and reduced access to ground water. With regard to the post-conflict negotiations on the water issue, it is clear that only forward caste people are in a position to conduct direct negotiations with the company authorities. The greater part of negotiations was carried out with the panchayat authorities, for the most part the elected representatives in the Perumatty Gramapanchayat. This is pointing to the importance of Panchayati Raj institutions in everyday life. Unlike the case of other villages in Kerala, political leaders has limited stake in the whole negotiation processes.

3.17 Coca Cola Company and Employment Opportunities in Plachimada

This section aim to give a picture of the job prospects in the Coca-Cola Company. The advent of company in Plachimada was justified with its ability to generate additional employment opportunities in the locality. The logic of employment opportunities was extensively projected at its initial stage. However, the field work had shown that out of the 77 percent ST population, 53 has applied for employment in the Company. The fact that OBCs and forward caste did not apply for a position in the company deserves special mention. The field survey shows that only nine percent of ST applicants got employment in the company. The survey also found that the local people were deliberately excluded from the employment opportunities and the company showed enthusiasm in giving employment to non-Plachimada people on political basis.

The limited employment prospects in the company rules out the prevalent argument that these kinds of industries are capable of generating employment to the local people. Being a good example for a capital-intensive industry, Coca-Cola Company has limited potential to solve the unemployment problem in the region. As said by Vilayodi Venugopal, one of the local leaders of Plachimada struggle, the Coca-Cola Company cheated the local population with respect to employment opportunities. In 1999, Hindustan Coca-Cola Beverages Private Limited was brought into Plachimada in the name of employment expansion. But only forty people from Plachimada got absorbed into the company. [5]

According to the company authorities, it is difficult to rely on the working skills of the Scheduled Tribe people. Thus majority of the workers were recruited on political party lines across the state while the local population was highly marginalized. The recruited persons from the locality were mainly from the OBC and SC category. Most of them were all wage labourers and had been working for very low wages (such as ₹ 30-₹ 40 per day) in the nearby villages. A greater part of these wage labourers joined the company during the very first year itself.

It is important to note here that these people were absolutely unaware about the advent of company before the inception of company activities in Plachimada. Initially the workers got the same pay scale of daily wage labourers, but when the struggle started their wages increased up to ₹ 75-₹100 per day. Usually, the workers have to work from 7 am to

3 pm. But they can overwork for one or two hours with double wage. The work they indulged in the company were not hazardous in nature. At many times the local people were given cleaning, loading, unloading works. They have regular jobs for all the days in a month within the company. The author documented some union and political party activities among the factory workers. The survey among them shows that only a minority of the workers is not against the struggle in Plachimada. They hold the view that the struggle is genuine.

When the factory was closed majority of the workers made a protest in front of the factory for opening it within the shortest possible time. The absorbed employees were given jobs even when the factory was not functioning. During the struggle they occasionally go the factory for cleaning purposes at least once in a week. Some of the employees revealed that they are ready to quit their factory job in case of reliable alternatives. According to the author's observation they gave preference to job than commitment to the company. Soon after the prevalence of water depletion issue in Plachimada the company started supplying water to the workers in tanker lorries on a daily basis. They believed that the company could exist if it supplies water to them. Henceforth they expressed a sense of satisfaction over the existing arrangements.

End Notes

1. (1) The establishment of building and material should be based on a proper plan. Prior consent is required for any amendment, new installation and construction activities. (2) The building wall should be in the minimum height of 2.5 meter. (3) The used water should keep out from pollution. (4) The machines should be equipped with protective coverings. (5) The factory should abide factory laws and public health requirements. (6) Cleaning activities should be established. (7) Dispose the waste materials. (8) Emergency doors should establish in an openable form to meet an emergency situation. (9) First aid medicines and kits should be kept in the factory. (10) In case of violating the aforesaid conditions, the factory approval must be cancelled immediately. (11) The final consent letter should collect before

starting the operation of the company (Keraleeyam, 2005).

2. Central Ground Water Board and the State Ground Water Department (2004), *Report on the Dynamic Ground Water Resources of Kerala as on March 2004,* pp. 14-20. The categorization of safe area, semi-critical, critical and overexploited was based on two criteria–(a) stage of ground water development and (b) long term trend of pre and post monsoon water levels. Thus, there are four categories based on the above norms, (1) s*afe-areas* which have ground water potential for development (development means, extraction); (2) *semi-critical areas* where cautious ground water development is recommended; (3) *critical-areas* and (4) *over-exploited* areas where there should be intensive monitoring and evaluation and future ground water development be linked with water conservation measures and micro level studies.
3. It should make it clear that the utilization of water in the case of the bigger landholding households far outstrips the water utilization patterns in a low landholding household.
4. Interview with Mayilamma, a local level leader of the struggle. She received wide media attention for putting up a brave struggle. She passed away in 2007.
5. Interview with Vilayodi Venugopal. He was a local level leader at the forefront of the struggle.

References

BBC (2003), *Report* published on 25/07/03 at 17:51:55GMT, BBC MMIII, p. 8.

Centre for Water Resource Development and Management (CWRDM) (2005), Report, *Investigations on the Extraction of Ground Water by M/S Hindustan Coca-Cola Beverages Private Limited at Plachimada,* Calicut, p. 4.

Eva Wrammer (2004), *Fighting Coca-Colonization in Plachimada: Water, Soft Drinks and Tragedy of Commons in an Indian Village,* Human Ecology Division, MKU, 131, p. 30.

Indian National Trust for Arts and Cultural Heritage (INTACH), (2004), Report, *The Adverse Environmental Impact of the Hindustan Coca-Cola Beverages Private Limited,* Thiruvananthapuram.

Integrated Rural Technology Centre (IRTC), (2002*), Report***,** Calicut, pp. 1-3. MPN or Most Probable Number is a method for finding the presence of bacteria (such as Coliform) in water.

Keraleeyam Magazine, January 2005, Kokkale, Thrissur.

Kerala State Pollution Control Board (KSPCB), (2003), Report, *Presence of Heavy Metals in Sludge Generated in the Factory of M/S Hindustan Coca-Cola Beverages Private Limited*, p. 5.

Kerala Water Policy 2007, Water Resource Department, Government of Kerala, Thiruvananthapuram.

Panchayat Report, *Matters related to the issue and cancellation of license to Coca-Coal Company*, (License Number, A3-463/99 dated 27/1/2000), p. 1.

Paul, Antonio (2005), *Water Insecurity and Livelihood Strategies, A Study of the Livelihood Dynamics in Plachimada Village of Palakkad District, Kerala, India*, Centre for Development Studies, Thiruvananthapuram, p. 70.

Sajan, Thomas (2008), *The Clash of Domestic Economies: Micro credit and Household Economic Processes in the Migrant Settlements of Kerala, India*, M.Phil. Thesis, Department of Social Anthropology, University of Bergen, Bergen.

Tenth Five-Year Plan (2002-2007) *Development Report, Perumatty Panchayat*, Palakkad, p. 1.

VAK (2004): *Report, Coca-Cola: Quit Plachimada: Quit India: The Story of Anti-Coca-Cola Struggle at Plachimada in Kerala*, Vikas Adhyan Kendra, Mumbai.

Yuvajanavedi (2002), Report, The Environmental and Social Problems Raised by the Coca-Cola and Pepsi Companies in Palakkad District, pp. 3-14.

Websites

http://keralawater.org/policy.html, accessed on 20/11/08.

http://www.kerenvis.nic.in/isbeid/water.html, accessed on 21/11/08.

4

Private Monopolies in Surface Water Exploitation: A Case Study of Sheonath Issue in Chhattisgarh

4.1 Introduction

The Plachimada case in Kerala is a good example for the privatization of groundwater. However, the water privatization issue in Chhattisgarh is the privatization of surface water. At the outset, there is a need to give a brief note on the patterns of two different cases of water privatization in India. While groundwater privatization through appropriation largely involves overexploitation of the existing groundwater sources by private players, the privatization of surface water is nothing but the allocation of exclusive rights for the private companies to control a public water source like river. Both patterns of privatization involve different kinds of political questions. This chapter intends to discuss the case of Sheonath river privatization in Chhattisgarh against the backdrop of the Plachimada case in regard to ground water privatization.

Sheonath is a semi-perennial river that flows through Durg district in Chhattisgarh. Chhattisgarh, a state in central India formed when the sixteen Chhattisgarhi-speaking south-eastern districts of Madhya Pradesh gained statehood on 1st November 2000. The passing of the Madhya Pradesh Reorganization Bill to create Chhattisgarh state fulfils a long-standing demand of the local people. The history of the movement for Chhattisgarh state can be traced from the launching of Chhattisgarh Mukti Morcha (CMM), a trade union movement, in the late 1970s. The agitation for statehood got momentum with the struggle organized by the Chhattisgarh Rajya Sangarsh Morcha (CRSM) once the National Democratic Alliance (NDA) government failed to introduce the bill in the budget session of

Parliament. Sociologically, the demand for a separate state is traced to the need felt by the ex-Malgujas [1] to become numerically powerful under a new state. The landless labourers and poor peasants were apparently not excited about the formation of Chhattisgarh state (Venkatesan, 2000).

The history of Chhattisgarh goes back even before 11th century. The term Chhattisgarh is not coined by the official rulers in the history. For Marathas, the area was either under Ratanpur (around present Bilaspur) or Raipur states. For the early British administrators, the eastern area of the present Chhattisgarh, along with a 12 states falling under the districts of the present western Orissa, formed a group of 18 states, what was then called 'Garhjaat States'. States of present Chhattisgarh area which were the part of this Garhjaat States are—Jaspur, Udaipur (Dharamjaigarh), Raigarh, Sakti, Sarangarh and Phuljhar. The next administrative change was when the State of Central Province came into being incorporating these six states, the rest going to the state of Orissa and Bengal in 1936.

During the post-Independent period the mineral rich regions of the present day Chhattisgarh contributed significantly to the state domestic product of Madhya Pradesh. High levels of industrialization made this region a distinct socio-political landscape. The region's economy is fuelled by the presence of the Bhilai Steel Plant, S.E.C. Railway Zone, BALCO Aluminium Plant (Korba), NTPC (National Thermal Power Corporation Limited) Korba, and S.E.C.L. (South Eastern Coalfields Limited). The rapid economic development of the newly born state of Chhattisgarh is highly attributable to the existent industrial economic base.

The state of Chhattisgarh has a geographical area of 1,37,360 sq. km. Geographically, the northern and southern parts of Chhattisgarh are hilly, while the central part is a fertile plain. Forests cover roughly forty-four percent of the state. The state is divided into 5 river basins. Mahanadi Basin drains out 75546 sq. km., Godavari Basin 39577 sq. km., Ganga basin

18808 sq. km. and Narmada basin 2113 sq. km. of the catchment area in the state. The central part of the state lies in the fertile upper basin of the Mahanadi and its tributaries, with extensive rice cultivation. The upper Mahanadi basin is separated from the upper Narmada basin to the west by the Maikal range, part of the Satpuras, and from the plains of Orissa to the east by hilly ranges. The population of Chhattisgarh is notable for its high proportion of Scheduled Tribes and in specific regions the Scheduled Castes constituted the demographic majority. The percentage of Scheduled Tribes against the total population of Chhattisgarh (32.5 percent) is significantly high among other Indian states.

4.2 Water Scenario in Chhattisgarh

The following is a brief note on the water scenario in Chhattisgarh. The main sources of water in the state are rivers, tanks, ponds and groundwater. The state has a history of tanks built in villages since Kalchuri Kings and nearly every village has a small tank for the daily needs of villagers. The state has important rivers such as Mahanadi, Sheonath, Indravati, Arpa, Hasdeo, Kelo, Rehar etc. providing a lifeline to the socio-economic development of the state. Nature has been kind to Chhattisgarh in terms of rainfall as compared to several other north-Indian states. Chhattisgarh gets an average rainfall of 1400mm per year and about 90 percent of the total rainfall occurs in the monsoon season i.e. July to September. But due to large variation in the yearly rainfall, agriculture of the state, which is mainly paddy, is affected. The groundwater availability of the state is at 1,56,340 cubic meters. The annual surface water flow in Chhattisgarh is estimated to be 59,900 cubic meters and the dependability is at 75 percent. Out of this the usable surface water wealth is 41.72 thousand million cum. and only about 7.50 thousand million cum. is tapped at present.

The usable water wealth in the state has been assessed as 41720 million cubic meter out of which, 7603 million cubic meter of water is being utilized by completed and ongoing projects in the state. The total potential of 1.55 hectares has been created as on 31st March 2004. At the time of formation of the state, the created potential was 1.328 million hectares. Thus additional potential of 0.222 million hectares has been created after the formation of the state, up to March 2004. The irrigation percentage to net sown area is 32.10 percent and with respect to gross sown area is 26.78 percent. Following the formation of Chhattisgarh, special attention has been given to the development of irrigation facilities. The irrigated area in the state is about three-fourth of the total cultivated area whereas potential exists to bring nearly one-fourth of the cultivable area under irrigation. About 75 percent irrigation in the state is by canals and the rest is by wells, tanks and tube wells.

Recent neglect of traditional water preservation practice has led to recurrent droughts in the state. This has forced the state government to take up irrigation projects on top priority with an ultimate aim of achieving 75 percent of the irrigation potential. There are 3 major, 30 medium and 2067 minor completed irrigation projects and 7 major, 8 medium and 748 minor projects are under construction in the state as on March 2004. [2] Budget provision for 2004-05 plan works is ₹ 756.08 crore. The ceiling for 10th Plan (2002-07) has been fixed for ₹ 2455.62 crore for Water Resources Department as against state plan of ₹ 11000 crore which is about 22 percent of state ceiling. The target for creation of additional irrigation potential has been fixed as 3,60,000 hectares during 10th plan. The irrigation projects are being funded by various agencies like National Bank for Agriculture and Rural Development (NABARD) and Accelerated Irrigation Benefit Programme of Government of India (AIBP). The incomplete minor projects are being funded by NABARD under Rural Infrastructure Development Fund (RIDF).

Similarly, incomplete major/medium projects are being funded under AIBP. Nearly 87 projects have been completed till March 2004 and balance projects are being completed in phased manner. In a similar fashion 5 projects viz. Hasdeo Bango Major project, Jonk Division Major project, Sheonath Division Medium project, Kosarteda Medium project and Barni Medium projects received financial assistance under AIBP, out of which Sheonath diversion medium project has been completed.

The remaining projects are also being completed in phased manner. In addition to this 18 anicuts are under construction in rain-shadow districts of the state. [3] Anicuts are important in the rivers of Chhattisgarh to prevent the flowing water and making it available for domestic purposes. Now the government is planning to build 9 anicuts from Durg to Somgav for ₹ 22 crore and the work has already begun. They are in Chikli, Bhatgav, Gheghari, Khamhariya, Dhamadha and Somanath. It was during 19th and 20th century that the British Government constructed dams and anicuts for irrigation purposes. The Ahmedabad dam in Tandula river, Rudri dam in Mahanadi, and Madamsilli dam in Silgiri Canal was constructed in 1954.

The Rajghad jute mill was the first company using river water for industrial purpose. But after the beginning of thermoelectric industry in Korba, water was used in large amount for industrial purposes. Later a dam in Bango river and a dam in Hasdeo river were built. Today water is being given to units of electric zones by National Thermo Electric Corporation established in Korba region. In 1955, the construction of Bhilai steel plant has begun and the flow of various rivers were blocked by construction of dams. In spite of all these, waste materials were dumped into the river that polluted the river. Besides industries like vegetation industry, paper industry of Mahadi, alcohol factory in Kharoon, the various factories in Bhilai and various thermoelectric units of Hasdeo polluted the river waters. Pollution of river water is always an issue in Chhattisgarh and protests are going on.

4.3 Water Policy of Chhattisgarh

As the water sector in the world undergoes a change, Chhattisgarh too is not left untouched by this trend. Immediately after the formation of Chhattisgarh, the state formulated a policy of its own on a number of subjects like, minerals, energy, tourism, education, culture, women, etc. The water policy of Chhattisgarh was formulated with the following objectives:

1. Planned development of water resources in environmentally sustainable manner.
2. Efforts for the development of water resources in drought-prone and rain-shadow areas.
3. Supplying water for potable, agricultural and industrial purposes on practical rates, so that at least maintenance and operational expenses are recovered.
4. Encouraging private investment in the development of water resources.
5. Ensuring participation of representatives of water users in the development and maintenance of water resources.

The other elements in the water policy are water resource planning, water resource management, rationalization of water rates, water conservation, legal initiatives, increasing institutional reforms and capability. The water policy was prepared on the lines of National Water Policy (2002) and it contained technical description of the steps for its implementation. It is clear that the official policy of state and union government underlines the need of inviting private participation in water sector especially in the management and distribution system in industrial areas. At the same time it mentions about the participation of farmers and water users in the management of irrigation systems (Singh, 2004).

The state has also prepared a Chhattisgarh Vision-2010 document with the help of Price Waterhouse Cooper (PWC), an internationally known financial-consultancy company. Besides, PWC carried out a survey of organized water delivery system in 42 towns of Chhattisgarh. The Report says that most of these systems are outdated and need infrastructure and institutional renovation. It identified the following root causes of underperformance in water sector.

1. Low utilization of developed water resources.
2. Inequitable development of resources.
3. Low coverage for urban water supply.
4. Low funds for operation and maintenance.
5. Limited capacity of the government to fund development.
6. Poor revenue recovery and low tariffs.
7. Higher manpower costs.
8. Limited skill tests.

Moreover the Vision 2010 has identified certain targets before the government. They are:

1. 200 percent increase in created irrigation potential.
2. 100 percent coverage of safe drinking water supply.
3. Each village to have at least one perennial water source.
4. Tariff rationalization to cover operation and maintenance cost.
5. Coverage to urban water supply as per prescribed norms.

In a nutshell, the water policy of Chhattisgarh is aimed at developing a strong rationale for the privatization of water resources in the public domain. The manner in which the vision document identified the root causes of under performance in water sector is a good example for it. The scarcity of infrastructural development that exists in the water sector is proposed to be rectified by limited government intervention. The policy contains a greater degree of internal contradiction; a major hallmark of the policy is the co-existence of mutually conflicting objectives such as increased access to water resources, greater participation of private players, etc.

4.4 Socio-economic Profile of Durg District

Durg is a populous district located in the central part of Chhattisgarh. The district is formed on 1st January 1906. Durg city is the headquarters of Durg district. This city is a municipal corporation and lies about 11 km. from Bhilai and 35 km. from the state capital Raipur. Durg district occupies the south-western part of the Chhattisgarh plain and possesses belts of hilly country in the south, southwest and northwest, bestowed with mineral resources and forests. Durg lies between 20° 23` N and $22^{o}$ 02` N latitude and 80° 46` E and $81^{o}$ 58` E longitude. The total geographical area of the district is 8701.80 sq. kms. The district occupies the south-western part of the upper Sheonath-Mahanadi valley and the bordering hills in the south and southwest. Physiographically, the district can be divided into two divisions, viz. the Chhattisgarh plain and the Southern plateau. The Chhattisgarh plain occupies the largest area in the district.

The general slope of the district comes under Mahanadi river slope and is towards the north and northeast and locally in some places towards east. The main tributaries of Mahanadi river are Sheonath, Kharun, Tandula, Kharkhara and Aamner. Sheonath and Kharun rivers contribute the most in the drainage system of the district. All the small rivulets and rivers are the tributaries either of Sheonath river or Kharun river. Sheonath river flows nearer to the western border of the district whereas river Kharun forms the eastern border of the district, which ultimately joins Sheonath river. The river Sheonath itself forms the part of big Mahanadi basin. The people in the district depends the rivers for drinking, household, and agricultural purposes including livestock bearing. Durg has sub-tropical climate characterized by hot summer and monsoon rainfall followed by hot dry and cold winter season. The onset of monsoon is usually from 2nd week of June and the season extends up to September with monsoon peaking during July and August. Maximum, average and minimum rainfall in Durg district is, 1477.2, 1071.16 and 781.5 mm respectively per annum.

Durg has a total population of 28,10,436 consisting of 50.45 percent males and 49.55 percent females (2001 Census). The population of Durg constitutes 13.47 percent of the state's total population and it is the second most populous district after Raipur. The decade 1991-2001 witnessed a population growth of 16.9 percent against the state average of 18.1 percent. Literacy rate of Durg district is much higher i.e. 75.6 percent as compared to 64.7 percent in a state as a whole. The literacy rate of female population is 64.6 percent whereas the literacy rate of SC and ST population stands at 71.1 and 73.3 respectively. The rural population of the district constitutes 62 percent of the total population. Out of the total population of Durg 12.8 percent belongs to Scheduled Castes and 12.4 percent belongs to Scheduled Tribe population. Most of the Scheduled Tribe population is concentrated in Dondi Lohara and Dondi blocks. The major communities in the district include Sahus, Satnami and Kurmi. The major religions in Durg district are Hinduism, Islam, Christianity and Sikhism.

From Table 4.1 it is clear that around 62 percent population of Durg district is engaged in agricultural activities. Out of the 3.88 lakh farmers in the district 55.9, 22.52, 14.7 and 6.9 percent belongs to marginal, small, medium and large farmer's category respectively. The SC and ST farmers account for 12.8 and 12.4 respectively. Work participation rate is 41.4 percent and is slightly lower than the state average. Proportion of cultivators to the total workers is 34.4 percent in the district. Agricultural labourers constitute 30.2 percent of the total workers in the district. Mining and industrialization in few parts of the district have significantly influenced the traditional occupational pattern of local population partly because of direct or indirect employment opportunities in these enterprises and partly because of the loss of agricultural land through land acquisition by the government.

The cropping intensity of the district is 145 percent, which is 20 percent higher than the state average. Although rice is the main crop in Kharif and covered 4.15 lakh hectare of the total cultivated area, soyabean has also emerged as a major cash crop during the last five years. Wheat, lentil, mustard, gram, arhar and urad are other major crops cultivated in this area.

Table 4.1: Demographic Profile of Durg District

Demographic indicators	Unit	Durg district	Chhattisgarh
Total population	No.	28,10,436	20,795,956
Male		14,17,865	10,452,547
Female		13,92,571	10,343,409
Rural population	%	62	79.9
Urban population	%	38	21.1
SC population	%	12.8	10.5
ST population	%	12.4	28
Population density	Person/Km^2	328	153
Sex ratio		982	985
Literacy rate Persons	%	75.62	64.7
Male		86.4	77.9
Female		64.6	52.3
ST		71.1	52.1
Male		84	65.2
Female		58.2	39.3
SC		73.3	64
Male		85.6	64
Female		61.6	27

Source: www.chhattisgarh.nic.in.

The major horticultural crops are banana and papaya. During rabi season the river water is lifted through pumps for irrigation purpose. In this district 41 percent of the land is possessed by 79 percent of marginal and small farmers, whereas, 59 percent land is held by 21 percent of the farmers belonging to semi-medium, medium and large category. This indicates the uneven distribution of land resources. Durg district is ideally located for development of inland fishery activities like, fish seed production, cultivation, etc. A river length of 84 kilometres is available in the district for fisheries.

4.5 Privatization of Sheonath River

Sheonath is the main river of Durg district, which originates from Panabaras Hill and flows towards northeast. This river flows through the middle of Durg district through Raipur, Bilaspur and Janjgir-Champa before merging with the Mahanadi at Shivrinarayan. River Kharun joins it on the midway. Sheonath is the main tributary of Mahanadi river. The Sheonath and Mahanadi rivers contain 58.48 percent of the state's water resources. Sheonath river collects 40 percent of total water catchments of Mahanadi.

The total length of Sheonath river is 345 km. The length of Sheonath river in Durg district is 120 km. Sheonath has number of tributary rivers, namely Amner, Haanp, Maniyari, Arpa, Kharkara, Tandula, Kharman, Jamniya, and Khorsi in which Tandula river is the main one. Tandula river originates from hills situated in the north of Bhanupratappur in Kanker district. After covering a distance of 34 km., this river joins Sukhanala. Tandula river joins Sheonath river in the southwest of Durg in a distance of approximately 13 km. The total length of this river is 96.6 km. A dam is constructed during the period 1905 to 1921 at the joining point of Sukhanala and Tandula river.

Sheonath river, flowing into the Mahanadi river, has been a source of livelihood to farmers and fishermen for centuries. It meanders through the verdant lands of Chhattisgarh and is important in terms of the drainage it offers. The name of the Chhattisgarh state comes from the 36 forts, of the Kalchuri dynasty, that existed on the banks of Sheonath river in the then southern Kosal. 18 forts on either bank totally make 36, which in Hindi is called 'Chhattis' and 'Garh' means fort. Thus the area around the Sheonath river can be considered very important in the history of the state of Chhattisgarh. The Sheonath river in Chhattisgarh also has socio-religious importance even in modern times. Devotees of Lord Parshwanath celebrate 'Snan Mahotsav' and 'Kaalash Jatra' during the Mahavishek on the banks of Sheonath river.

They collect waters of 108 rivers of India and follow the rituals on the banks of this holy river in Chhattisgarh. The popular picnic spot, Dewarghata, is situated on the confluence of Sheonath river, Lilagarh river and Mahanadi river and attracts thousands of people every year.

In Durg district, Sheonath river flows through Borai, where a special industrial area has been established. Borai is a newly developed industrial hub, promoted by the Chhattisgarh State Industrial Development Corporation (CSIDC). The region is rich in natural minerals and lies at a reasonable distance from Raipur airport. As Bhilai steel plant is near, Borai industrial area gets surplus power at a reasonable cost. Most of the industries located here are water intensive by nature–distilleries, sponge iron units and thermal power plants. This issue is about the handing over of a stretch of Sheonath river near Borai to a private firm for supplying water to the Borai Industrial Area, lying between two districts head quarters, Durg and Rajnandgaon. Chhattisgarh is the first state where private companies have been given the right to supply water to industrial units. The first step of privatization of water in Chhattisgarh was the contract made by CSIDC with sponj-iron factory for 22 years to construct an anicut (15 kilometre away from Raipur) for the supply of water. But due to protest the water distribution system was taken jointly (Das and Pangre, 2006).

Sheonath project known as *Rasmada* scheme is not the only such projects in Chhattisgarh. There are four other projects where stretches of rivers have been awarded to private and government agencies. They are, Kharun river to Madhya Pradesh Audyogig Kendra Vikas Nigam Limited (MPAKVN), Kelu river to Jindal Group, Sagri river to S. R. Group. The 95 km. long Kelo river passes through Raigarh and is its lifeline. In 1996, Jindal Steel and Power Limited made a bid to lift water from Kelo, but the government refused, saying that it would cause a drinking water shortage.

When Jindal persisted, the government allowed to take

water from the Kelo and also to erect a stop dam that enabled it to lift 35,400 cubic metres of water every day from the river. Water levels in ponds have dropped and the villagers have little water even for drinking purposes. When the villagers of Bonda Tikra and others on the banks of the river felt water scarcity they began to protest. The farmers of Bonda Tikra and Gudgahan were most affected because their lands had been taken over in the name of another irrigation project and the only way they could irrigate their fields was from the water of Kelo. The battle against Jindal Steel resulted in marches, demonstrations and rallies.

Apart from Kelo, the Kurkut river too has been affected by various plants that Jindal has erected. Villagers of Rabo village decided not to allow their village to be sacrificed for a dam constructed by Jindal group. Public protest forced the Chief Minister to order for the stoppage of construction and the work on the dam was stopped on November 4, 2004. Jindal, however, ignored the instructions of the Chief Minister and resumed work after a week. Moreover a large part of the Shabri river that flows through Naxalite-affected Dantewada in Bastar district is under the occupancy of Essar Steel Chhattisgarh Ltd. Essar has a pipeline network from Dantewada to the port of Vishakhapatnam in Andhra Pradesh. It plans to send iron-ore through this pipeline with the force of the water from the Shabri river. Industrial houses such as Monnet Ispat and Neco Jaiswal have private dams on the Kharoon river in Raipur. Neco Jaiswal lifts 3 mgd (million gallons daily) and Monnet Ispat 2 mgd water from the Kharoon. Lafarge India possesses rights to 0.75 mgd of water of the Sheonath river. Bajrang Ispat and Power Ltd, SKS Ispat, and M/s South Asian Agro Ltd. are in queue for signing contracts with the government for getting proprietary rights over these rivers.

Besides the government of Chhattisgarh again thought of building new stop dams, anicuts on Sheonath river and its tributaries at a cost of ₹ 200 crore. The objective of this project is to facilitate farmers to withdraw water for irrigation through their own pumps. Under this project construction of an anicut at Bhatgaon, Durg District was approved by the Water Resource Department. Besides, the government is planning to build 17 anicuts in Durg district alone in order to solve the problem of water scarcity. The industrial department found that by stopping the flowing water of Kharoon river more than 10 industrial units could be given water. But it is found that the water levels in many rivers are decreasing. This will bring problems in irrigation.

The story of Sheonath river privatization goes back when the ₹ 9 crore Sheontah river project was formalized on 5th October 1998, between MPAKVN and Radius Water Limited (RWL) [4] on a Build, Own, Operate and Transfer (BOOT) basis. This was effective from October 4, 2000 to 4 October, 2020. The project, India's first river privatization experiment handed over to RWL by the then Madhya Pradesh government, pleading a lack of sufficient funds for the distribution of water to the newly developed industrial area at Borai. The contract signed for the construction of a barrage on the Sheonath river was to supply water up to 30 Million Litres per Day (MLD) to the Borai Industrial Growth Centre (Sethi, 2006). As per the contract, MPAKVN should purchase water from RWL and sold it to the industrial units in Borai.

The Borai Industrial Growth Centre, situated on the banks of Sheonath, came up in 1989 and the water for it was to be drawn from the same river. However, since Sheonath is not a perennial river, the Madhya Pradesh Government had committed to release water to the industrial units, which it did from the Kharkhara reservoir between September and July. But to store the water for further use, it was necessary to build a barrage at a cost of ₹ 1.10 crore. Since the Government was not in a position to release funds, the project was put off. In 1992, pressure by the industrial units to revive the project forced the Madhya Pradesh government to set up the Madhya Pradesh Audyogik Kendra Vikas Nigam (now called the

Chhattisgarh State Industrial Development Corporation Limited) as the nodal agency and to re-estimate the project. As the cost had escalated four times, to ₹ 4.5 crore in three years, the project was shelved once again.

Later the demand for water increased up to 3.75 MLD (Million Litres a Day), including 3.6 MLD from a single consumer, M/s Hindustan Electro Graphite (HEG) for which an agreement was also executed between the consumer and the nodal agency in 1996. A feasibility study was done once again and a technical sanction for ₹ 7.5 crore was given by the M.P. Audyogik Kendra Vikas Nigam Limited. Since it did not have funds to undertake the work on its own, it asked HEG to share 50 percent of the cost of the barrage construction and get water at a fixed rate for a long period and adjust their share against water bills.

HEG initially agreed to the proposal but backed out later. The nodal agency was under obligation to supply the agreed quantity of water to this bulk consumer and did not have sufficient means to implement the project with its own resources, hence involved the private sector for creation of infrastructural facilities. Finally, the agreement for 22 years was signed with Radius Water Limited for providing water.

As the new state Chhattisgarh was formed in November 2000 the contract was transferred from MPAKVN to Chhattisgarh State Industrial Development Corporation (CSIDC). The CSIDC is trying to make Borai as the hub for all water-based industries. By the contract RWL secured exclusive access to a 23.6 kilometres stretch of the river. The contract was for twenty years that can be extended further. The company got monopoly rights over the supply of water to all sectors of the Borai Industrial Growth Centre and RWL became a service partner of CSIDC. Moreover, CSIDC was obliged to provide all land for the industrial units in Borai.

The RWL built a 4-meter high dam in Sheonath river near Borai through a technique called Flood Regulating Barrier System along a 3.5 kilometres stretch at a cost of ₹ 4 crore.

The anicut built by RWL started just after the anicut built by the government in Mahmara village during 1957-58 to provide water to the cities. Water from this anicut is collected and pumped to filter plants and tubes and then supplies to cities. The water holding capacity of this anicut is about 100 million cubic feet which has now become half, due to sedimentation. About 24 million-litre water per day is supplied to Durg city from this anicut. Usually water becomes scarce in summer season.

The total cost of Sheonath project is ₹ 9 crore for producing 6 million litres per day. After the construction the barrage has a supplying capacity of 6 MLD, but CSIDC bought only 4 MLD due to lack of demand from the industrial area. The supply was started on November 2000 and CSIDC purchased water at a rate of ₹ 12.60 per kilolitre initially. In reality only 2 MLD water is required. No enquiry was done in order to find it. The CSIDC entered into the contract on the assumption that new industries would come up with demands for more water. However the contract says, 'the company requires a minimum guaranteed purchase of 4 MLD water quantity by the corporation. In case the demand reduces below 4 MLD, the payable bill shall be for 4 MLD from the applicable first tier of tariff'. Earlier termination of the agreement is possible only by 'reimbursing all outstanding loans and credits of the project and by compensating the likely profit that the project company is expected to earn in the balance concession period'.

Borai has only two large and medium scale industries and their combined water requirement is between 1 and 1.5 MLD while the CSIDC paid for 4 MLD everyday as per the contract in order to ensure the profitability of RWL. For those years that it has worked, CSIDC gave money from its exchequer irrespective of it's loses because of lack of demand for water. There has never been a demand of 4 MLD water, as the growth of industry did not catch up the way it was expected. Thus, everyday at a rate of ₹ 12.60 per kilolitre a payment of ₹ 50,

400 were made to RWL.

For a month this figure becomes ₹ 15,12,000 and for a year ₹ 1.81 crore, for at least 4 years. Besides in order to ensure the profitability of RWL, the government has instructed the industrial financial branch of the State Bank of India, Bhilai that it should reserve the monthly minimum guaranteed amount to RWL and ensure that regular payment to RWL is being made.

For this purpose they opened a joint escrow account. The cost of water is measured by RWL spread on intake well, pump house, electrical sub-system, store, staff quarters, main pipe, treatment plant, distribution line, etc.

The CSIDC sold water to the industrial units for ₹ 10 per kilolitre. Thus, it is clear that the company is at a loss. As per the contract, a 12 percent increase can be made in the water rate as such for the past four years RWL has increased the tariff rate 3 times (October 2000- ₹ 12.60, November 2004- ₹ 16.76. Table 4.2 will depict these facts). But CSIDC sold it to industries in low cost. In this system for the last four years RWL achieved ₹ 8.52 crore, but CSIDC got only ₹ 2.62 crore from the industrial units. Thus, it had a loss of ₹ 5.90 crore.

The private firm still continues to manage the barrage and supply water to industries. In the case of the termination of contract the government is obliged to give a lump sum amount to the company as compensation. This may be the reason behind the continuation of the project in Durg.

When Ajith Jogi was Chief Minister he tried to cancel the contract in a cabinet meeting held on 2nd April 2003, but the cancellation was not made into action. When the issue becomes controversial the legislative assembly of the state set up a Public Accounts Committee (PAC) to investigate matters relating to the privatisation of the Sheonath river.

Even before this, it examined the agreement and inspected the area. The PAC was headed by Dr. Ramchandra Singh Deo in 2005-06 and in 2006-07 by Ravindra Choube. The committee in its report tabled in the state assembly on 16th

March 2007 asked the government to cancel the deal and initiate criminal action against Radius Water Limited and the former managing directors of the Madhya Pradesh Audyogik Kendra Vikas Nigam Limited.

Table 4.2: Tariff Rate of Water Supplied to CSIDC

Year	Price escalation @ 10 percent per year (as per agreement in ₹)	Rate @ per cubic meter (decided by RWL in ₹)	Payment made by CSIDC as per 4 MLD guaranteed purchase (as per agreement in crore)	Actual water supplied by RWL @ 1.8 MLD
A	B	C	D	E
2001	--	12.60	1.839	657
2002	1.26	13.86	2.023	657
2003	1.38	15.24	2.225	657
2004	1.52	16.76	2.446	657
Total			8.533	

Contd...

Year	Actual water supplied by RWL @ 1.8 MLD	Rate @ per cubic meter (CSIDC charging from industries)	Revenue collection by CSIDC from industries by selling water which is supplied by RWL in crore)	Difference (D)-(G) = money of CSIDC
A	E	F	G	H
2001	657	10.00	0.657	1.182
2002	657	10.00	0.657	1.366
2003	657	10.00	0.657	1.568
2004	657	10.00	0.657	1.789
Total			2.628	5.905

Source: Water Resource Department, Chhattisgarh.

The committee also asked CSIDC to take possession of all assets associated with the ₹ 9 crore project and sought to scrap the build-own-operate-transfer project within one week after the report's submission. The PAC criticized the then managing director of MPAKVN for manipulation and forgery of documents. But the government has not yet initiated any action.

4.6 Impacts of Sheonath River Privatization

The privatization of Sheonath river had negative impacts

on Durg people in a multitude of ways. For instance, after the construction the owner of RWL, Kailash Nath Soni, imported a motorboat from Hong Kong and made trips in the anicut through the water declaring that the water is his property where his eye reaches. He allowed the people to take water as a privilege granted by him, only for 6 months, in a year. From January to June the company authorities never allowed the people to take water from the river, on the reason that water supply will get reduced during the summer season.

The storage area of the dam is 3.6 km. In this length RWL constructed spring fence around this area in order to prevent access to river. They had taken possession of thousands of square feet of land apart from the 176 acres adjoining the river bank. Even domestic animals didn't get water. Land on the banks of the river which was used for cultivation, has been submerged following the hoarding of water for the anicut. A board has come up stating 'bathing and fishing in this river are strictly prohibited. It may cause danger to your life'. He held that the company has full authority over the river water and it is their privilege to give water to others.

After the implementation of the agreement, many villages, both upstream and downstream–Durg, Mohlai, Mahmara, Samoud, Siloda, Jhola, Pulgav, Peeperchhadi, Bharni, Rasmara, Malood, Khapri, Tirga, Changeri, Belodi, Chikhlai, Nagpura, Jherni, Jewra Sisra, Patharia-were affected adversely as their access to river water and its use was completely restricted. All the water was concentrated in the upper reaches because of the dam, causing the lower portion of the Sheonath to dry up. Initially, the locals, including Scheduled Castes and Scheduled Tribes were not aware about the contract, as the RWL was not provided any prior information. Later, the RWL personnel informed the local fishermen that they were no longer permitted to fish in the 200m zone from the barrage for safety reasons. As such the nets of the fishermen were cut and confiscated by the company workers. The employees of Radius Water did not allow the farmers who owned land near the river to lift water from the river and forcibly took away their pumps.

This ban had the endorsement of district administration that also banned the installation of tube wells on the ground that it will reduce the inflow to river. Usually during summer season, for one and half months, CSIDC itself with the help of district administration stopped the intake of river water for irrigation. The most affected region is near to the Borai industrial area. Here, the farmers lost their agriculture because of water scarcity and now they are searching for alternatives. The RWL held that taking water from the upstream area would reduce the quantum of water for supply to industrial units in Borai, as such villagers have been completely stopped from taking water from the river. People from downstream villages reported that the groundwater table had plummeted and therefore affected the water level in their wells.

This is because the anicut reduced the flow of river to the downstream. Farmers forced to stop their vegetable cultivation on the banks of the river in Rasmara and Mohlai villages. Fisher folk constituting large number of families in these villages has become jobless as fishing has been stopped by RWL. Thus the villagers were forced to abandon their jobs and consequently it affected their livelihoods and productivity. Besides, RWL banned washing of cloths at the banks of river, on the ground that it will increase pollution. Right to collect sand from the river was also banned by RWL as such the Panchayat lost its ₹ 90,000 revenue per year (Singh, 2004). The RWL prevented all sorts of negotiation with the people and said that it needs permission from CSIDC.

Moreover the company asked the corporation that it should collect an amount from farmers who used this water. The company once attempted to take legal action against the farmers for defamation. In this matter CSIDC found that 27 farmers used 2 million litres of water from the dam. Anyway this does not affected the water supply of the dam. The RWL claimed that restriction above the dam for 200 meters is for security. They complained to the CSIDC that the villagers are taking water from the control area by using motor pumps.

So the corporation has to recover the amount from villagers to the company. So a meter should be fixed to measure the amount of water. If this is not possible then the corporation should give compensation to the company. The RWL authorities claimed that if the farmers need water they have to pay the fees. As a response to these problems the local people initiated protest at various levels. Following the struggle the government took various measures to appease the people. On 27th February 2002, government lifted the ban. Following it, the access of villagers to river water has been reinstated (Lakshmi, 2003).

4.7 Legal Problems in the Contract

There are a number of irregularities in the contract. At the time of agreement no drawing design, survey report and other technical details of project were submitted by the RWL. The company prepared all these documents after the award of the contract. Moreover before implementing the project no communication was made with the Grama Panchayat. Besides, the government approved the cost of the project without conducting any scientific enquiry. The cost of the project was calculated for the supply of 30 MLD. The CSIDC guaranteed that it would ensure from Water Resource Department that RWL receives an assured supply of 30 MLD water at the maximum. Moreover under BOOT agreement the government does not have any responsibility. But in Sheonath project CSIDC became an agent of RWL.

It collected the monthly bills from the industrial units. In case of any disagreement and litigation between CSIDC and industrial units over the quantum of water supplied and charges made in the bill it will be the responsibility of CSIDC to recover the bill and incurring expense over the litigation while the RWL has simply escaped from all these provisions (Putul, 2009). An instance in this regard is that, the Hindustan

Electro Graphite (HEG), which buys 90 percent of the CSIDC's total water sales, has refused to pay its dues. The others are, LNG Bhilwara and Khoday Distilleries (Jain, 2003).

There were some other legal problems against RWL. The company was not adhering to the terms and conditions of the contract. According to BOOT contract, the project company would undertake construction and maintenance work with its own resources within a specified period. However, the construction did not started on time because of lack of funds. Thus a decision was taken to the effect that of the total cost of ₹ 9 crore, ₹ 6.5 crore would be loaned to the firm and the remaining ₹ 2.5 crore would be in the form of equity. The AKVN was given a relaxation to invest up to ₹ 50 lakh within six months under this equity. The loan has not repaid yet. Besides before getting approval the company started works of ₹ 2.75 lakh. During the construction itself, the company got many privileges from the government. The AKVN handed over its entire infrastructure in Borai, and assets worth ₹ 5 crore, to Kailash Soni, for a token ₹ 1, for establishing the water supply project on BOOT basis. Thus the company got intake well, pump house, overhead tank, pipeline, old motors and even water treatment plant.

In the contract there were no provisions for imposing a ban on the intake of water by the villagers. The water minister claimed that the ownership of the river is not given to the company by the contract. The RWL claims that their technical efficiency cannot be achieve by the CSIDC. As per the contract, after 20 years the project with such technical efficiency will go to the hands of CSIDC as per the BOOT agreement. Regarding water supply RWL claimed regularly that they are distributing water to the industries up to 3.4 MLD. But the industries demanded only 1.5-2 MLD of water. They claimed their water rate is less compared to other parts of India. The RWL argued that they spend a minimum of ₹ 4 lakh per month for its operation and maintenance (Krishnakumar,

2003).

Kailash Soni is of the view that the river is under RWL ownership and the company has the right to allow or deny access of villagers to river. He claimed that his decision to enter into the business was taken after a detailed study and cost-benefit analysis of companies engaged in the business of water throughout the world.

He was extremely happy about the way he has shaped privatization of water in Durg district as well as for converting wasteful flow of river water into a neat monetary profit. He pointed out that water resources worth ₹ 15,000 crore are lying useless owing to official inefficiency and leakage alone causing a loss of ₹ 36,000 crore. He justified the Sheonath project on the ground that, after the project water table in neighbouring areas has increased up to 9 meters.

In addition to this, CSIDC will ensure that pollution from industrial units located at Borai does not reach the anicut supplying water to Borai. In case of water being polluted, RWL has a right to recover the additional cost incurred on treatment of this polluted water from the polluting agent, i.e. the industrial units.

The RWL has also been given the right to increase tariff of selling water, if there is an increase in electricity rates or inflation. Moreover RWL has never taken any permission from Water Resource Department for utilizing the water from Sheonath river though it was mandatory. In case RWL has not made any specific agreement with Water Resource Department in this regard, then the withdrawal of water from Sheonath river merely on the basis of the contract with CSIDC is illegal.

The department started investigations on the total quantum of water used by RWL. This is being done on the basis of payments made by the industrial units to CSIDC. They collected detailed monthly bills from the concerned departments. Madhya Pradesh government issued an order on 29th April 1998 regarding the water tariff. According to this order, the rate of withdrawal of water from natural resources is

30 paisa per cubic meter and from storage facilities of government is ₹ 1 per cubic meter. So the Water Resource Department considered imposing a fine on RWL, along with charges for withdrawal of water at a rate of 63 paisa per cubic meter from the date of its operation (Putul, 2009).

Another instance related to Water Resource Department is that when the Department invited tender for the construction of 285m anicut in Bhatgaon village, RWL protested against it. They argued that it has already taken permission from Water Resource Department to construct a barrage at Nagpura, and the two proposed anicuts are close by. They said that the proposed region is under their control and the government does not have the authority to construct a new anicut there. In addition, for the last four years RWL did not produce the agreement before the Water Utility Committee of Chhattisgarh and take permission for using water (Mumtaz, 2006). There were some technical irregularities in the agreement. For instance, the height of the gate constructed at the river is only 3 meter, but for showing an increased storage capacity 3 meter underground is also added.

Besides, government employees were posted at this plant before it was handed over to RWL and they were transferred to Chhattisgarh after its formation. At the time of agreement it was agreed that RWL will be responsible for their wages. But RWL has not paid wages to them and they continued to receive wages from government. The government hence comes under increasing nationwide criticism appointed a high power committee to look into this issue. Various representations were made by the concerned citizens, non-governmental organizations, etc.

4.8 Findings of Field Survey

This section discusses the findings of field survey conducted by the author in Chhattisgarh in March-April 2006. The objective of the field survey was to understand the socio-economic profile of the people near to Sheonath river in Durg district, to estimate the water availability and utilization pattern in the villages, to explore the changes took place in access to water and utilization pattern since the Sheonath project and finally to find out the impacts of Sheonath river privatization among the people. The survey was conducted among the villagers on the banks of Sheonath river in Durg district. The villages are, Durg, Mohlai, Samoud, Siloda, Peeperchadi, Rasmara, Kapri, Nagpura, Jherni and Jewra Sisra. During the first phase a pilot study was conducted. It was during this time the author got familiar with the villages near to Sheonath river and Durg town. The field, the people, the river, the anicut and the construction associated to it were well observed. In this time a sample survey was conducted with the help of ad-hoc open-ended questionnaire. By the end of this study the study area, the number and category of households were selected through simple random sampling.

The second visit was held on April 2006. During this phase the final survey was conducted with a close ended questionnaire. The impact of Sheonath river privatization and the nature of the struggle were made clear through the survey among households. Interview with local political party leaders and leaders of the struggle, were also conducted. In addition to this, primary data related to the project, its operation details were collected. The empirical data were statistically analyzed, while other kinds of primary data were put into qualitative analysis. Regarding the study area the estimated population comes around 4800. The total number of households in the study area is around 800 and the average household size is six. Out of the 800 households in the study area, a survey among 85 families was conducted. Among the 85 families there are 12 farmers, 3 petty businessmen and 39 fishing folk. The remaining 31 constitute the agricultural and other daily wage labourers.

4.9 Demographic Pattern of the Study Area

Socially and economically the study area was backward though it belongs to the Durg municipality and only 4 km.

away from the Durg town. Economically the population shows a mixed character. Unlike the case of Plachimada, majority of the respondents in Chhattisgarh were males (73 percent). The most important reason for having the greater share of male respondents is the introvert nature of the female population in the study area. It is worthwhile to note here that the obtained female response was the result of intense persuasion and request to cooperate with the study. At many times, both male and female respondents formed small groups to respond to the survey questionnaire. There are even occasions in which the males responded to the questions asked to the female population in Durg. Except few instances the female respondents did not take initiative to answer the questions raised by the author.

Majority of the respondents were either middle-aged or people with more than fifty years of age. This is because of the fact that the youngsters in Durg went to nearby region for manual works. In a sense the presence of 36-50 and 51-65 age groups was a blessing for the study. The respondents belonging to these age groups had been in a position to answer the survey questionnaire in a comparative and historical perspective. Most of them compared the water availability scenario in Durg during different time periods in the last twenty-five years. A major section of the survey questionnaire was aimed to collect the monthly income pattern of the respondent population in Durg district.

The occupational pattern (Table 4.3) of the study area holds special relevance to the study. The author divided the population of the study area into agricultural and other daily wage labourers, fishermen, petty businessmen or traders and farmers. The wage labourers and fishing men constitute the majority in the study area. Even though the petty businessmen and farmers were less in number they contribute significantly to the region's political economy. From the table it is evident that fishing, agricultural labour and other wage labouring constitute the most important income source of the respondent population.

Table 4.3: Occupational Pattern

House holds	Agri & other wage labourers	Fishermen	Petty business -men or traders	Farmers	Total
Number	31	39	3	12	85
Percentage	36	46	4	14	100

The dependence on fishing has special relevance in this case. Unlike the groundwater issue of Plachimada, the people at Durg depend upon the Sheonath river in a wide array of things, such as drinking water, washing, bathing, fishing, irrigation, etc. The very fact that 46 percentage of the respondents lived solely on fishing highlights the multifaceted dependence on Sheonath river by the villagers. Agricultural labour and other kinds of labour form the additional major sources of livelihood.

The landholding patterns (Table 4.4) in Durg have close relation with the water availability in Sheonath river. In contrast to the general North Indian scenario, small scale landholdings is a major attribute of the study area in Durg district. Out of the total respondents 70 percent of them hold land between two and ten cents. While those hold land between ten cents and two acres comes around twenty-five percent. A very few proportion of the respondents are holders of more than two acres of land. In fact the complexity of landholding pattern has crucial effects on the Sheonath issue. The dependence of nearly all categories of the population in the study area on river water is largely an outcome of the landholding patterns in Durg.

Regarding the educational background of the respondents in Durg, there are some interesting patterns. More than one-third of the sample (36 percent) constituting the fishermen and labourers together are illiterates. The remaining respondents either have lower or upper primary education. But the author has not found a respondent whose educational background is at the college level. Regardless of the relatively poor educational statistics of the region, it seems that the people have good understanding about the privatization issue of the river and its aftermath. Although this understanding is in no way comparable to the awareness level in Plachimada, the author observed that most of the respondents in the study area were informed about the basic facts of the water right struggle.

Table 4.4: Land Holdings across Population

Land holdings	Agricultural & other wage labourers (31)	Fishermen (39)	Petty businessmen or traders (3)	Farmers (12)	%age
2 - 10 cents	24	34	-	-	68.24
10 cents – 2 acres	7	5	3	7	25.88
2 - 10 acres	-	-	-	5	5.88

4.10 Water Availability in the Study Area Until 1999

Given that the functioning of Sheonath project since 1999 had impacted upon the water availability in the villages in Durg District, the author collected information regarding the water availability and rainwater availability.

A greater part of the selected respondents in the study area were of the opinion that water availability was not an issue before the Sheonath river privatization. It should be noted that the limited responses towards in regard to the non-availability of water largely emanates from the general water scarcity in the region.

Most of the villagers stress the point that it is the river water availability that kept them secured from the general water scarcity in the region.

Moreover, majority within each group of respondents opined that the region received normal rainfall during the last ten years. Many of them raised apprehensions about the river water shortage in case of a less rainfall. Some of them even said that the Sheonath river survives only because of the abundant rainwater availability. They are worried about the fact that if the rainfall reduces beyond the normal stage they will face the detrimental consequence of river privatization in a higher degree.

4.11 Sources of Water

Similar to the Plachimada case, in order to look into the sources of water till 2000, the author made a three-fold classification of the water sources in Durg. They are drinking water sources, water sources for household purposes and water sources for agriculture. To begin with it should make clear that these three categories are not the resultant of a clear-cut classification as there are numerous instances of overlap between the three. This classification is just for the analytical convenience. The aforementioned overlaps between the three categories have ramifications in regard to the access and utilization of water and will be discussed in due course.

Regarding drinking water sources (Table 4.5) one fourth of the population depends on the public water sources. Except farmers and traders most of the labourers and fishermen rely on Sheonath river for drinking purposes. This dependence is in addition to the own wells, public/bore wells and pipeline. At the same time river water dependence on petty businessmen/traders and farmers are negligible in number. The direct dependence on Sheonath river bear ample testimony to the fact that river water constitute one of the most important source of drinking water till 1999.

The people of Durg have access to a variety cf household water sources (Table 4.6) such as, own wells and public wells, pipelines and water from the Sheonath river. Despite the relatively good accessibility to non-river water sources the people in Durg extensively depends on Sheonath river for their daily needs. This is mainly because of two reasons–socio-cultural and infrastructural. It seems, the respondents in the study area assign a certain degree of intrinsic value for the river water.

Table 4.5: Drinking Water Sources until 1999

Source	Agricultural labour & other wage labourer (31)	Fishermen (39)	Petty business or trade (3)	Farmers (12)	%age
Own wells and ponds	4	5	1	10	23.53
Public wells and bore wells	5	10	2	2	22.36
Pipeline	12	12	-	-	28.23
Sheonath river	10	12	-	-	25.88

Table 4.6: Household Water Sources

Sources	Agricultural & other wage labourers (31)	Fishermen (39)	Petty business men or traders (3)	Farmers (12)	%age
Own wells and ponds	3	5	2	10	23.53
Public wells and bore wells	4	2	1	-	8.23
Pipeline	5	6	-	-	12.95
Sheonath river	19	26	-	2	55.29

The water from Sheonath river is found to have a greater degree of instrumental value (such as satisfying the big-scale water needs of households), but their dependence on river is mostly determined by socio-cultural factors. Taking water from the river is an indispensable part of the local culture in Durg. Henceforth the advent of alternate water resources does not reduce the river water dependence of the population under study. It is pertinent to note here that public water supply through public wells and pipeline gets disturbed in lots of occasions.

A detailed account of the cultivation pattern in Durg is important for understanding the political economy of the study area. Apart from fishing the local people rely considerably on cultivation in the river basin area. There are predominantly two types of cultivation. A limited number of the farmers are indulged in paddy cultivation. But majority of the farmers invested in fruits and vegetable cultivation. Sheonath river holds a central role in the irrigation requirements of the region. Out of twelve farmers interviewed, only two of them uses water from own wells and ponds for the agricultural purpose. Majority of the farmers were of the opinion that the agricultural production in Durg is directly correlated with the water level in Sheonath river (Table 4.7).

Table 4.7: Agricultural Water Sources

Sources	Agri. and other wage labourers (31)	Fishermen (39)	Petty business or trade (3)	Farmers (12)	%age
Own wells and ponds	5	4	-	2	12.95
Sheonath river	26	35	3	10	87.05

Given that paddy, fruits and vegetables are relatively water intensive crops, any small scale reduction in the river water level will have detrimental consequences for the region's agricultural economy. One farmer informed the author that the increasing irregularity in rain water availability during the last few years compelled the Durg people to depend the Sheonath river for agricultural purposes in an unprecedented manner. Moreover other than farmers, fishermen, traders and labourers in the region have vegetable and fruits cultivation for the household purposes. They heavily depended on Sheonath river for the irrigation. Thus the table on agricultural water source in Durg bears ample testimony to the fact that Sheonath river is critical to the agricultural economy of the region.

4.12 Impact of Sheonath River Privatization

Tables 4.8 and 4.9 are based on the water scenario in Durg since the privatization of Sheonath river. The given tables are based on the responses of different categories of the Durg population regarding the detrimental impacts of river privatization. The focus of the survey was on denial in water access, impact on water intake and negative impacts on the economy. The survey was intended to find out the detrimental consequences of company activity in Durg especially in regard to the privatization of a Common Property Resource.

Table 4.8: Denial in Access to Sheonath River

Ban on	Agricultural & other wage labourers (31)	Fisher-men (39)	Petty businessmen or traders (3)	Farmers (12)	%age
Taking water, sand mining, washing clothes and bathing	28	1	2	2	38.82
Pumping water from wells, digging new wells	3	5	1	10	22.36
Fishing	-	33	-	-	38.82

As already mentioned in the first session, the most important aspect of Sheonath river privatization is the construction of a barrage (anicut) of 3.6 kilometres. Even though the river privatization agreement does not contain an absolute ban in accessing the water from Sheonath river, most of the villagers revealed that they were completely isolated from the river water. There was even ban on bathing, washing and fishing activities in Sheonath. The company authorities appointed securities to prevent any intrusion of the villagers into the Sheonath river. There are cases in which the company authorities had confiscated the pump sets of villagers. In order to make the policing of the company a more effective one, they constructed fences in the river premises. The worth mentioning fact is that the company even imposed checks on Durg people with respect to pumping water from the existing wells. There was also a complete ban on the digging of new wells.

Table 4.9: Impact on the Intake of Water

Reduced the water intake for	Agricultural labour & other wage labourer (31)	Fishermen (39)	Petty business or trade (3)	Farmers (12)	%age
Drinking purpose	3	4	-	-	8.24
Household purpose	4	2	3	2	12.94
Drinking and household purpose	24	33	-	-	67.06
Agricultural purpose	-	-	-	10	11.76

The table shows that the intake of river water for drinking, household and agricultural purpose reduced substantially since the inception of company activity in Durg. A greater number of the respondents in all categories stated that the water intake, both for the drinking and house hold purposes declined considerably during the project period. The farmers expressed the opinion that the intake of river water for agricultural purpose declined during period.

The economy in Durg faced a near total collapse following

the company activities. All sectors in the economy were affected detrimentally during the project period. Both the agricultural and daily wage labourers were victims of river privatization. In the case of agricultural labourers the decline in the area under cultivation has taken away much of their jobs. Given that the daily wage labourers were compelled to spend most of their time in collecting water from other sources, they have really little time to spend for daily work. All the fishermen in Durg mentioned about an absolute stoppage of fishing activity in the river. It should be noted that these detrimental impacts paved the way for stagnation in the region's domestic economy. The author is of the opinion that the privatization of Sheonath river is not the sole causal factor behind the collapse of Durg economy.

Despite having close proximity to the Borai industrial area, industrial sector did not have any considerable contribution towards the economy of the selected villages in Durg. Lion's share of the village population directly depend on primary sector such as, agriculture, fishing and petty business. As happened in the case of a large number of developing societies across the world, the primary sector in Durg had adversely affected with the emergent global transformations such as climate change, fluctuating agricultural prices, etc. According to many of the respondents things had gone to such extent that the income from agriculture, fishing and petty trade did not become sufficient for meeting the day-to-day livelihood needs. The privatization of Sheonath river made the things much worse as the existent struggling economy gets deteriorated in a multitude of ways.

From the study it became clear that the pre-company water availability scenario is reinstated following the opening up of Sheonath river. Only very few people mentioned that water was not available even after the termination of the ban imposed by RWL. This is pointing to the fact that the company had prevented access to a greater part of the river in Durg district at the cost of water availability in Durg. The study also highlights the fact that in contrast to the arguments made by the company people, the privatization of Sheonath river acted detrimentally upon the day-to-day water needs in Durg.

Moreover, the few responses in regard to the present-day non-availability of water emanates mostly from the general scarcity of water in the study region. Even though one can find a wide array of differences with that of the Plachimada case the water privatization issue in Sheonath also generated considerable negotiations at various levels. The affected people conducted negotiations with the municipal and district authorities and people's representatives.

Unlike the Plachimada case, where the farmers conducted negotiations with the company authorities at various time periods, the Chhattisgarh case is peculiar for the complete absence of the company officials for negotiation. As a matter of fact the authorities of Radius Water Limited were unapproachable for the local people. This is the reason why all sections of the population are engaged in extensive discussions with the municipal and district authorities. This also points to the extensive potentiality of local self-governing bodies in addressing the issues at the grassroots level. As already explained above in the preceding paragraph, the municipal and district authorities were at the centre of the negotiation scene. Accordingly lion's share of the people in study area thinks that the problem was solved because of the intervention of municipal and district authorities. The decision to reinstate the water access came from the state government, but the home work was set by the district and municipal authorities. People's representatives also played an important role; however it was mostly through the municipal and district authorities.

End Notes

1. Ex-Malgujas are communities of rich peasants, who ad the right to collect land revenue on behalf of the Maratha and British rulers.
2. The completed major projects include Tandula, Kodar and Pairy and major projects under construction include Hasdeo Bango,

Mahanadi Reservoir, Sondur, Jonk, Kelo, Rajeev Samoda and Tandula Lining.

3. Anicut is a dam or mole made in the course of a stream for the purpose of regulating the flow of a system of irrigation.
4. RWL is part of Kailash Engineering Company, Raipur. Kailash Engineering Company was engaged in construction works under the name of Kailash Construction Company. Kailash Construction Company later became Kailash Engineering Company.

References

Agreement for Borai Industrial Growth Centre Water Supply on BOOT (Build, Own, Operate, Transfer) Basis. (The contract of Sheonath river Privatization).

Chhattisgarh Government Scraps Privatized Water Supply Deal, available at, http://smgwp.com/news/10.pdf, accessed on 6/2/09.

Das, Binayak and Pangare, Ganesh (2006), *In Chhattisgarh a River Becomes Private Property, Economic and Political Weekly,* 18 February 2006, Mumbai, pp. 611-612.

Durg Comprehensive District Agriculture Plan, District Vision-2020, Submitted to District Planning Committee, Durg, Prepared by PRIA (an International Centre for Learning and Promotion of Participation and Democratic Governance).

Faulty Water Privatisation Deal Haunts Chhattisgarh State, available at, http://www.asiawaterwire.net/node/270, accessed on 20/3/09.

Jain, Sonu (2003), A *River Gone Private is Drying Up,* available at, http://www.indiaresource.org/news/2003/3583.html, accessed on 15/1/09.

Janhith Magazine (2003), AIYF Publication, Durg District Council.

Janasatta Magazine, 9 January 2003 and 24 November 2000, Raipur.

Krishnakumarmar, Asha (2003), *People's Battle for a River,* Frontline, Volume 20, Issue 22, October 25-November 07, Chennai.

Lakshmi, Rama (2003), India: Water Privatization Draws Indians' Ire: Villagers Resist New Approach to Sacred Resource, *available at,*

http://www.waterconserve.org/shared/reader/welcome.aspx?linkid=28074, accessed on 16/4/09.

Mumtaz, Rifat (2006), *Rivers for Sale: Common Property in Peril,* http://en.wikipedia.org/, accessed on 5/7/08.

Putul, Alok Prakash (2007), *Sheonath Deal Slammed, No Action Yet*, Down to Earth, 31 May 2007, New Delhi.

Putul, Alok Prakash (2009), *Privatization unlimited: Rivers for Sale in Chhattisgarh,* available at, http://infochangeindia.org, accessed on 13/12/09.

Putul, Alok Prakash (2009), *When Rivers are Sold for a Song*, available at, http://www.commodityonline.com/crops-weather, accessed on 2/2/09.

Sarvodaya Press Service Bulletin, 2 April 2003 and 18 May 2003, Raipur.

Singh, A. K. (2004), *Privatization of Sheonath River*, Combat Law, June-July, Mumbai, pp. 74-75.

Singh, A. K. (2004), *Privatization of Rivers in India*, Vikas Adhayn Kendra, Mumbai, p. 40.

Sethi, Aman (2006), *Private Water, Public Misery*, Frontline, 21 April 2006, Chennai, pp. 10-11.

V. Venkatesan (2000), *Chhattisgarh: Quiet Arrival*, Frontline, Volume 17, Issue 17, Aug. 19-September 01, 2000, Chennai.

Websites

http://en.wikipedia.org/, accessed on 5/7/08.

http://chhattisgarh.nic.in/, accessed on 12/7/08.

http://chhattisgarh.nic.in/, accessed on 23/7/08.

http://chhattisgarh.nic.in/, accessed on, 9/9/08.

http://durg.nic.in/DistrictProfile.html, accessed on 18/8/08.

http:/www.mapsofindia.com, accessed on 20/9/08.

http://smgwp.com/news/10.pdf, accessed on 6/2/09.

http://bluegold.rediffiland.com/blogs/2006/11/30/MONGRY.html, accessed on 24/2/09.

http://www.asiawaterwire.net/node/270, accessed on 20/3/09.

http://www.manthan-india.org/article25.html, accessed on 2/4/09.

http://www.waterconserve.org/shared/reader/welcome.aspx?linkid=28074, accessed on 16/4/09.

5

Water Right Struggles in Plachimada and Sheonath: A Comparative Analysis

This chapter intends to present a comparative exploration of the water rights struggles in Plachimada and Sheonath. The author's basic intention is to compare the two cases against the backdrop of the historical account on socio-political movements in Kerala and Chhattisgarh. The theoretical framework used to compare the Kerala and Chhattisgarh cases would be the Political Opportunity Structure (POS) thesis, which perceives social movements as resultant of expanding political opportunities. Besides attempting to bring out the parallels between both struggles, this chapter primarily intends to understand the broader structural factors that determine the outcome in Plachimada and Sheonath. The crux of the argument is that the stark difference in the movement culture of Kerala and Chhattisgarh paved the way for differential successes in the Plachimada and Chhattisgarh cases. While both struggles resulted in partial termination of company activities in the region, the pattern and outcome of success differed in both cases. The initial section is a historical account of the socio-political movements in India.

5.1 Socio-Political Movements in India

Indian sub-continent has witnessed the emergence of a wide variety of social movements even before the country obtained independence from the British colonial power. The cultural, social, political and economic diversity of Indian society has for centuries, allowed the emergence of varied forms of voluntary activities by people at the local level. Much of the detailed evidence is from the nineteenth and early twentieth centuries when India was under British colonial rule.

This period also marked the beginning of several social reform movements such as those focusing on religious reform, ending child marriage and improving the status of women, the lower castes, peasants and tribal groups.

Many of these movements included mobilization of people at the grassroots level. With increasing resistance to policies of the colonial administration, many of the movements for reform and resistance were incorporated into the nationalist struggle against British imperialism. The Indian national movement was widely regarded as an umbrella movement that contains within itself a wide array of grassroots based local struggles.

The first two decades after Independence from British rule in 1947 was a sort of honeymoon period for the Indian state. This period were marked by few movements of resistance against the state. In keeping with the constitutional principles of equality, liberty and social justice as well as secularism, socialism and democracy the Government of India instituted several laws granting equal rights to all disadvantaged groups and launched numerous plans for economic development and modernization. Nevertheless the state-orchestrated and uneven capitalist economic development and the liberal democratic model of politics have largely benefited the middle and upper castes and classes and few segments of the poor lower castes and classes.

By the late 1960s and early 1970s there was increasing realization by people from various marginalized groups that they were being left out of the development and democratic processes. Moreover, it was also becoming clear to many that the government lacked both the political will and resources to initiate and implement major policies. Lower castes, small and poor peasants, landless agricultural workers, women and people from different religious, linguistic and tribal groups started organizing and mobilizing for inclusion in the political and economic process.

The aforementioned one-to-one correspondence will not be sufficient enough to examine the evolution of social movements at the local level. The emergence of grassroots movements in India is also interlinked with the revitalization of civil society following the totalitarianism during the emergency period. This socio-political scenario provided fertile ground for the emergence of organizational initiatives that would reshape the concept of civil society and shift the focus from welfare and charity to development, empowerment and social change. Many of these organizations were a curious mixture of Gandhian and Marxist idealism.

By the early 1980s, the civil society arena had grown big and diverse and the most prominent development during this phase is the emergence of non-governmental organizations (NGOs). This shift is strongly reflected in the changing terminology used to define civil society organizations–from voluntary sector in the 1970s to the present development sector or NGOs clearly indicates the changing character of the civil society institutions that now work as professional organizations instead of the Gandhi-inspired voluntary efforts for social and developmental work. The 1990 saw the growth of professional intermediary organizations focusing issues like capacity building, research, advocacy and networking.

There is a need to mention about a parallel trend in the civil society arena. It was the development of socio-political action groups and social movements. Rajni Kothari and Harsh Sethi classified these groupings as non-party political formations. Such movements do not have party affiliations and work largely through political mobilization of disadvantaged communities, often occupying the anti-state space, criticizing the dominant mainstream paradigms and strategies of development from the perspective of ordinary people. Despite their localized support base and local character, these movements have often been able to affect policy making at the macro level. The author is of the opinion that any comparison of social movements in Kerala should consider the broader movement framework of India.

5.2 Political Opportunity Structure Thesis

Regardless of the fact that 1960s witnessed a proliferation in various kinds of social movements and revolutions, research on social movements languished in the backwaters of sociology and social psychology until the late 1960s and was largely ignored by political scientists. But the flowering of the civil rights and student movements in the US and of the new social movements of Western Europe in the 1970s led to a resurgence and normalization of this field. Della Porta's (2006) study in this tradition relate to the movements in regard to political processes. She used the key concept of the structure of political opportunity to show how some of the movements that emerged in the late 1960s were integrated within the political process, while others gravitated towards political violence. In fact the extensive conceptualization of the political environments that movements face has been an exciting development in recent research on social movements. This has largely taken the form of 'political opportunity' or political process approaches.

As per the narrow political opportunity thesis, social movements emerge as a result of expanding political opportunities. As Tarrow writes in *Power in Movement*, 'the main argument of this study is that people join in social movements in response to political opportunities and then, through collective action, create new ones'. Tarrow here loosens the narrow political opportunity thesis by emphasizing that social movement, once they have emerged, can further expand the political opportunities that allegedly gave rise to mobilization in the first phase. The passage nonetheless suggests that neither intense grievances nor extensive resources are sufficient or even necessary for movement mobilization to occur. Collective-behaviour and resource-mobilization theories had not been sufficient to give a proper definition. What is necessary and it would seem, virtually sufficient for social movement mobilization to occur is the opening up of political opportunities. The POS argument identifies political opportunities instead of genuine grievances as the most important contributory factor for the emergence of political movements.

The following is a brief elaboration of the *Political Opportunity Structure* thesis. The concept of POS will be critical in analyzing the outcome of social movement such as environment/resource struggle. The POS refers to the general political, economic and socio-historical context at both national and international level in which politics of repatriation take place. The POS is concerned with the dimensions of political environment, which either encourage or discourage people from collective action. Political opportunity structures refer to not necessarily permanent or formal configurations of political institutions and historical precedents for social mobilization, which protestors can exploit to promote collective action.

This model differs from those explored above in various ways, but the major distinction is its ability to adopt a comparative approach which the other frameworks cannot. While the neo-Marxism of new social movement theory can demonstrate links between the socio-economic stage of development and the emergence of social movements, it cannot explain why similar movements might have dissimilar outcomes. Resource mobilization concentrates primarily on internal variables of the movement including recruitment, goal formation, internal organization and the establishment of alliances. The POS on the other hand, examines how the emergence and methodologies of the movements relate to external institutional constraints specific to distinct political systems.

There are already attempts to deploy POS to explore the structure and practices of environmental movements. The ability of some environmental movements to wield power in global political fora is based on their established position within domestic POS. The fact that western environmental movements operate against a background of established political opportunity structures undoubtedly propelled western environmental movements on to the global stage. Although emerged as a radical social movement within the broader climate of political protest of the late 1960s, western environmental movements have gradually become institutionalized. One key factor promoting this has been mass memberships (both active and passive), which have provided the necessary resources to make use of the established and entrenched political opportunity structures of western democracies. Institutionalization has also promoted the convergence of policy discourses–notably in relation to ecological modernization–between some of the larger western environmental movements and structuring political and economic elites.

The early literature on political opportunity frameworks focused on political institutions and their practices as major structuring devices, which conditions the possibilities for success and failure of collective action. More recent POS theorizing has emphasized the extent to which non-institutional structures as well as political and cultural arrangements affect the possibilities for collective action. The cultural challenge to political opportunity structure research includes a developing focus on social movement context i.e. 'interactions between overall structures of power and argumentative strategies' and the specific setting in which collective action occurs. Context, as per Edmondson's argument, focuses primarily upon argumentative structure and content which is closer to a cultural than an institutional conception of factors shaping opportunities for collective action; yet she grounds her understanding in the recognition that, notions of politically acceptable argument in a given setting define the limits of its politically practicable world. The context dimension is critical for the author in regard to the comparative exploration of the cases in Kerala and Chhattisgarh.

Another worth mentioning fact about POS is that like civil

societies and social movements the POS was conceived in terms with the national government. The political opportunities open to social movements can increase when the state is opening up to give greater access to power or when divisions emerge between ruling elites. An open POS may encourage social movements to engage in conventional action repertoires, whereas a closed POS may encourage a more contentious action repertoire of direct action. Conflicting political opportunities may, however appear at the local, national and global levels. Before going into a comparative appraisal of Plachimada and Sheonath on the basis of POS, the author thinks it is appropriate to provide an elaboration on the struggle which took place in Plachimada and Chhattisgarh.

5.3 The Plachimada Struggle

The Plachimada struggle was formally inaugurated on 22nd April 2002. During the first four months itself regional organizations such as *Adivasi Samrakshana Sangham* (Tribal Protection Group), *Haritha* Development Association, *Janakeeya Poratta Vedi* (People's Struggles Forum), *Viplava Sthreevedi Prasthanam* (Revolutionary Women's Movement), *Porattom,* People's Union for Civil Liberties (PUCL), Youth League of National Alliance People's Movement, *Pattikajathi-Pattikavargha Samrakhshana Munnani* (Scheduled Caste Scheduled Tribe Protection Alliance), *Gandhi Yuva Mandalam* (Gandhi Youth Forum), etc. were integrated into the struggle. Notwithstanding the fact that struggle got support from a wide array of organizations, mainstream political parties were antagonistic to the anti-investment struggle.

Except the Communist Party of India (CPI), all the prominent political parties detached from the initial struggle phase. Moreover Communist Party of India (Marxist), Janata Party, Congress and Bharatiya Janata Party took a position in favour of the company. Most of the parties were of the opinion that lodging struggle against companies like Coca-cola will affect the general investment climate in the state. There is a general feeling that Kerala has been hostile to industrial investment. Given that neighbouring states like Tamil Nadu and Karnataka are preoccupied with a pro-investment policy by giving incentives to domestic and multinational corporations for generating a good investment climate, the mainstream political parties were not in a position to support the anti-water privatization struggle.

However, the Perumatty Panchayat lead by Janata Dal (S) took radical position since the second year of the struggle. During the first year of the struggle Perumatty Panchayat did not extend any support to the local people who were active participants in the struggle. It is the Communist Party of India and Solidarity movement supported the struggle in the initial year of its commencement. The food materials provided by the Solidarity people to the participants of the struggle contributed to the sustenance of the struggle in a considerable degree. But very soon the political parties which were active at the panchayat level became aware of the importance of the struggle within the region's political economy. In a sense the struggle dynamics emerged as a critical political force which no political party can afford to ignore.

The situation has emerged in such a manner that even if one political party ignored the struggle it becomes suicidal for their political future, especially at the grama panchayat level. This is best reflected in the fact it is the Perumatty Grama Panchayat which took the initiative to cancel the license of the company. The panchayat also initiated a legal struggle against the company for the final termination of company activities at Plachimada.

It is pertinent to note here that the Perumatty Panchayat got support from M.P. Veerendra Kumar, state leader of Janata Dal and Member of Parliament for its operations against the Cola giant. He intervened in the Plachimada struggle both at ideological and operational levels. He is of the opinion that the struggle in Plachimada is not just a local protest aimed at reinstating water access to the affected people. According to him, Plachimada struggle is a good example for resistance against the globalizing neo-liberal economic forces. Many national and international organizations were involved in the agitation at different times.

Though the struggle has a global representativeness the *Coca-Cola Virudha Samara Samithi* (CVSS) showed a kind of homogeneity, they are close to one another, and belongs to same caste and sub-caste, manifest some sanction system, reduces free-rider problem (Nair, 2008).

Before the advent of Panchayat, the struggle was initiated with Veloor Swaminathan as convener and Vilayodi Venugopal as Rakshadhikari (patron). It is during this period the National Alliance of People's Movement (NAPM) under the leadership of Medha Patkar decided to start their national agitation against globalization and privatization from Plachimada. The commencement of *'Deshbachao Deshbanao Abhiyan'* (Movement for Protecting and Building the Nation) started from Plachimada on January 26, 2003 gave a new phase to the Plachimada struggle.

It should be noted that even at this stage mainstream political parties were not ready to align with either Anti-Coca-Cola Struggle or with other environmental organizations. On April 22, 2003 Dr. Vandana Shiva visited Plachimada and participated in the three-day anniversary celebrations. In the same month itself NAPM took over the struggle. Its leader Medha Patkar said that Plachimada struggle was fought for protecting the natural resources. It was a model for similar struggles in different parts of the country. Sri M. P. Veerendra Kumar and Dr. Vandana Shiva took the initiative to conduct World Water Forum in Plachimada during 21-23 January 2003. In this forum the CPI (M) and Janata Dal joined together in their fight against Coca-Cola Company.

This forum accepted the Plachimada declaration on water rights. In the meanwhile a *Plachimada Aikyadardya Samiti* (Plachimada Supporters Group) was formed under R. Ajayan, a well-known social activist. His involvement was instrumental in popularizing the struggle all over the state. In short, within a short span of time the political parties were compelled to extend their support to the individuals and organizations that took part in the struggle.

For the past years, the Anti-Coca-Cola Struggle Committee and Plachimada Supporters Group primarily stand for four main demands. They are:

1. To close down the Coca-Cola company in Plachimada after giving compensation to the local people for destroying their habitat.
2. To ensure the proper trial of HCBPL for its involvement in polluting the Plachimada region.
3. To give legal powers to the Gramasabhas for enabling the protection of natural resources.
4. To amend the pollution control laws and Panchayati Raj Acts for not repeating more Plachimada cases.

When court decisions became delayed the Anti-Coca-Cola Struggle Committee demanded to the Kerala government the appointment of a high level committee to solve the Plachimada issue. The Water Resources Department has then constituted an expert committee to study the nature and extent of losses suffered by the people of Plachimada. The panel submitted its report recommended the Kerala government to take steps to realize Rs.200 crore as compensation in damages from the multinational company. The following is a chronology of the political events associated with the Plachimada struggle.

5.4 Chronology of Political Events

June 3, 2000: HCBPL started production in Plachimada.

April 22, 2002: Anti-Coca-Cola struggle was inaugurated.

April 17, 2003: Temporary closure of the factory as per the order of Perumatty Panchayat. [1]

June 12, 2003: LSGD stayed the order of Perumatty Panchayat.

August 2003: KSPCB found that cadmium was present in the solid waste more than the permissible limit.

August 7, 2003: KSPCB asked the company to establish the solid waste disposal mechanism.

October 3, 2003: LSGD ordered the Panchayat to conduct scientific investigation. [2]

December 16, 2003: High court judgment against HCBPL in consequence to the petition filed by Perumatty Panchayat president. [3]

January 7, 2004: High Court order for scientific investigation in Plachimada by CWRDM. The court order was in consequence to company's petition.

February 4, 2004: Publication of Joint Parliamentary Committee Report. [4]

February 2004: Kerala government banned the extraction of groundwater by HCBPL till June 15. The ban was on the basis of the report of Palakkad district Collector. [5]

February 23, 2004: KSPCB cancelled the authorization of the company as it did not construct the solid waste disposal mechanism.

March 9, 2004: HCBPL is closed on the basis of government and High Court order.

March 11, 2004: Perumatty Panchayat issued license with three conditions. HCBPL rejected it, but LSGD stayed this intervention of Perumatty Panchayat. [6]

August 14, 2004: Supreme Court Monitoring Committee report published. [7]

February 11, 2005: CWRDM report published recommending safe withdrawal of five lakh litres of water per day by HCBPL.

April 7, 2005: Based on the CWRDM report the Kerala High Court permitted to draw 5 lakh litres of water per day.

April 26, 2005: Perumatty Panchayat decided not to renew the license of HCBPL. [8]

May 6, 2005: Supreme Court issued notice to HCBPL, Kerala Government and KSPCB. [9]

June 6, 2005: On the basis of court order Perumatty Panchayat issued 3 month license to HCBPL with 13 conditions. However, the company rejected the proposal on multifaceted grounds. [10]

August 19, 2005: KSPCB ordered the stoppage of production in the HCBPL plant. [11]

November 16, 2005: High Court asked the Perumatty Panchayat to reissue license within January 6.

January 4, 2006: Perumatty Panchayat issued a license with 17 conditions. As happened earlier the company rejected these proposals.

August 10, 2006: Kerala Government banned the production and sale of Coca-Cola and Pepsi. [12]

August 20, 2006: As a note of victory the tribal people of Plachimada called off their 1,588 days agitation.

September 26, 2006: Kerala High Court stayed the ban of Coca-Cola and Pepsi. [13]

October 12, 2007: Plachimada struggle completes 2000 days with a seminar, public meeting and installation of a sculpture.

October 14, 2008: Kerala Ground Water Authority found that the functioning of the company leads to environmental destruction. [14]

February 24, 2009: Plachimada struggle completed its 2500th day.

June 20, 2009: The Water Resources Department has constituted an expert committee headed by Additional Chief Secretary K. Jayakumar. [15]

March 22, 2010: The expert committee submitted its report recommending for a compensation of ₹ 216.26 crore to the people. [16]

April 20, 2010: Plachimada Coca-Cola Viruddha Samara Samithi submitted a memorandum to Chief Minister and demanded for the constitution of the tribunal as suggested by the expert committee.

April 22, 2010: The eighth anniversary of Plachimada struggle was inaugurated by writer Sukumar Azhikode.

May 24, 2010: The comment by Principal Secretary

(Industries and Commerce) T. Balakrishnan on the circumstances leading to the closure of the Hindustan Coca-Cola Beverages plant at Plachimada has become a controversy. [17]

June 27, 2010: The Department of Law has given consent to the formation of the tribunal as suggested by the Jayakumar Committee. [18]

June 30, 2010: The Kerala Cabinet decided to set up a tribunal to adjudicate on compensation claims from people affected by the operation of the Coca-Cola plant at Plachimada in between 2000 and 2004.

The aforementioned legal events had crucial impacts on the course of the Plachimada struggle. At many occasions the interventions of courts and governments acted as a detrimental factor for the struggle. For instance, when the Kerala Government banned Coca-Cola in August 2006, the leaders withdrew the struggle. Nevertheless when the court stayed the government decision the struggle regained its momentum.

It is not an exaggeration to say that the leaders of the struggle framed its strategies as per the external factors such as court orders and government decisions. The heavy reliance on external factors has resulted in the undermining of local participation in decision-making and hijacking of the struggle by outside organizations. There was also competition within the outside organizations and there were occurrences in which the individuals and organizations deliberatively utilized the Plachimada struggle for their publicity.

5.5 Analysis on the Findings of Field Survey in Plachimada

This section is based on the findings of field survey conducted by the author in Plachimada. The thrust of the field information pertains to the nature of social movement that emerges in Plachimada following the functioning of HCBPL since 2000. Both the participants and non-participants in the Plachimada struggle found a place in the selected sample. A separate section in the questionnaire is devoted to understand the nature and course of the struggle. The author also took special care in interviewing the important personalities who are directly and indirectly associated with the struggle.

The survey proved that the tribal population constitutes most of the struggle participants. The sheer majority of these victimized population in the struggle makes it a good case for the resistance from the below. The aloofness of the forward caste in the locality from the struggle does not prevent the Scheduled Tribes and Castes from their participation in the struggle.

During the survey the author found that the Other Backward Class (OBCs) and forward caste had always shown non-interest towards the anti-Coca-Cola struggle. Even though most of the participants in the struggle are Scheduled Tribe population, the Plachimada struggle cannot be branded as mere a tribal struggle. The most important reason for the cross-cultural non-participation in the struggle was non-interest in the modus-operandi of anti-Coca-Cola struggle. This non-interest of OBCs and forward castes is particularly due to their capacity to find alternatives to the ground water depletion and pollution caused by the company. It reiterates the fact that struggle is the last resort of people who do not have other options.

An analysis on duration of participation is critical in understanding the nature of water right struggle in Plachimada. Unlike many of the similar struggles across the country, the Plachimada struggle proves that continuous participation over the years is not a simple process. Eighty four percent of the participants belonging to ST category have participated in the struggle all through the last six years.

The local political activists play a facilitational role in mobilizing the victimized population constantly for the struggle. On many occasions it was found that these activists had managed to provide subsistence allowance for the affected population (Table 5.1).

Table 5.1: Duration of Participation: Day-wise

Duration	ST	SC	Percentage
All days, without going for job	11	-	11
Alternative days, without going for job	84	5	89

Notwithstanding the fact that there are daily and alternate day participants nearly all participants had involved in the struggle even after compromising their jobs. In the case of SC and ST population, all the struggle participants had stopped going for jobs. During the survey it could be noticed that many of the respondents expressed optimism about the ultimate termination of company in Plachimada. The author has also noted a sense of over activism among certain participants in the struggle. They demanded huge compensation from the company. The modes of Plachimada struggle deserve special mention. It is worth mentioning that the participants of the struggle had utilized democratic means such as marches, demonstration and picketing to raise their protest. The non-violent Gandhian method constitutes the central strategy of the Plachimada struggle. Even though the substantial success in the legal battle acted as inspiration for the struggle, the leaders of the Plachimada struggle took special care to prevent the violent deviation of the struggle modes in most of the times.

During the fieldwork, the author has collected the details of the support, which the struggle participants received from inside and outside the village. It is really difficult to categorize the nature of support and the attempt to divide it into physical and moral is for analytical convenience. From the survey it became clear that the support received for the struggle from inside the village was mainly physical and moral. The best illustration in this regard is the unparalleled rigor in the struggle participation. Given the fact that the Plachimada struggle is mainly lead by downtrodden masses there was little response and physical support from inside. Moreover, the struggle participants did not receive any financial support from inside the village. This is because those who are capable of extending financial assistance (for example, the farmers) were non-participants and provided only moral support to the Plachimada movement (Table 5.2).

Table 5.2: Support to Struggle from Outside the Village

Types of support	ST	SC	Percentage
Financial support	35	-	35
Physical support	50	5	55
Moral support	10	-	10

As per the inputs received from the respondents the water right struggle in Plachimada received all types of support from outside the village. By outside support the author meant the support from outside villagers, political and non-political organizations, civil society groups, NGOs, etc. The support consists of financial help, physical assistance and moral support. The most significant aspect of the physical support is the active participation of nationally acclaimed environmentalists and social activists in the Plachimada struggle.

On many occasions the author found that the participants are receiving financial support from outside the village. Moreover the participants were coming to the protest site on a daily wage basis. There are instances in which the leaders of the struggle were indulged in some sort of hiring struggle participants from the neighbouring villages. In spite of this it is improper to call the Plachimada resistance as an orchestrated one. The local economy of Plachimada suffered serious disruption due to the company activity. The leaders of the struggle have no way other than assuring basic subsistence of the struggle participants. Considering the larger processes and goals of the struggle, there is no point in exaggerating these kinds of isolated instances.

5.6 Struggle in Chhattisgarh

The Sheonath river project started its working in November 2000. Within a short span of time the villagers began to face difficulties in accessing water from the Sheonath river. It is the All India Youth Federation (AIYF), which first initiated a struggle against the project. Majority of the local population participated in the struggle. During the earlier phase itself the participants of the struggle received support from the national as well as international environmental organizations. The best illustration of the external support was the organization of a Water Conference by Mayaram Surjan Foundation, Unity Council and Chhattisgarh Science and Technology Council on November 17-18, 2000.

Prominent participants in the seminar include noted environmentalist Medha Patkar and Chhattisgarh Finance Minister Dr. Ramachandra Singh Deo. Following the seminar a Water Conference core group meeting was convened at Ravishanker University. The core group consists of the then Finance Minister, Vice-Chancellor of Ravishanker University and a member of Amity Council. The Ravishanker University was asked to conduct studies in regard to the water problem in Chhattisgarh. The core group decided to draft a new water policy and the plan was named as Water Vision 2025. The core group also decided to form a water community in each district and it was intended to organize demonstrations to generate awareness.

In fact the interventions of the core group were critical in regard to the further course of the struggle. On 24th February 2003, a symposium was organized by the Sheonath Bachao Andolan (Sheonath Redemption Movement). This movement was started from the Sabarmati Ashram founded by Mahatma Gandhi and its intention is to assert society's right over water. Water activist Rajendra Singh, Gautam Bandhopadhyay (coordinator of River Valley Entrenchment Unity Council), Communist Party of India (M) State Secretary C. R. Bhakshi, and Deshbandhu Chief Editor Lalit Surjan delivered speeches during the symposium.

On the last day social activists Medha Patkar and Sandeep Pandey visited the anicut at Mohlai village and addressed the symposium. Further in order to express support to the Sheonath cause the National Water Alert Travel visited the anicut in Sheonath river on March 1, 2003.

During the later phase the struggle participants formed an organization called Nadi Ghadi Sangarsh Samithi (River Valley Entrenchment Movement). In consequence, a group of organizations submitted memorandum to the Governor requesting his interference in the issue. These organizations include All India Farmer's Committee, Fishermen's Union, Progressive Writer's Union, Ipta, Dalit Study Circle, All India Peace Unity Organization, All India Students Federation (AISF), All India Women's Federation, National Alliance of People's Movements, Youth Federation, Ekta, Kisan Sabha, Action Aid, Progressive Writer's Union, People's Union for Civil Liberties, etc. They also demanded a report on the issue.

On August 20, 2003 the second phase of AIYF's Sheonath Bachao Andolan was begun. They organized a semi-nude demonstration near Kachhari on September 3. They have started this movement because even if the government agreed to cancel the contract no cancellation has been done so far.

A charity walk near the riverbank and a mass meeting in Durgav village were organized during the second phase. The organizers also arranged street plays to put across the relevance of Sheonath struggle. It is during this time that the CPI General Secretary A.B. Bardhan explained that nobody has ownership right on the Sheonath river. On September 24, 2003, AIYF organized a charity walk from Mohlai village to Durgav against the privatization of Sheonath river. The charity walk got good reception during the public meetings from the local people.

The success of the charity walk is attributable to the heterogeneity of the members who participated in the rally. The participants include the rank and file of political parties, farmers, villagers, social workers and noted environmentalists. On 1st November 2003 the agitators under the leadership of AIYF and more than two dozen progressive organizations organized a picketing to push for the cancellation of privatization agreement. The picketing was arranged at the front of district office in Durg. Deshbandhu, one of the popular newspapers in Chhattisgarh which actively supported the struggle from its initial stage by giving wide news coverage, played a commendable role in extending the outreach of the struggle to local people. They arranged a signature campaign in order to get support for the Sheonath Bachao Andolan. Finally the agitators submitted a signed memorandum to the district collector asking prompt action on the issue.

On April 5, 2005 Sheonath River Valley Entrenchment organized a 'water satyagraha' in Kachhari junction to protest against the river privatization. This satyagraha was organized on the 75th year of Gandhiji's Dandi march and salt satyagraha. It should be noted that hundreds of villagers from neighbouring districts also participated in the satyagraha. The points raised by the satyagraha participants were more of a general nature such as the destruction of water resources and increase of water pollution. They had indulged in protest modes like burning an effigy at Gandhi Chauk.

The agitators had resorted to innovative struggle modes during this period. On April 14, 2005 AIYF organized a cycle rally to protest against the privatization of Sheonath river. Slogans against the privatization of water were one of the most important hallmarks of the rally.

Sheonath Bachao Andolan coordinator Sunil Meshram took the leadership of the rally. Members of organizations such as Rajya Etek, Ipta, Dalit Study Circle, Action Aid, River Valley Entrenchment Movement, Kissan Sabha, etc. came to Raipur by cycle. The representatives of the agitation handed over a memorandum to Governor K.M. Sethi demanding intervention in the matter.

5.7 Analysis of Findings of Field Survey in Chhattisgarh

This section discusses the findings of the field survey conducted by the author in Chhattisgarh during 2006. One of the most important objectives of the field survey was to understand the nature of social movement in Chhattisgarh. The survey sample consists of participants and non-participants in the struggle against Sheonath river water privatization. There is a separate section in the questionnaire pertaining to the nature and course of struggle. As part of the field survey, scheduled interviews were conducted with most of the eminent personalities and struggle leaders. The following discussion is based on the data collected from the field survey in Chhattisgarh.

The data on participation in the water struggle at Sheonath has close correlation with the impacts of Sheonath river privatization. The most prominent group participated in the struggle were fishermen, the group which was severely hit by the advent of Radius Water Limited. The fences constructed by the company on the banks of Sheonath river obstructed the access of the fishing folk in Durg district. The participation of farmers and agricultural labour in the struggle can shed light on over arching destruction caused by the company activity in Sheonath (Table 5.3).

Table 5.3: Duration of Participation: Year-wise

Duration	Agricultural & other wage labourers (31)	Fishermen (39)	Petty business or trade (3)	Farmers (12)	Percentage
1-2 year	5	4	2	5	18.83
2 year	20	32	1	4	67.06
More than two year	6	3	-	3	14.11

The duration of participation holds special relevance in understanding the nature of Sheonath struggle. Unlike the

Plachimada case, the struggle participants in Sheonath were solely concerned about the threat on their livelihood. The people in Durg limit their concern to reinstate the water access scenario before the company operations. This is best reflected in the sharp decline in the number of participants who completed more than two years in the struggle. Following two years of struggle and government intervention the company allowed the villagers to access the river water in a considerable degree. More specifically by 2002 the villagers were in a position to access and utilize the Sheonath river as they availed it for centuries. However, as happened in the case of Plachimada the ideological struggle against privatization of river water still continues in Sheonath.

The main thrust of the post-2002 struggle was to cancel the privatization agreement with Radius Water Limited; the struggle leaders are not satisfied with just reinstating water access in Sheonath river. But the mass participation in the Sheonath struggle reduced considerably when the struggle took an ideological turn. It seems the Durg people were just concerned about their day-to-day lives and were not politically empowered when compared to their counter parts in Plachimada. It is worth mentioning to note that there had not been any significant decline in participation in the Plachimada struggle following the temporary closure of Coca-Cola factory. But Lalit Surjan, Chief Editor, Deshbandhu and Dr. Ramachandra Singh Deo held another view point. Though the participants are less in number compared to its initial phase, the struggle does not lose its momentum. The nature of the struggle portraits that, it is not only a struggle against water privatization, but also a resistance against national and multinational water corporations.

The analysis on modes of struggle will give a profile of the nature of Sheonath movement. Participation in various demonstrations and marches constitute the most significant struggle mode. From the table it is evident that more than half of the sample population participated in all types of marches.

Picketing forms the second most important mode of struggle in Sheonath. It is pertinent to note that there is no reported arrest bearing cases in connection with the Sheonath privatization issue. One of the important hallmarks of Sheonath struggle is the considerable participation of agricultural labour, fishermen and farmers in the struggle. In the meanwhile there were few people who did not participate in the struggle at any point of time. During the interview with the non-participants the author observed that most of them extended their moral support for the Sheonath cause. A considerable number of the non-participants kept away from the struggle due to personal reasons. There is a need to make it clear that unlike the Plachimada struggle, financial assistance for the struggle was less in Sheonath (Table 5.4).

Table 5.4: Support to Struggle from Outside the Village

Types of support	Agricultural labour & other wage labourer (31)	Fishermen (39)	Petty business or trade (3)	Farmers (12)	Percentage
Physical support	6	10	1	4	24.70
Moral support	25	29	2	8	75.30

The analysis on outside support to the struggle was done on the basis of the responses given by the sample population in Durg. By outside support the author meant the support from outside villagers, political and non-political organizations, etc. When comes to the outside support majority of the respondents were of the opinion that there was considerable amount of moral support to the struggle from other villages. However, the author observed the absence of financial support though it received much physical support from non-political organizations. The most significant aspect of the physical support is the active participation of nationally acclaimed environmentalists and social activists in the Sheonath struggle. Similar to the previous one, the efficiency of political parties in addressing the problem is also based on the response from Durg villagers. It points to the fact that nearly half of the people believe that the intervention of political parties was efficient in regard to finding a solution to the water access problem. The other half of the respondents was of the opinion that political parties were not effective in mitigating their grievances. It is difficult to make observations from the response, as the political literacy among the Durg people is low when compared to the Plachimada people and the forces that supported them in Kerala. There is every chance that the above-mentioned response of the Durg people may have emanated from the lack of political awareness.

5.8 Comparison of the Water Right Movements in Kerala and Chhattisgarh

As the author already mentioned, Plachimada and Sheonath are cases of ground and surface water privatization respectively. Henceforth, the nature of privatization and its consequences on the local population differed significantly in both cases. More specifically the cases of Plachimada and Sheonath also differed in regard to the impact of national, regional and local political contexts on mobilization and its outcomes. In this section the author attempts to identify the comparative features of water right struggles in both cases. The following subsections attempts to conceive the Plachimada and Sheonath case against the backdrop of the divergent movement characteristics of Kerala and Chhattisgarh.

5.9 Plachimada: A Global-Local Movement

Socio-political and religious movements form an important causal factor of the exceptional developmental trajectory of Kerala. Kerala development model is largely a post-facto generalization of an experience, historically evolved, but promoted by public action (which *inter alia* includes socio-religious reform movements, wide and active press, adversarial politics) and sustained by social demands. The political activity in the state is evolved as a sort of local group demands that habitually expressed through conscious collective struggle. These bottom-up struggles, particularly from underprivileged groups (at many times for a better social system itself), had limited options of democratized state to supply basic services. This way of democratization has created too many stake holders, more in a participatory sense, for the development process. Consequently, any initiatives, which deprive the local population's livelihood rights, are doomed to be responded with grassroots movements. The interventions of such grassroots movements are highly facilitated by the high density electronic/print media and a relatively literate society. The aforesaid attributes of Kerala society are critical in exploring the Plachimada case.

In a sense the Plachimada movement has close allegiance largely on the movement culture of Kerala. The leaders and participants of the struggle were not just lodging a struggle against the company activities in Plachimada. One of the important aims of the struggle was to mobilize public protest against the state's policy of allowing private monopolies to control the extraction and utilization of water. Henceforth, the targets of the struggle were both the state and the HCBPL Company. Moreover, the Plachimada struggle is a best illustration of the positive use of communication to make the local people aware about functioning of HCBPL and its disadvantages in Plachimada. Apart from giving wide publicity to the struggle through new papers, the organizers of the struggle tried to circulate poems and booklets among the people to make them aware of the hazards of water privatization. These poems and booklets were important inspirational source all through the struggle phase. The following widely circulated pamphlet [19] is aimed at uncovering the atrocities committed by the company, which claimed itself as a responsible corporate citizen.

1. The company has started its operations before acquiring the required sanctions for the starting up of company activities.
2. Even after estimating that the production processes in the company will trigger environmental pollution, the government gives permission for the inception of company activities in Plachimada. This is regardless of the fact that Plachimada is a densely populated and agriculturally rich region. Following numerous reported occurrences of environmental pollution, the company is now indulged in forging new arguments to claim its innocence.
3. The company authorities are fully aware of the fact that the solid waste from HCBPL contains poisonous materials. Notwithstanding this realization the company relentlessly sold the solid waste as agricultural manure. The company has also deposited the solid waste in riverbanks. The presence of solid waste from the company has affected the quality of water in the public and private wells. If this situation is allowed to continue the Plachimada village will be suffocated with the over presence of toxic wastes.
4. Ground water is a precious natural resource. It is formed through generations and thus is a natural right of the forthcoming generations. In order to generate profits through producing socially unimportant goods, the company is exploiting water resources in an environmentally unsustainable manner. The *grama sabha* and *oorukoottam* [20] in Plachimada consistently asked for the stoppage of company activities in the region. But the company took a provocative position that they are giving back more water when compared to extracting volume.
5. The ruling class and scientific institutions are expected to address the complaints of the people in an objective manner. But the company people are trying to gain their support through conscious manipulations and illegal means. It was the means through which the company

authorities tried to defeat the local people who were lodging struggle against atrocities caused by the company.

6. The company deliberatively attempts to conceal the crucial facts on the ownership of the company; toxic solid waste materials emerges out in the production processes; the income-expenditure figures of waste disposal; details of environmental impacts; profit share, etc. Through concealing these important details the company is trying to hide the much-needed information in regard to the negative impacts of company activity in Plachimada.

Even though the Plachimada struggle is largely fought on locally specific causes, this case is exceptional for the global-local inter-linkages. Plachimada had become the location of national and international struggle against the privatization of water and the most important event was the World Water Forum (WWF) that took place in Plachimada and Puthuserry on 21-23 January 2004. The forum was a meeting place of activists from France, Candada, United States of America, Sweden, Finland, Germany and Italy. The forum ended on 23rd January with the acceptance of a declaration, which is considered as the Magna Carta of water rights struggle. The following is the full draft of Plachimada Declaration.

- Water is the basis of life; it is a gift of nature; it belongs to all living beings on earth.
- Water is not a private property. It is a common resource for the sustenance of all.
- Water is the fundamental right of all people. It has to be conserved, protected and managed. It is our fundamental obligation to prevent water scarcity and pollution and to preserve it for generations.
- Water is not a commodity. We should resist all criminal attempts to marketise, privatise and corporatise water. Only through these means we can ensure that the fundamental and inalienable right to water for people all over the world.
- The Water Policy should be formulated on the basis of this

outlook.

- The right to conserve, use and manage water is fully vested with the local community. This is the very basis of water democracy. Any attempt to reduce or deny this right is a crime.
- The production and marketing of the poisonous products of the Coca Cola, Pepsi Cola corporates lead to total destruction and pollution, which also endangers the very existence of local communities.
- The resistance that has come up in Plachimada, Pudussery and in various parts of the world is the symbol of our valiant struggle against the devilish corporate gangs who engage in piracy of our water.
- We, who are in the battlefield in full solidarity with the tribal people who have put up resistance against the tortures of the horrid commercial forces in Plachimada, exhort the people all over the world to boycott the products of Coca Cola and Pepsi Cola.

Coca Cola-Pepsi Cola "Quit India".

The inter-linkage between the processes of local and national struggle is of great importance. Dr. Vandana Shiva rightly pointed out that in Plachimada a local government is in struggle not only against a multi-national corporate giant but also against the ruling dispensation in the native place. The Plachimada movement is not only endowed with a heterogeneous group of struggle participants but also characterized by the prevalence of more than one targets. To a great extent, the Plachimada movement has an ideological orientation and at many times the struggle has gone beyond practical objectives. The above given movement characteristics are in sharp contrast to the unfolding of water rights movement in Chhattisgarh.

5.10 Sheonath: A Pragmatic Movement at Work

Unlike the Plachimada struggle the water right movement

in Sheonath is more of a pragmatic kind. Notwithstanding the fact that the Sheonath movement witnessed the participation of people from various backgrounds, the cross sectional participation does not contribute to the rigor of the movement. During the fieldwork the author found that people from several villages, including Mohlai, Kekro Koli, Bedwa Pathra, Vagrum Nala, Basik Hai and Chatarri, have joined the struggle. However, there has not been any indication of any ideological orientation for the protestors as occurred in the Plachimada case.

A greater part of the struggle participants were concerned about the day to day necessities of life and the dimension of ideological struggle against anti-privatization is alien to them. This is best reflected in the fact that mere reinstating the river access prompted a major chunk of struggle participants to terminate their participation. The positive outcome of the struggle took place is largely due to the legal intervention of the government. The following is a brief note on the course of legal developments in the Sheonath issue.

With the protests intensifying, the former Chief Minister, Ajit Jogi, decided, in April 2003, after a ministerial meeting, to cancel the contract. The state government agreed to terminate the contract within the legal framework and pay compensation to the company for the lease period after the Law Department and the Advocate General had given their opinions. According to him, the government is ready to pay any amount to end the contract, but it will at no cost allow the privatization of natural resources. According to the State Legal Committee, to which the issue was referred, if the government ends the contract with Radius Water Limited, it has to pay a compensation of ₹ 400 crore.

However, the government pointed out that as the company had not taken the approval of the State Water Utilization Committee as mandatory; it might not be eligible for compensation. In April 2003, the government assured the protestors of its intention of terminating the contract, but nothing seems to have happened since then. The RWL continues to manage the barrage and the frequency of public protests has declined and so has their impact.

Similar to the Plachimada case, the Chhattisgarh case has also fought at the High Court level. The controversial privatization of the Sheonath river has later been challenged through the filing of Public Interest Litigation (PIL) in the state High Court. The PIL contends that selling the river to a private company seven years ago has adversely affected the livelihoods of local fishermen as well as the supply of irrigation and drinking water in the area.

The petition was filed by the Forum for Fact-finding Documentation and Advocacy, a civil society organization based in Raipur, capital of Chhattisgarh. The petitioner argues that the agreement between Radius Water Limited and the state of Madhya Pradesh goes against the central government's water policy. The Forum for Fact Finding Documentation and Advocacy has sought the High Court's directives to quash the agreement between the state of Madhya Pradesh and RWL. However, unlike Plachimada case, the legal battle and the local struggle has not been inextricably intertwined to a substantial degree.

The last two subsections intended to give a brief outline of the key aspects of water rights struggle in Kerala and Chhattisgarh. The following subsection will be based on a comparison of two movements in the light of the Indian movement history in general and political opportunity structure in particular.

5.11 Experience of Water Right Struggles

As the author made it clear in the initial section, the concept of *Political Opportunity Structure* (POS) will be the central theoretical framework for comparing the Plachimada and Sheonath cases. The fundamental proposition of POS is that the critical factor that determines success or failure of social movements is their interface with political opportunities.

This interface can happen in two ways. Social movements can either struck its root by making use of the existing political opportunities or through creating new political opportunities in nature. In the conventional POS literature emphasis has been given to the political opportunities linked with the institutionalized politics. However, the author's standpoint is akin to the recent theorizations that also gave primacy to the non-institutional structures and political/cultural arrangements affect possibilities for collective action. After elaborating the five comparative points regarding the political opportunity aspects in Plachimada and Sheonath, the author will conclude this chapter by mentioning the water right movements within the wider context of Indian social movement history. The following are the five comparative points.

5.11.1 Differential Engagement of Political Parties: The engagement of political parties with the Plachimada struggle is an interesting dimension to be looked into. It is worthwhile to mention here that the Plachimada movement has begun outside the purview of institutionalized political activity in Kerala. The rise and progress of Plachimada movement was largely with the support of civil society groups which is outside the political party processes. The individuals and institutions that supported the Plachimada struggle had not been associated with the established political parties in Kerala. Moreover, most of the political parties took an antagonistic position to the struggle during the initial days. Their rationale was that this anti-privatization struggle would affect the general investment climate in the state. Kerala is lacking an industrial climate. It is not surprising to find that prominent political parties such as CPI (M) and Congress supported the company during the initial phase.

However, the intensity of the struggle and the extensive attention that the Plachimada movement attracted within the national and international forums compelled the political parties to rethink on the issue. Cutting across party lines, a considerable number of political leaders started supporting the

Plachimada struggle. For the most part, the Plachimada issue has turned to be a pet issue for the oppositional party leaders. The most prominent leader in this regard is V.S. Achuthanandan during his tenure as the leader of the opposition (2001-2006).

Following the order of the Kerala State Pollution Control Board [21] the State Government tried to implement the order of the Pollution Control Board (PCB) to close down the Coca-Cola bottling plant at Plachimada immediately. V.S. Achuthanandan even argued that the ruling government is pursing an anti-people attitude in this issue. The Congress Party, the most important opposition in the present set up, extended its support to the Plachimada movement. Several important leaders of the Congress party even criticized the present ruling Left Democratic Front government for failing to take urgent action against Coca-Cola Company. Some of the Congress leaders demanded collecting compensation packages from the Coca-Cola Company. In short, the Plachimada issue emerged as an inevitable issue for all mainstream political parties in the state.

Even though there is a whole host of organizations involved in the Sheonath struggle, unlike the Plachimada case, none of these organizations is endowed with the capacity to sustain the water right struggle without political support. The civil society organizations are not in a position to utilize the existing political opportunities or create new ones. The ability to positively engage with political opportunities contributes to the adaptability of Plachimada movement when compared to the Sheonath case.

5.11.2 Legal Battle and Movement Outcomes: Legal battles against the company forms one of the common struggle strategies in both cases. At the outset it should be noted that considering the present context of judicial activism in India, particularly the unparalleled interest of Supreme Court and High Courts in environmental issues, there is great scope for pursing a successful legal battle against the company. The following interpretation given to the Article 48 (A) by the Supreme Court is highly significant in regard to the Plachimada and Sheonath cases. It is constitutional duty not only of the state but also of every citizen to protect and improve the environment and natural resources of the country. In short, the legal battle is not just an issue of a constitutional remedy, but more a political opportunity. But there is a sharp difference in the manner in which the legal option utilized in the Kerala and Chhattisgarh cases.

The social movement in Plachimada has been fuelled by the verdicts and observations of judicial authorities. The Perumatty panchayat, the complaining body in most of the cases, fought the case against HCBPL in a systematic manner. The leaders of the struggle utilized the court interventions for strengthening their cause against the company. At many times the court observations regarding people's right to water resources shaped the ideological orientation of the Plachimada movement. However, the legal battle in Sheonath was merely aimed at reinstating the status quo in accessing the river water. Unlike the Plachimada movement there has not been any deliberate attempt to embark on the political opportunities unleashed by the intervention of the judicial system in India.

5.11.3 Proactive Role of Local-Self Governing Bodies: The Plachimada question raised an important issue regarding the power of panchayat over natural resources. The Kerala Panchayat Raj Act (1994)–the Act passed by the state government to implement the 73rd constitutional amendment regarding local self-government–increased the power of panchayats over public properties. Section 218 of the Act vests the authority over public water resources [22] in Panchayat bodies. But it excludes ground water as it is considered to be the sole property of land owner. The Third Schedule of this Act stipulates the maintenance of traditional drinking water sources and preservation of ponds and other water tanks as two of the mandatory functions performed by the village panchayats. The fairly successful implementation of Panchayat

Raj Act in Kerala enabled the Perumatty Panchayat to fight the case against the corporate giant when the well-being of the local people is at stake. [23] The absence of well-functioning Panchayat Raj institutions limits the political opportunities of the struggle participants in Sheonath. It is pertinent to note here that the Radius Water Limited is a less mighty corporate when compared to the Coca-cola company.

5.11.4 Substantial and Peripheral Legislations: As the author explained in the second chapter, concrete and comprehensive ground water legislation is inadequate in India. In 1970, the Central Government circulated a model bill to state governments. As per this Bill, Kerala has enacted its law in 2002 namely, The Kerala Ground Water (Control and Regulation) Act 2002. As per this Act the entire power to control ground water use is vested in the Ground Water Authority. Section 6 of the Act says about notifying areas for the control and regulation of ground water development. It reads like this, "the Government may, if satisfied on the recommendation of the authority, that it is necessary in the public interest to regulate the extraction or use of ground water of any area, declare by notification in the Gazette, such area as notified area or the purpose of this act with effect from such date as may be specified therein".

The Act also contain provisions such as granting permit to extract and use ground water, registration of the existing wells in the notified area, registration of ground water users, protection of public drinking water sources, etc. All these provisions aimed to exert control over the use of ground water and public water sources. The Act also says about the creation of a State Ground Water authority with adequate power to intervene in water related issues. The Authority shall have the power to measure the quantity of water; to inspect public and private wells; to make it mandatory for the ground water users to install water measuring instruments in their supply machinery; to seize the equipments and instruments in the case of malpractices like unauthorized digging and so on. Even though the Kerala Ground Water Authority has yet to achieve its full potential; it can provide checks on instances of ground water exploitation like Plachimada.

There are certain fundamental differences in regard to the legislations enacted in Kerala and Chhattisgarh. As mentioned in the preceding paragraph the scope of legislations in Kerala is much more when compared to the Chhattisgarh case. The legislative interventions in Chhattisgarh were mostly aimed at temporary solutions. For instance, the legislations enacted in Chhattisgarh against the backdrop of the Sheonath issue were primarily intended for reinstating the access into the river. But the legislations in Kerala are characterized with addressing the water right issue in a concrete and long-term perspective. The author is of the opinion that this difference is attributable to the political opportunities existing in Kerala's civil society. The redistributive social demands in Kerala often provide more political opportunities for the civil society organizations to positively engage with the state. Consequently, unlike the Chhattisgarh case, the governments in Kerala are not in a position to neglect the demands arising in the civil society.

5.11.5 New Social Movements and Political Opportunities: The Plachimada case is pertinent in regard to the exploration of the political opportunities set out by the new social movements. The inception of water rights struggle in Plachimada is concomitant of the emergence of a wide gamut of grassroots based movements outside the domain of institutionalized politics. These movements have emerged on the tribal, land and related subaltern issues. However, unlike many of these movements the Plachimada struggle have succeeded in exploring the political opportunities associated with the selective engagement with institutionalized politics. It should be noted that the Plachimada movement always kept the political parties at an arm's length. One cannot find such a complex interface between institutionalized and non-institutionalized politics in the Sheonath case. In contrast to the Plachimada case, concrete attempts were less in Sheonath to form linkages between likeminded new social movements.

A comparative exploration of two cases of ground and surface water privatization is indeed a challenging task. The diametrically opposite political processes, in particular the varied movement culture, of Kerala and Chhattisgarh, make this comparison a more difficult endeavour. While the state of Kerala is endowed with a globally acclaimed history of social movements, Chhattisgarh does not inherent a vibrant movement culture. The political opportunities in both states directly correlate with the degree of vibrancy of the movement culture. In a sense, the global inter-linkages of the struggle are also closely related to the specifities of the state-specific social processes. The comparative exploration of Plachimada and Chhattisgarh case is important in analyzing the complexities associated with the privatization of CPRs, especially the water resources.

End Notes

1. When the license cancelled the company filed a case (O. P. No. 13513/03) in the Kerala High Court and on 22nd April the court asked the company to reply to the show cause notice. HCBPL produced the reply before the panchayat on 30th April and the personal hearing was conducted on 6th May. But panchayat decided to cancel the license from 17th May and the company closed temporarily. The KHC in its order on 16th May asked the company to give an appeal in the concerned higher authorities. As per this order the company filed its appeal in Local Self-Government Department (LSGD) and the first trial was conducted on 11th June 2003. On the next day LSGD stayed the cancellation order of Perumatty Panchayat (No. 22501/C2/03/LSGD).
2. On 3rd October LSGD finalized the company's appeal. It found that the panchayat did not conduct any scientific studies before cancelling the license. As such the panchayat cannot claim that the water scarcity was due to the company's overexploitation of water. Besides LSGD ordered the panchayat to conduct a scientific investigation with an expert team within three months and for that period the company can continue its operation.

3. On 29th October Perumatty Panchayat president A. Krishnan filed a writ petition against the LSGD order in Kerala High Court. The judgment on this petition was come on 16th December 2003. Justice K. Balakrishnan Nair directed Hindustan Coca-Cola Beverages Private Limited to find out alternative sources of water for its bottling plant at Plachimada in Palakkad in a month. He also held that ground water belongs to the people and the Government had no right to allow a private party to extract such a huge quantity of ground water which is "a property held by it in trust" (Petition number, WP (C) 34292/03).
4. It recommended the State Government should bring in necessary amendments to the groundwater laws making it mandatory for those using water for commercial purposes to recharge groundwater to the maximum extent possible.
5. Though this order was upheld by the KHC the company continued its production. Later, the division bench of High Court approved the decision of Kerala Government to close the factory till monsoon. Then the factory closed on 9th March 2004. Meanwhile on 21st February government declared Palakkad as drought affected area and ordered closure of the factory.
6. On 11th March the panchayat send notice to the company for renewing the license with three conditions in consideration of the job opportunities for the local people. But the company openly rejected the conditions saying that the panchayat does not have the power to impose such conditions. As such the panchayat cancelled the license of the company and company filed its appeal in LSGD. Like the earlier decision LSGD stayed the order of panchayat and panchayat filed its writ petition in High Court, The Hindu, March 12, 2004.
7. As per the Supreme Court Monitoring Committee Report KSPCB formed a local environmental protection committee in the next month.
8. The Court on 7th April directed the panchayat to consider the application of the company seeking renewal of license for the coming year or if such application was filed within two weeks. But on 26th of this month Perumatty Panchayat decided not to renew the license because of two reasons; (1) the company has not submitted the KSPCB clearance. (2) the company has not produced the documents as per the Factories License Act.
9. The division bench of SC did not cancel the KHC order on the

reason that the company was not allowed to reopen with the panchayat's decision. Soon the company filed its appeal in High Court against the panchayat order of 26th April and the same division bench judged again in favour of the company. Moreover the judgment asked the Panchayat to give license within ten days otherwise the company can function for two years without permission.

10. Report, Perumatty Grama Panchayat, 'Matters related to the issue and cancellation of license to Coca-Cola company, 2005. The conditions are, that the company should produce a fresh clearance certificate as required under the Hazardous Waste (Management and Handling) rule, 1989 before 1 August also, the company would not be permitted to bring water from outside or store it without obtaining the requisite license under the Kerala Panchayat Raj Act or Rules framed there under, the company should inform the panchayat about the withdrawal and use of the quantity of water fixed by the High Court, the High Court had allowed the company to draw five lakh litres a day, of which one lakh should be made available for distribution to the public, another condition is that the company shall submit a detailed plan regarding the social security schemes ordered to be implemented by the High Court and intimate the same to the panchayat within a period of one month from Monday any violation of these 13 conditions "will entail cancellation of license issued subject to the order of the Supreme Court, which had already been approached by the Panchayat", The Hindu, 7 June 2005.
11. KSPCB ordered stoppage of production at the Plachimada plant for failure to comply with pollution control norms and the directives of Supreme Court Monitory Committee to distribute water to the local population. The Board observed that the presence of cadmium in its sludge was 400 to 600 times above the permissible limit. It also did not carry out the directive, given by the Board and the Committee, to set up modern facilities for purifying the liquid effluents from the plant. The unit had been asked to set up treatment facilities that used reverse osmosis or similar process.
12. The ban was being imposed as the colas contained substances harmful to health of the people. The Government had received reports from the department in charge of enforcement of Food

and Adulteration Act on the colas. Several studies had shown that the cola products contained harmful substances. On the next day two writ petitions came up before Justice S. Siri Jagan, counsel for Hindustan Coca-Cola Beverages Private Limited and PepsiCo India Holdings Private Limited argued for a stay on the order.

13. The bench held that the State Government have no powers to pass orders prohibiting the manufacture and sale of Coca-Cola and Pepsi, as a reply to the writ petition filed by Coca-Cola and Pepsi against the ban order. Allowing writ petitions the court held that powers to prohibit the manufacture and sale of products under the provisions of the Prevention of Food Adulteration Act were vested with the Union Government. The Bench pointed out that if state legislatures and Parliament had concurrent powers on a matter, the executive power of the State Government was subject to the executive power of the Centre.
14. Besides the Authority headed by K. Jayakumar pointed out that the loss in Plachimada is not confined to groundwater problem. The sub-committee appointed by the authority found the destruction caused to environment, livestock, agriculture, etc. The sub-committee cleared that it is not powerful to find out the scope of losses in different fields. It is in this situation that the committee suggested the creation of another committee (bahuthala samithi) consists of the representatives from different departments.
15. The 14 member committee consists of other members like expert in Community Medicine C.R. Soman, Ecologist S. Faizi, the former Sessions Judge T.K. Raman, Chairman of the State Pollution Control Board, Director of Health Services, Director of Animal Husbandry and officials from the Central Ground Water Department, Kerala Agriculture University and Kerala Water Authority.
16. Breaking up the amount, the report said that up to ₹ 84.16 crore was being charged for causing agricultural damages, ₹ 62.10 crore for polluting water sources, ₹ 20 crore each for cost of water provided and wage-loss opportunity cost and ₹ 30 crore for causing various health problems. The panel has also recommended the formation of a tribunal which the people of Plachimada could approach seeking compensation for the damage. The tribunal can be formed through state legislation on

the lines of the Environmental Tribunal Act of 1995 or under Article 323 B of the Constitution. Tamil Nadu has already put in place an Act and constituted an authority for payment of compensation for environmental damage to people and places caused by industries. The Report says that the company has violated the Water (Prevention and Control of Pollution) Act, the Environment (Protection) Act, the Factories Act, Hazardous Waste (Management and Handling) Rules, the SC and ST (Prevention of Atrocities) Act, Indian Penal Code, Land Utilization Order, the Kerala Ground Water (Control and Regulation) Act and Indian Easement Act.

17. Principal Secretary, Industries Department T. Balakrishnan had said at a public forum that he regretted that the plant could not be saved from closure triggered by environmental issues. The Cabinet resolved to convey its displeasure over the matter to the official by saying that his stand did not represent that of the State Government. The Chief Minister of Kerala took an open stand against this bureaucrat and clarified that it was not the policy of the government to encourage indiscriminate exploitation of ground water. While referring to the issue on 27 June 2010, V.S Achuthanandan openly declared that the Coco-Cola Company betrayed both the state and people of Kerala. The Industries Department's stand is that there was no unusually high exploitation of groundwater in the Perumatty Panchayat. The area experienced water shortage mainly on account of a dry spell during 2001-02 and increased use of water by coconut growers in the locality which has a flourishing toddy tapping industry.
18. But the Industries Department informed that the Tribunal does not have the legal validity as Industrial Department opposed the findings of the committee. Instead The Department suggested the government to pay the compensation. Consequently T. Balakrishnan in his exhaustive note on the K. Jayakumar Committee report on the subject, contended that Coca-Cola had not over-exploited the groundwater resources in the area and that the ecological damage said to have been caused by the company was insignificant or of a scale that could be tackled through legal means.
19. English translation of a campaign pamphlet collected from the struggle site.
20. *Gramasabha* is the meeting of villagers of a revenue village.

The meeting is organized under the auspices of the grama panchayath. *Oorukoottam* is the gramasabha of tribal people in a village.

21. The Kerala State Pollution Control Board on 19 August 2005 ordered stoppage of production at the Plachimada unit of the Coca-Cola Company in Palakkad district for its failure to comply with pollution control norms.
22. *Public water sources include the beds and banks of river streams, irrigation and drainage channels, canals, lakes, back waters, etc. The Kerala Panchayati Raj Act, 1994, Department of Local Self-Government, Government of Kerala, Thiruvananthapuram.*
23. But it should be noted that the PRIs in Kerala are functioning within the political and bureaucratic constraints. For instance in Plachimada the power of grama panchayaths over industrial licensing was superseded by LSGD, KSPCB and other ministries.

References

Beckwith, Karen (1997), 'Movement in Context: Women and Miner's Campaigns in Britain', in Ricca Edmondson (ed.), *The Political Context of Collective Action: Power, Argumentation and Democracy,* Routledge, London and New York, p. 3.

Behar, Amitabh and Prakash, Assem (2004), 'India: Expanding and Contracting Democratic Space', in Muthiah Alagappa, *Civil Society and Political Change in Asia: Expanding and Contracting Democratic Space,* Stanford University Press, Stanford, pp. 197-199.

Carter, Neil (2007), The Politics of the Environment: The Ideas, Activism, Policy, *Cambridge University Press,* Cambridge, p. 99.

Engel, Stephen M. (2001), The Unfinished Revolution: Social Movement Theory and the Gay and Lesbian Movement, *The Press Syndicate of the University of Cambridge,* Cambridge, p. 183.

Fagin, Adam and Tickle, Andrew (2002), 'Environmental Movements, Nation States and Globalization', in Francis W. Carter and David Turnock (ed.), *Environmental Problems of East Central Europe,* Routledge, London and New York, p. 46.

Goodwin, Jeff and Jasper, James M. (2003), 'Caught in a Winding,

Snarling Vine: The Structural Bias of Political Process Theory', in Jeff Goodwin and James M. Jasper, *Rethinking Social Movements: Structure, Meaning, and Emotion*, Rowman and Littlefield, Lanham, pp. 3-6.

McAdam, Doug et al. (1996), 'Introduction: Opportunities, Mobilizing Structures and Framing Processes–Toward a Synthetic, Comparative Perspective on Social Movements', in Doug McAdam et al. (ed.), *Comparative Perspectives on Social Movements: Political Opportunities, Mobilizing Structures, and Cultural Framings,* Cambridge University Press, Cambridge, p. 2.

Nair K. N., Antoniyo Paul and Vineetha Menon (2008), *Water Insecurity, Institutions and Livelihood Dynamics. A Study in Plachimada India,* Centre for Development Studies, Danish Books, New Delhi.

Oommen, M. A. (ed.) (1999), *Rethinking Development: Kerala Development Experience*, Vol. 1, Concept Publishing Company, New Delhi.

Porta, Donatella Della (2006), *Social Movements, Political Violence, and the State: A Comparative Analysis of Italy and Germany,* Cambridge University Press, Cambridge, p. 7.

Rombouts, Heidy (2004), Victim Organizations and the Politics of Reparation: A Case-study on Rwanda, *Intersentia NV,* 2640 Mortsel (Antwerpen) Belgium, p. 501.

Sekhon, Joti (1999), 'Grassroots Social Action and Empowerment in India: The Case of Action India Women's Program', in Jill M. Bystydzienski and Joti Sekhon, *Democratization and Women's Grassroots Movements,* Indiana University Press, Bloomington, Indiana, pp. 26-27.

Shiva, Vandana (2006), *Earth Democracy: Justice, Sustainability, and Peace*, Zed Books, London, p. 170.

Tarrow, Sidney G. (1998), *Power in Movement: Social Movements and Contentious Politics*, Cambridge University Press, Cambridge.

Tharakan, Michael P. K. (2004), 'Historical Hurdles in the Course of the People's Campaign in Kerala, India', in John Harris et al (ed) *Politicizing Democracy: The New Local Politics of Democratization,* Palgrave Macmillan, New York.

Varkey, Shaji and Thomas, Sajan (2005), *Kerala Development Experience in a Technological Age*, in ISDA Journal, Vol. 15,

Number 4, October-December 2005, Thiruvananthapuram, pp. 273-281.

Websites

http://www.hindu.com/2005/08/21/stories/2005082102260500.htm, accessed on 12/12/08.
http://www.hindu.com/2010/06/28/stories/2010062858960400.htm, accessed on 28/06/10.

6

Conclusions and Major Findings

6.1 Conclusions

The comparison of water rights movements in Kerala and Chhattisgarh brought out many of the emerging trends in the politics of social movements in India. It is highly improper to view the grassroots based movements in Plachimada and Sheonath as mere protest movements or local uprisings. They are also not just organized responses to the interruption of status quo in water access by a private corporation. Although one can find huge differences in the modus operandi and outcome of water rights movements in both states, these two struggles herald the emergence of certain new trends in Indian politics. This work is an attempt to explore some of these trends in detail and rest of them in synoptic perspective.

It is true that grassroots based struggles of local people against the exploitation of natural resources has not been an isolated phenomenon. Beginning from the colonial times, endeavours of the Indian state to take control over the natural resources had met with protest from the local population. Because at that period a wide array of social practices was prevalent through out communities which aimed at protecting and ensuring the sustainable use of CPRs. Private ownership had not been the dominant mode of protecting CPRs within a given locality. But it should be noted that most of the community ownership systems existed in India were not all-inclusive in nature, because of the caste-based access regime prevailed in India over centuries.

The prevalence of caste system affected detrimentally the public access to CPRs in a multitude of ways. For instance, a greater number of the Indian population was denied access to public water sources due to their lower caste origin. There are lots of documented instances in which the higher caste population deny the right of lower caste people's access to village ponds, public wells, etc. Moreover, there were also documentations regarding the existence of segregation within the lower caste groups. The fundamental point is that notwithstanding the existence of socially determined modes of CPR ownership there were widespread occurrences of exclusion on the basis of caste, gender, etc.

The post-colonial Indian state had initiated steps to strike down the anti-egalitarian bias of the Indian social system. In addition to abolishing the practices of caste system, the modern Indian state had strived for ensuring state control over the CPRs. In a sense, the interventions of the post-colonial state have ensured the public access to CPRs that were essential to meet the livelihood. But it should be noted that the state denied public access to certain CPRs for meeting the global environmental standards. The community management systems had not been wiped out by the intervention of the state through legislations and other forms of surveillance tactics. The best example in this regard is the water scenario in India. Ever since the initial years of independence, the successive governments have enacted a wide array of legislations to regulate the control and use of public water sources in an egalitarian manner.

However, various types of community management systems still proved to be critical for the Indian population. The relevance of governmental legislations often arises in the wake of conflicts among people or different water management regimes. It is worthwhile to note here that the above mentioned hybrid forms hold relevance mostly in the rural context as the state water management systems veiled an over arching control in the urban areas. The role of water authorities at the state level is a pertinent case of this rural-urban difference.

While protests against the British state were largely subsumed by the national independence struggle, the post-independent phase witnessed the emergence of numerous protest movements. The post-Independent Nehru government embraced a developmental schema that gave primacy to the implementation of big projects such as dams, to facilitate agricultural production. Industrial plants also found prominence in the nation-building project. Mass displacement and deforestation was the detrimental impact of most of these projects and there were significant protests at the local level.

The fact that most anti-environmental programmes implemented by the post-Independent Indian state did not meet with immediate local opposition, was probably because of ignorance and lack of political consolidation. Again green revolution was characterized with the exorbitant use of artificial fertilizers and it had proved to be detrimental to the land and water resources. However, the rationale of increasing food production to combat the existent food shortage was more or less appreciated by the Indian people. The author is of the view that the oppositional movement witnessed in Plachimada and Sheonath was drastically different from the protest dynamics till 1990s.

However, it can be found that 1970s is the appropriate benchmark for analyzing the water right movement in Kerala and Chhattisgarh. The selection of this benchmark is not only because of the emergence of a wide spectrum of movements that can be clubbed under the category of environmental movements. It is during this period environmental issues emerged across the world as an important aspect which no national government can neglect while framing its development policies. In a sense, the Indian movements like Chipko and Narmada indebted heavily to the settling in of environmental consciousness across the globe. This is regardless of the fact that the Indian state took a pessimistic attitude towards the shooting up of environmental consciousness across the state. Even though there are considerable differences with regard to the nature of environmentalist groupings emerged in 1980s and 1990s, there is lot much in common between these groups.

The LPG (Liberalization, Privatization, Globalization) framework is appropriate for capturing the intricacies of the environmental movements in 1990s. Notwithstanding the fact that there are environmental movements limitedly interlinked with the effects of LPG, a greater part of the environment-based grassroots uprisings are resultant of the paradigm shift in India's political economy. Ever since the New Economic Policy of 1991, LPG has become the development mantra of national and state governments. One of the major policy shifts in this regard is related to the privatization of Common Property Resources (CPRs). To a large extent, the LPG has resulted in the reinvention of the erstwhile exclusionary management regime existed in India which was partially corrected through the state interventions.

However, there is a sharp difference between the exclusion prevalent under caste hierarchies and the emerging exclusionary regime during the LPG phase. Unlike the systems of caste-based exclusion, the emergent CPR management regime under LPG has in effect triggered class-based divisions. Even though one can find different patterns of private property ownership systems, the vesting of control and management of CPRs to private players forms the order of the day. The aforesaid different patterns of private property ownership emanates from the existence of hybrid varieties of state and community CPR management systems. By hybrid varieties, the author meant the new patterns of CPR management which is evolved out of the state intervention in the existent community management regime.

Contemporarily, the private ownership-based water management systems are penetrating extensively into the rural and urban areas. While the penetration in urban centres is largely through the privatization of water supply system, water privatization in rural areas have a different pattern. The limited water supply institutions of the state governments and local self-governments notwithstanding the water supply and distribution system in the Indian rural areas, was mostly organized in community lines. Henceforth, water privatization in rural context refers mostly to the official issuance of extraction rights of ground and surface water to private monopolies. The instances of water privatization in Plachimada and Chhattisgarh are good cases in point. The author would like to place the water right movements in India within the general context of environmental movements, but this work took a position that the contemporary understanding of Indian environmental movement contains serious lacunae with regard to exploring the case of water right movements.

6.2 Major Findings of the Study

The study succeeded in realizing most of its objectives. In order to realize these objectives the author has undertook both qualitative and quantitative analysis as per the situation demands. The work finds that globalization and water privatization have brought forth new theoretical issues with respect to Common Property Resources, social movements and human rights. The study also found that water privatization in developed as well as developing countries cause serious environmental hazards. In most of the countries water access was restricted due to higher water tariffs which violated the people's right to water. Notwithstanding the fact that developing an alternative theoretical schema did not come under the scope of this study, the author attempted to raise few significant theoretical issues brought about by the globalization process.

The study points to the need of conceptualizing the CPR problem against the backdrop of the emergent global and local transformations. The CPR problem–*Tragedy of Commons*-identified by Hardin has greater applicability during the period of liberalization, privatization and globalization. *Tragedy of Commons* becomes a common phenomenon in all resource management regimes in the globalization era. The ineffective regulatory mechanisms in all management regimes resulted into *Tragedy of Commons.* In some cases the regime change was deliberate and formal but in some other cases the original intention was not the regime change as suggested by Hardin.

The former is visible in the case of Plachimada where private enterprises using the CPRs like ground water are not for the management sake. It should be noted that the sanctioning of HCBPL to extract ground water in Plachimada is not based on the realization that privatization is more effective than the public water management system. The district grama panchayath gave green signal to the water bottling plant on the assumption that it would generate employment opportunities and thus would emerge as a major contributor to the region's development. In the case of Sheonath river privatization, the project was aimed at ensuring better management of water distribution to provide river water to the Borai industrial area. In effect water privatization in Sheonath river became a management solution though its sole purpose was to facilitate regional development.

Moreover, it is a well established fact that the Coca-Cola Company in Plachimada extracted groundwater in relentless manner, over and beyond the limits prescribed in the license agreement. The unscientific ground water exploitation has seriously affected the water table in Plachimada and adjoining regions. Moreover the hazardous waste deposited by the company has resulted in the pollution of soil and surface water in Plachimada. By no means, the extraction of groundwater and its aftermaths in Plachimada is regarded as a sustainable utilization of CPRs. Both the principles of intra-generational and inter-generational equity were compromised due to the functioning of HCBPL in Plachimada.

In the case of Chhattisgarh, the Radius Water Limited utilized water from Sheonath river in an unsustainable manner. There are even occurrences in which the company acted in sharp contradiction to the provisions in the river privatization agreement. The operation of privatization agreement had resulted in restricting the local people from accessing the river for their day-to-day needs. As already mentioned in the third and fourth chapter, local economic activities were also detrimentally affected by the advent of two companies in Plachimada and Sheonath.

The overexploitation under private regime in Plachimada and Sheonath points to the fact that *Tragedy of Commons* is in fact open to all property management regimes or systems. According to Hardin's theory *Tragedy of Commons* is a major attribute of the open access and collective property regime. As per his theoretical schema, *Tragedy of Commons* will be rectified when the management of CPRs gets handed over to private players or governmental authorities. But the empirical findings from Plachimada and Sheonath are in sharp contradiction to the outcomes as expected by Hardin in his path breaking theoretical intervention. What matters are the control and effective regulatory mechanisms for the functioning of private and public CPR management regimes. Henceforth, the study points out the fact that *Tragedy of Commons* is integral to all property management regimes in the absence of effective regulatory mechanisms. It is found that regime change is of limited use with regard to manage CPRs in a sustainable manner.

The study finds that the human right framework has become central in exploring the case of water right movements related to the management of Common Property Resources. The issue of universal access is turn to be indispensable for human flourishment as CPRs are undergoing substantial depletion. Consequently, the CPR issue is well qualified to consider as a human right question. Because universal access had been an important attribute in the ground water case of Plachimada. Even, as majority of the households in Kerala depended upon individual household wells, the villagers in Plachimada relied on common/public wells.

Henceforth the availability of sufficient ground water level and universal access to the same is critical for the sustenance of the Plachimada village itself. Given that the functioning of

HCBPL affected detrimentally on the availability and access to ground water, the Plachimada issue is well qualified to term as a human right question. In the case of surface water privatization in Sheonath, the issue is more complicated. Besides, the fulfilment of drinking and related water needs, the Durg people utilized the Sheonath river extensively for income-generative activities like fishing and agriculture. Following the operation of water privatization agreement, a greater part of the local population was deprived of their sources of livelihood income. Accordingly, human rights framework will be an apt one to explore the multi-dimensional consequences of the river water privatization in Chhattisgarh.

The study also points to the need of integrating the water rights question into the human right discourses. The existing human right discourses mostly cluster around topics such as state sponsored violence and the direct violence committed by the non-state actors. The exclusion of different social segments from the state-directed welfare schemes is yet another important area in the discussions of human rights. Issues pertaining to the deprivation of water rights are hardly debated within the human rights discourses.

The two cases of water privatization demonstrate that the denial of water rights can be perceived as a human right violation. One of the worth mentioning aspect of the development/social change discussions in Kerala is the high inculcation of human right dimension. Most of the emergent discourses on land alienation, tribal exclusion, domestic violence against women, etc. are collared with the human right dimension in a multitude of ways. Developments have gone to such an extent that only the inculcation of the human right frame work will qualify for an issue to get public attention. Contemporarily, the electronic media portray majority of the social justice issues as good cases of human right violations. A good example in this regard is the ongoing dalit struggle against land alienation in Chengara. However, issues pertaining to the right of general public over ground and surface water were limitedly interlinked with the human right discussions. The relatively scant attention that the Plachimada struggle received within the human right discourses is a clear illustration of the afore-mentioned trend.

The lop-sided nature of the human right discourses is also evident in the Chhattisgarh case. Despite being a newly formed state, lots of human right issues were reported from Chhattisgarh. The high incidence of under development and the increasing challenge posed by the naxal group turned Chhattisgarh a good case for looking at the human right question. The outcome of the recent formation of Salwa Judum by the Chhattisgarh government to compact the naxal threat occupies a major position within these human right discussions.

Another discussion which dominates the Chhattisgarh human right discourse is the recent arrest of Dr. Binayak Sen, who is an activist defending the human rights of tribal and other poor people. The point here is that even after the continuing violation of water rights by Radius Water Limited, there had not been any significant initiative on the part of civil society to bring the human right perspective. Unlike the Kerala case, the instance of water privatization in Chhattisgarh points to the serious disconnect between the existing discourses on water right and human right frameworks.

The study finds that there exist an inextricable link between land rights and water rights. At the practical level, there hasn't been any separation between land and water rights. Consequently, the land owner enjoys dominance over the underground water. Given the absence of an institutional mechanism to monitor and regulate ground water use, the land owners extract as much as they want. This has resulted in a situation in which the land lords are in the possession of multiple water sources. In addition to the private wells and ponds they enjoy control over small streams passing through their land.

On contrary, regardless of the grassroots struggles for

water, common people were denied of access to pure water in most of the times. Safe drinking water is also not assured for those who posses minimal land. Thus, the quantity of land is also important–when extent of land increases chances of getting water also increases. In this regard land right can be viewed as a basic condition for water right. Moreover, given the absence/inefficiency of a public water supply system, possession of land becomes the most important variable determines the access to water sources. This fact is evident in both Plachimada and Sheonath cases. This interlinkage between water and land rights in both the study areas mostly emanates from the nature of land holding pattern and the absence of a centralized water supply system. No wonder, in case of a scarcity situation, those with minimal or no land become the worst sufferers.

Another finding of the study is with respect to the issues of stratification within the water rights framework. Similar to most of its human right counter parts across the world, water rights are also highly stratified as per the divisions in society. Access and control over water resources are very much determined by factors of social stratification such as caste, class and gender. Even though water right struggles provide a common platform irrespective of the social stratifications, there are certain issues of stratification that needs to be addressed at the theoretical and policy level. In other words, the immediate and most serious problem of water scarcity can be tackled at a macro level without considering different sorts of social stratification. But stratification of water issues is important in solving the micro level issues emerging out of the underlying social divisions.

The most important factors of social stratification in Plachimada and Sheonath are caste, class and gender. In both cases lower caste and lower class people were to be the most affected sections of water privatization. When people began protest, Dalits are on the forefront of the struggle in both places. On many occasions these struggles were identified as

Dalit struggles. This identity showed by Plachimada and Sheonath struggle bear ample testimony to this fact. Gender is yet another stratifying factor. Given that women are the prime collectors and users of water at the household level, they are the most affected group of water privatization. In Plachimada, the tribal women have to go miles to collect water and the use of polluted water for long time in house hold activities caused many health hazards among them. The increased participation and leadership of women in Plachimada struggle is a clear indication of this fact. When water became scarce due to Sheonath river privatization women were forced to collect water from distant places.

Examining the nature of grassroots movements emerged against water privatization is a pivotal objective of this work. This was a theoretical cum empirical challenge because these grassroots movements do not get due mention in the mainstream social movement literature. It is true that this work did not offer any substantial breakthrough with respect to understanding the nature of these grassroots movements, but the comparative exploration of Plachimada and Chhattisgarh cases offered critical insights in understanding the movements sprung up against the privatization of CPRs.

The agitations received substantial support from domestic and external forces. The author is of the opinion that arriving at any conclusion on the efficacy of grassroots resistance movements against water privatization is a difficult enterprise as external actors hijack the local struggle and manipulate its course and outcome at different points of time. The work finds that the political processes and movement culture in Kerala has crucial bearing on the sustenance of Plachimada struggle as compared to the Sheonath case. Keeping this work objective in mind, the author took special care in comparing and analyzing the Plachimada and Sheonath cases within the broader socio-political processes of respective states.

The study finds that the water rights movement occupies a unique place among the environmental movements in India.

The dynamics of water rights struggles are more complicated than that of the post-1970 Indian environmental movements, because, movement for a basic livelihood resource is more intense and crucial in its nature and course of its development. Unlike most of the Indian environmental movements, the ideology and praxis of water right struggles are mostly indigenous that takes into account the regional and communal specific variations.

These campaigns based on conflict over natural resources are response to very concrete local problems than perceived distant problems like in western environmental campaigns. For instance the Plachimada struggle continues despite the closing down of company operations. But this continuing enthusiasm of Plachimada people in the struggle is largely shaped by the unparalleled movement culture in Kerala. But in the case of Sheonath river privatization, the absence of a movement culture comparable to that of Kerala adds a special significance. The struggle participants in Durg took a sort of utilitarian perspective towards the struggle. Regardless of the high struggle participation during the initial phase, the Sheonath movement witnessed a massive fall in the number of struggle participants following the reinstation of universal access to Sheonath river. Unlike an ideologically oriented environmental movement, the Durg people were just indulged in a struggle to reinstate their livelihood requirements.

The study gives clear indication that water right movements are resultant of the inappropriate exercise of state power. This is evident because most of the water right movements demand a major shift in the policy of the existing governments and political parties at the national and provincial levels. At another level, they can be viewed as a resistance against globalization which unfolds itself through directing the policy priorities of national and state governments in lieu with liberalization and privatization. The global inter-connectedness of water right movements through its associated organizations and its pro-left posture reiterates this fact.

These two features can be interpreted in such a manner that water right movements in association with environmental movements are gradually becoming a global pressure group. The globalization of water right struggles and its pressure group potential has been a positive factor in regard to the exposition of the water cause. The global pressure group politics has played a greater role in the integration of the two water right struggles in Plachimada and Sheonath towards the international level. Its efficacy as a pressure group also contributed to stagnation of the anti-people industrialization activities in both Plachimada and Sheonath.

Like other environmental movements in Asia Plachimada and Sheonath struggles show an apolitical nature and also run by citizen action groups of social activists. It is the institutional failure of politics which call for this apolitical struggle. The people lost their faith in conventional party politics and other democratic institutions. Thereby the struggles stuck as groups of party-independent civil society movements. This non-partisan nature of the struggles invited the involvement of environmental and human right activists world wide. They succeeded in their effort by influencing the decision making system with out the help of political parties, but with the combined effort of alienated global mass.

The water right movements are marginalized from the mainstream political parties in Kerala and Chhattisgarh. Even the opposition parties detached from the struggle in the initial stage. In the case of Plachimada, the depoliticized nature of the struggle helped to keep its objectives static after eight years unlike other diverted political struggles. The tribal people are not confined to any particular political party or organization as such it still remains untouched by party politics.

Judiciary can also play a greater role in determining the nature and course of environmental movements. Though judiciary has limitations it's less populist approach and limited vote bank concerns are important in environmental/human right issues. The legal battle between Coca-Cola and the local people/panchayat get boosted when the single bench of the Kerala High Court ruled on 16 December 2003 that the company would have to seek alternative sources of water for its bottling plant in Plachimada. The High Court maintained that ground water belongs to the people and that the government did not possess the right to allow a private party to extract it in such huge quantities, it being 'a property held by it in trust'. The legal battle between a corporate giant and local grama panchayath received wide national and international attention though court has turned its stance on many circumstances.

It is true that a comparable positive judicial interpretation is absent in the Chhattisgarh case, but the Chhattisgarh case is also a clear illustration of the fact that judiciary is a major stake holder which determine the nature and outcome of environmental movements in India. The wide currency of Public Interest Litigation (PIL) got in the legal circle facilitated this process in a wide gamut of ways. For instance Forum for Fact-finding Documentation and Advocacy, a civil society organization based in Raipur, challenged the Sheonath privatization agreement through a Public Interest Litigation.

6.3 Policy Suggestions

The transformation from state property regime to private property regime has ramifications in the policy point of view. The transfer of ownership from public to private players brings out critical changes in the access to Common Property Resources. Policy formulation during the phase of state-private regime transformation should regard the indigenous water management systems existing at a given locality. For instance, in the case of a heterogeneous society like India indigenous systems of CPR management does not get affected considerably because of the state-private regime change. This means that whatever may be the legal/governmental changes taking place at the peripheral level, alternate management systems are still working at the grassroots level.

Contemporarily, public-private partnership has emerged as a buzz-word in the development discourse. Likewise, there are greater prospects for public-public participation in the water sector. By public-public participation the author meant that the participation between state and general public at the grassroots level. Here government and the local community constitute the hyphenated concept of public-public participation. Considering the emerging grassroots activism generated by the functioning of self-help groups and local government institutions, public-public participation can resolve CPR management issues at the wider scale. It is an undisputable fact that the aforesaid grassroots institutions are producing substantial transformations in the day-to-day lives of the Indian population. The extensive penetration of these institutions make them good choices for implementing innovative strategies for managing CPRs such as water.

Ever since the constitutionalisation of Panchayati Raj system in 1993, there are lots of policy studies that looked at the impact of local self governments in the socio-economic development at the grassroots level. But there had not been any serious attempt to look into the possibilities opened up by Panchayati Raj institutions regarding the management of Common Property Resources. It should be noted that this lacunae exists regardless of the fact that the Plachimada struggle brought out the various dimensions of the intervention of local self-government in the management of CPRs.

The Plachimada issue points to the importance of amending the Kerala Panchayati Raj Act, 1994 in such a way that grama panchayats will get more power over natural resources in general, and water in particular. In the case of Kerala, institutions such as KILA (Kerala Institute of Local Administration) can conduct policy related studies linking CPR with human rights and decentralization processes. In the case of a state like Chhattisgarh or other north Indian states where the Panchayati Raj system implemented only in a limited degree, there should be policy related enquiries pertaining what can be done under the existing institutional frame work. Such explorations will amplify the potentialities of LSGIs in CPR management.

The term water privatization does not refer to a homogeneous process. The nature of privatization varies according to the sources which are selected for privatization. As the case studies in Plachimada and Sheonath illustrates, the nature of ground and surface water privatization is found to have diverse consequences. Similarly, the nature of privatization differs when it comes to the arena of extraction and distribution. Given that water privatization is a multi-faceted process there is an urgent need to set up an institutional mechanism to regulate the extraction in the water sector. This should not be a bureaucratic body, similar to the institutional bodies existing under the state governments. Apart from bureaucratic and scientific personnel, there should be members from all walks of life such as social activists, panchayath representatives, local civil society leaders and local party members. Moreover The Kerala Ground Water (Control and Regulation) Act 2002, which became effective since 16 December 2003, needs to be amended to provide power and effectiveness.

Given the determining role played by the Indian judiciary in regard to the water right struggles there is an urgent need to constitutionalise universal access to livelihood related CPRs. It is true that such an overarching constitutional amendment cannot be made in a single stroke, as it requires comprehensive discussion among the scholarly and political circles. To begin with, the author suggests that the national government can initiate steps to amend the Constitution for making *Right to Water* a fundamental right. The incorporation of right to water within part III of the Constitution will enable affected individuals and small-scale protest groups to seek constitutional remedies through speedy and cost-effective means such as Public Interest Litigation. Moreover the elevation of water right as a fundamental right may increase the responsibility of government which may develop the water infrastructure facilities even in drought prone areas.

6.4 Final Estimate

This work is based on a comparative exploration of two water right struggles in India—Plachimada and Sheonath. The author's attempt was to compare cases from Kerala and Chhattisgarh within the context of Liberalization, Privatization and Globalization (LPG). Such a comparative analysis is important in two distinct but interrelated ways. First, only through a comparison of select cases it is possible to arrive at any holistic conclusion about the grassroots level impact of LPG. Second, comparative investigations are proved to be pivotal in capturing the community and region wise variations that are critical in regard to LPG's micro level impact. The author is of the opinion that theoretical insights from Political Science is of great importance in understanding water based struggles as the question of rights, justice and equality are directly involved.

There is a near unanimity among the scholars that expansion of global capital has critical effects on the protection of human rights and management of Common Property Resources (CPRs). However, the globalization-human rights and globalization-CPRs discourses are compartmentalized to a great extent and there exist a serious scholastic lacuna regarding the interlinking theoretical and empirical questions. The fact that there has not been any worth mentioning study which looked into the human rights dimension of CPR privatization is a good illustration in this regard. One of the major attempts made in this work pertains to the invocation of social movement theory and *Political Opportunity Structure* (POS) framework.

This work took a position that the triggering of social movements to resist privatization and reinstate access to CPRs makes the human rights question a more relevant one. Even though one can find stark differences, water rights struggles in

Plachimada and Sheonath illustrate that human rights are not something emanate at legal parlours. The case of water rights shows that only those human rights which are capable of getting articulated in the civil society by victims themselves have sustenance and impact potential. It should be added that this articulation in civil society is depended on the extent to which the social movement make use of political opportunities existing in a society at a given point of time.

The water right struggles in Kerala and Chhattisgarh also shed light on the changing dimensions of social movements in India. Movements associated with environmental questions are not a new phenomenon, but movements that resist the privatization of CPRs are unique in many respects. The rights, justice and equality questions espoused by these resistance movements vary considerably from other socio-political movements in India. The findings of the work deal not only with conceptual issues but also on the need for emphasizing public policy formulation. The comparative exploration of Plachimada and Sheonath cases also bring about a wide array of issues that are critical from a public policy perspective.

Bibliography

Bibliography

Adve Nagraj (2004), 'Rising Struggles, Falling Water: Anti-Coca-Cola Agitation Picks up in Kaladera, Rajasthan', available at http//www.indiaresource.com, accessed on 8/7/2010.

Agarwal, Aradhana (2006), 'Special Economic Zones: Revisiting the Policy Debate' in *Economic and Political Weekly*, 4 November 2006, Mumbai.

Agreement for Borai Industrial Growth Centre Water Supply on BOOT (Build, Own, Operate, Transfer) Basis. (The contract of Sheonath river Privatization).

Ahmed, Sara (2008), 'Gender and Integrate Water Resource Management in South Asia: The Challenge of Community-managed Alternatives' in Lahiri-dutt, Kuntala and Wasson Robert J. (ed.), *Water First: Issues and Challenges for Nations and Communities in South Asia*, Sage Publications, New Delhi.

Avritzer, Leonardo (2002), Democracy and the Public Space in Latin America, *Princeton University Press,* New Jersey.

Ballabh, Vishwa (2009), *Governance of Water: Institutional Alternatives and Political Economy,* Sage Publications, New Delhi.

Bargh, Maria (2007), *Resistance: An Indigenous Response to Neo-liberalism*, Huia Publishers, Wellington.

Barlow, Maude and Clarke, Tony (2003), *Blue Gold; The Fight to Stop Corporate Theft of Water,* Left Word Books, New Delhi.

BBC (2003), *Report* published on 25/07/03 at 17:51:55GMT, BBC MMIII.

Beckwith, Karen (1997), 'Movement in Context: Women and Miner's Campaigns in Britain', in Ricca Edmondson (ed.), *The Political Context of Collective Action: Power, Argumentation and Democracy,* Routledge, London and New York.

Behar, Amitabh and Prakash, Assem (2004), 'India: Expanding and Contracting Democratic Space', in Muthiah Alagappa, *Civil Society and Political Change in Asia: Expanding and Contracting Democratic Space,* Stanford University Press, Stanford.

Berkes, Fikrett (ed.) (1989), *Common Property Resources; Ecology and Community-Based Sustainable Development,* Belhaven Press, London.

Bhattacharya, Dwaipayan et al. (2004), *Interrogating Social Capital: The Indian Experience,* Sage Publications, New Delhi.

Boyle, Alan E. and Anderson, Michael R. (1998), *Human Rights Approaches to Environmental Protection,* Oxford University Press, New York.

Bromley, Daniel W. (ed.) (1992), *Making the Commons at Work: Theory, Practice and Policy,* Institute for Contemporary Studies Press, San Francisco.

Bromley, Daniel W. (1999), 'The Commons, Common Property and Environmental Policy', in Bromley, Daniel W. (ed), *Sustaining Development: Environmental Resources in Developing Countries,* Edward Elgar, Cheltenham.

Brubaker, Elizabeth (2001), *The Promise of Privatization,* Prepared for The Walkerton Inquiry, Energy Probe Research Foundation, 225 Brunswick Avenue, Ontario.

Bruns, Bryan Randolph and Meizen-Dick, Ruth S. (ed.), (2000), *Negotiating Water Rights,* Vistaar Publications, New Delhi.

Bryant, Raymond L. & Bailey, Sinéad (1997), *Third World Political Ecology,* Routledge, London and New York.

Brysk, Alison (2002), *Globalization and Human Rights,* University of California Press, Berkeley.

Calabrese, Andrew and Burgelman, Jean-Claude (1999), *Communication, Citizenship and Social Policy: Rethinking the Limits of the Welfare State,* Rowman & Littlefield, Lanham.

Campbell, Tom et al (2003), *Protecting Human Rights: Instruments and Institutions*, Oxford University Press, New York.

Carens, Joseph H. (1993), *Democracy and Possessive Individualism: The Intellectual Legacy of C.B. Macpherson,* Suny Press, Albany.

Carter, Neil (2007), The Politics of the Environment: Ideas, Activism, Policy, *Cambridge University Press, Cambridge.*

Cavanagh, John and Mander, Jerry (2004), *Alternatives to Economic Globalization: A Better World is Possible,* Berrett-Koehler Publishers, San Francisco.

Centre for Water Resource Development and Management (CWRDM) (2005), Report, *Investigations on the Extraction of Ground Water by M/s Hindustan Coca-Cola Beverages Private Limited at Plachimada,* Calicut.

Cesano, Daniele and Gustafsson (2000), Jan-Erik 'Impact of Economic Globalization on Water Resources; A Source of Technical, Social and Environmental Challenges for the Next Decade', in *Water Policy 2 (2000)*, Division of Land and water Resources, Royal Institute of Technology, KTH, 100 44, Stockholm, Sweden.

Chhattisgarh Government Scraps Privatized Water Supply Deal, available at http://smgwp.com/news/10.pdf, accessed on 6/2/09.

Claude, Richard Pierre (2006), *Human rights in the World Community,* University of Pennsylvania Press, Pennsylvania.

Conca, Ken (2005), *Governing Water: Contentious Transnational Politics and Global Institution Building,* The MIT Press, Cambridge.

Crate, Susan Alexandra (2006), *Cows, Kin, and Globalization: An Ethnography of Sustainability,* Rowman Altamira, Lanham.

D'Cruz, Sharon and Raikar, Avinash V. (2006), 'Democratic Management of Common Property in Goa; From

'Gaonkarias' and 'Communidades' to Gram Sabhas', *Economic and Political Weekly*, 4 February 2006, Vol. XLI, No. 5, Mumbai.

Dalby, Simon (2003), 'Globalization, Geography and Environmental Security', in Kofman, Eleonore and Youngs, Gillian (ed.), *Globalization: Theory and Practice*, Continuum Publishers, London.

Das, Binayak and Pangare, Ganesh (2006), *In Chhattisgarh a River Becomes Private Property*, *Economic and Political Weekly*, 18 February 2006, Mumbai.

Degaonkar, Chaya and Gills, Dong-Sook S. (2002), 'The Economic Reform and Feminization of Labor in Agriculture: The Case of Rural Village Women in India', in Gills, Dong-Sook S., Piper, Nicola, *Women and Work in Globalizing Asia,* Routledge, London and New York.

Déjeant-Pons, Maguelonne and Pallemaerts, Marc (2002), *Human Rights and the Environment,* Council of Europe.

Dhar, Subroto (2006), *Tapping Local Resources to Increase Panchayat Incomes*, *Economic and Political Weekly,* 8 April 2006, Mumbai.

Dhillon, Amrit (2010), 'Coca-Cola Suspected of Sucking the Land Dry', available at, http//www.indiaresource.org, accessed on 10/7/10.

Dierks, Rosa Gomez (2001), Introduction to Globalization: Political and Economic Perspectives for the New Century, *Rowman & Littlefield, Lanham.*

Doyle, Timothy (2004), *Environmental Movements in Minority and Majority Worlds: A Global Perspective,* Rutgers University Press, New Brunswick.

Durg Comprehensive District Agriculture Plan, *District Vision-2020*, Submitted to District Planning Committee, Durg, Prepared by PRIA (an International Centre for Learning and Promotion of Participation and Democratic Governance).

Eder, Klaus (1993), *The New Politics of Class: Social Movements and Cultural Dynamics in Advanced Societies,*

Sage Publishers.

Ekins, Paul (2003), 'After Seattle: What Next for Trade and Environment?', in Berkhout, France et al. (ed.), *Negotiating Environmental Changes; New Perspective from Social Science*, Edward Elgar, Cheltenham, UK.

Elian, George (1979), *The Principle of Sovereignty over Natural Resource,* Martinus Nijhoff Publishers, Netherlands.

Engel, Stephen M. (2001), The Unfinished Revolution: Social Movement Theory and the Gay and Lesbian Movement, *The Press Syndicate of the University of Cambridge, Cambridge.*

Eva Wrammer (2004), *Fighting Coca-Colonization in Plachimada: Water, Soft Drinks and Tragedy of Commons in an Indian Village,* Human Ecology Division, MKU.

Evans, Tony (1998), *Human Rights Fifty Years on: A Reappraisal,* Manchester University Press, Manchester.

Fagin, Adam and Tickle, Andrew (2002), 'Environmental Movements, Nation States and Globalization', in Francis W. Carter and David Turnock (ed.), *Environmental Problems of East Central Europe,* Routledge, London & New York.

Faulty Water Privatisation Deal Haunts Chhattisgarh State, available at, http://www.asiawaterwire.net/node/270, accessed on 20/3/09.

Fernandez, Luis A. (2008), *Policing Dissent: Social Control and the Anti-globalization Movement,* Rutgers University Press, New Brunswick.

Field, John (2005), *Social Capital and Lifelong Learning,* The Policy Press, University of Bristol, Bristol.

Finger, Matthias and Allouche, Geremy (2002), *Water Privatization, Transnational Corporations and the Re-regulation of the Water Industry,* Spon Press, London and New York.

Foweraker, Joe (1995), *Theorizing Social Movements,* Pluto Press, London.

Gaile, Gary L. and Willmott, Cort J. (2006), *Geography in America at the Dawn of the 21st Century,* Oxford University Press, New York.

Gills, Dong-Sook S. (2007), 'The Political Economy of Globalization and Grassroots Movements', in McGrew, Anthony G. and Poku, Nana K., *Globalization, Development and Human Security*, Polity Press, Cambridge.

Gilpin, Robert and Gilpin, Jean M. (2003), *Global Political Economy: Understanding the International Economic Order,* Princeton University Press, Princeton, p. 288.

Giugni, Marco G. (2002), 'Explaining Cross-National Similarities among Social Movement', in Smith, Jackie and Johnston, Hank, *Globalization and Resistance: Transnational Dimensions of Social Movements,* Rowman & Littlefield, Lanham.

Goldstone, Jack A. (2003), 'Bridging Institutionalized and Non-institutionalized Politics', in Goldstone, Jack A., *States, Parties, and Social Movements,* Cambridge University Press, Cambridge.

Goodwin, Jeff and Jasper, James M. (2003), 'Caught in a Winding, Snarling Vine: The Structural Bias of Political Process Theory', in Jeff Goodwin and James M. Jasper, *Rethinking Social Movements: Structure, Meaning, and Emotion*, Rowman and Littlefield, Lanham.

Guidry, John A. et al. (2000), 'Globalizations and Social Movements', in Guidry, John A. et al, *Globalizations and Social Movements: Culture, Power, and the Transnational Public Sphere,* University of Michigan Press, Ann Arbor.

Hall, David and Lobina, Emanuele (2002), *Water Privatisation in Latin America*, Public Services International Research Unit, University of Greenwich, Park Row.

Hamong Santono (2008), *Water Privatization in Indonesia and the Chance of PuPs as Alternatives*, available at, http://www.tni.org/water-docs/adbsantono.pdf, accessed on 16/608.

Hanagan, Michael (1998), 'Social Movements: Incorporation, Disengagement, and Opportunities–A Long View', in Giugni, Marco et al, *From Contention to Democracy: Social Movements and their Potential for Change*, Rowman and Littlefield, Lanham.

Hancock, Jan (2003), *Environmental Human Rights: Power, Ethis, and Law*, Ashgate Publishing, Surrey.

Hanna, Susan S. et al. (ed.) (1996), *Rights to Nature; Ecological, Economic, Cultural and Political Principles of Institutions for the Environment*, Island Press, Washington D.C..

Harawira, Makere Stewart (2005), *The New Imperial Order: Indigenous Responses to Globalization,* Zed Books Limited, London.

Hardin, Garret (1968), *The Tragedy of Commons, Science,* American Association for the Advancement of Science Publishers, Washington, 162 (1968).

Harvey, David (2005), *The New Imperialism,* Oxford University Press, New York.

Held, David et al. (1999), *Global Transformations: Politics, Economics and Culture,* Stanford University Press, California.

Holland, Ann-Christin Sjolander (2005), *The Water Business, Corporations Versus People,* Zed Books, London and New York.

Holton, Robert J. (1992), *Economy and Society,* Routledge, London and New York.

Hopper, Paul (2007), *Understanding Cultural Globalization,* Polity Press, Cambridge.

Indian National Trust for Arts and Cultural Heritage (INTACH), (2004), Report, *The Adverse Environmental Impact of the Hindustan Coca-Cola Beverages Private Limited,* Thiruvananthapuram.

Ingram, Helen M. et al. (1995), 'Interest Groups and Environmental Policy', in Lester, James P., *Environmental Politics and Policy: Theories and Evidence,* Duke

University Press, Durham.

Integrated Rural Technology Centre (IRTC), (2002), *Report*, Calicut, pp. 1-3. MPN or Most Probable Number is a method for finding the presence of bacteria (such as Coliform) in water.

Ishay, Micheline (2004), *The History of Human Rights: From Ancient Times to the Globalization Era,* University of California Press, Berkley.

Iyer, Ramaswamy R. (2003), *Water, Perspectives, Issues and Concerns*, Sage, New Delhi.

Iyer, Ramaswamy R. (2007), *Towards Water Wisdom: Limits, Justice, Harmony*, Sage Publishers, New Delhi.

Jain, Sonu (2003), A *River Gone Private is Drying Up,* available at, http://www.indiaresource.org/news/2003/3583.html, accessed on 15/1/09.

Jameson, Fredric and Miyoshi, Masao (1998), *The Cultures of Globalization,* Duke University Press, Durham.

Janasatta Magazine, 9 January 2003 and 24 November 2000, Raipur.

Janhith Magazine (2003), AIYF Publication, Durg District Council.

Jayaraman, Nityanad (2005), 'Water Wars and Bottle Battles', available at indiaresource.org, accessed on 27/8/10.

Jensen, Nathan Michael (2006), *Nation-states and the Multinational Corporation: A Political Economy of Foreign Direct Investment,* Princeton University Press, Princeton, New Jersey.

Joekes, Susan et al. (1994), 'Gender, Environment and Population', in Ghai, Dharam, *Development and Environment: Sustaining People and Nature*, Blackwell publishers/UNRISD, Oxford.

Johnston, Hank and Noakes, John A. (2005), *Frames of Protest: Social Movements and the Framing Perspective*, Rowman & Littlefield, Lanham.

Johnston, Hank et al. (1994), 'Identities, Grievances and New

Social Movements', in Laraña, Enrique et al., *New Social Movements: From Ideology to Identity,* Temple University Press, Philadelphia.

Kamieniecki, Sheldon (1993), 'Emerging Forces in Global Environmental Politics', in Kamieniecki, Sheldon (ed.), *Environmental Politics in the International Arena: Movements, Parties, Organizations, and Policy,* SUNY Press, New York.

Kerala State Pollution Control Board (KSPCB), (2003), Report, *Presence of Heavy Metals in Sludge Generated in the Factory of M/s Hindustan Coca-Cola Beverages Private Limited.*

Kerala Water Policy 2007, Water Resource Department, Government of Kerala, Thiruvananthapuram.

Keraleeyam Magazine, January 2005, Kokkale, Thrissur.

KGWCRA (2002), *The Kerala Ground Water (Control and Regulation Act) 2002*, The Law Department, Government of Kerala, Secretariat, Thiruvananthapuram.

Kirkpatrick, Colin and Lee, Norman (1997), 'Market Liberalization and Environmental Assessment', in Wilson, Frank A., *Towards Sustainable Project Development*, Edward Eglar Publishers, Cheltenham, UK, Lyme, US.

Kothari, Miloon 2004), 'Making Water a Human Right', *Combat Law*, June-July 2004, Mumbai.

Krapivin, Vladimir F. and Varotsos, Costas (2007), *Globalization and Sustainable Development: Environmental Agendas,* Praxis Publishing Limited, Chichester.

Krishnakumarmar, Asha (2003), *People's Battle for a River,* Frontline, Volume 20, Issue 22, October 25-November 07, Chennai.

Lakshmi, Rama (2003), India: Water Privatization Draws Indians' Ire: Villagers Resist New Approach to Sacred Resource, *available at,* *http://www.waterconserve.org/shared/reader/welcome.aspx?linkid=28074, accessed on 16/4/09.*

Landman, Todd (2006), *Studying Human Rights,* Routledge, London and New York.

Lee, Yok-shiu F. and So, Alvin Y. (ed.) (1999), *Asia's Environmental Movements: Comparative Perspectives,* M.E. Sharpe, Armonk NY.

Lynch, Katherine L. (2003), *The Forces of Economic Globalization: Challenges to the Regime of International Commercial Arbitration,* Kluwer Law International, Netherlands.

Manthan Adhyayan Kendra (2002), *Document on Water Privatization in India*, Badwani (M.P.).

Marks, Stephen P. (2004), *The Right to Development: A Primer,* Sage, New Delhi.

Marothia, Dinesh K. (2005), *Institutional Reforms in Canal Irrigation System: Lessons from Chhattisgarh, Economic and Political Weekly,* 9 June 2005, Mumbai.

McAdam, Doug et al. (1996), 'Introduction: Opportunities, Mobilizing Structures and Framing Processes–Toward a Synthetic, Comparative Perspective on Social Movements', in McAdam, Doug, et al. (ed.), *Comparative Perspectives on Social Movements: Political Opportunities, Mobilizing Structures, and Cultural Framings,* Cambridge University Press, Cambridge.

McDonald, David Alexander and Ruiters, Greg (2005), *The Age of Commodity: Water Privatization in Southern Africa,* Earthscan, London.

McGoodwin, James R. (1995), *Crisis in the World's Fisheries: People, Problems, and Policies,* Stanford University Press, California.

Mendieta, Eduardo (2007), *Global Fragments: Globalizations, Latinamericanisms, and Critical Theory,* SUNY Press, Albany.

Moore, Deborah and Sklar, Leonard (1998), 'Reforming the World Bank's Lending for Water: The Process and Outcome of Developing a Water Resource Management Policy' in Jonathan A. Fox and L. David Brown (ed.), *The*

Struggle for Accountability, The World Bank, NGOs, and Grassroots Movements, The MIT Press, Cambridge.

Mumtaz, Rifat (2006), *Rivers for Sale: Common Property in Peril,* http://en.wikipedia.org/, accessed on 5/7/08.

Nadkarni, M. V. and Monga, G. S. (2001), *Environment and Development,* Deep and Deep Publishers, New Delhi.

Nair K. N., Antoniyo Paul and Vineetha Menon (2008), *Water Insecurity, Institutions and Livelihood Dynamics. A Study in Plachimada India,* Centre for Development Studies, Danish Books, New Delhi.

Narmada Bachao Andolan vs. Union of India, AIR (2000) 10 SCC 664.

Nayar, Baldev Raj (2007), 'Globalization, Geopolitics and India', in Nayar, Baldev Raj (ed.), *Globalization and Politics in India*, Oxford University Press, New Delhi.

OECD Environmental Outlook (2001), Organization for Economic Co-operation and Development, OECD Publishing, Paris.

Oommen, M. A. (ed.) (1999), *Rethinking Development: Kerala Development Experience*, Vol. 1, Concept Publishing Company, New Delhi.

Oommen, T. K. (2004), *Nation, Civil Society and Social Movements: Essays in Political Sociology,* Sage Publishers, New Delhi.

Orend, Brian (2002), *Human Rights: Concept and Context,* Broadview Press, Peterborough.

Ostrum, Elinor (1999), *Governing the Commons: The Evolution of Institutions of Collective Action,* Cambridge University Press, Cambridge.

Page, Edward A. (2006), *Climate Change, Justice and Future Generations*, Edward Elgar Publishing, Cheltenham, p. 59.

Panchayat Report, *Matters related to the issue and cancellation of license to Coca-Coal Company*, (License Number, A3-463/99 dated 27/1/2000).

Pascual, Unai et al. (2009), *Water, Agriculture and Sustainable Well-being,* Oxford University Press, New York.

Paul, Antonio (2005), *Water Insecurity and Livelihood Strategies, A Study of the Livelihood Dynamics in Plachimada Village of Palakkad District, Kerala, India*, Centre for Development Studies, Thiruvananthapuram.

Pearce, David (1995), *Blueprint–4, Capturing Global Environmental Value*, Earthscan Publishers, London.

Perkins, Stephen J. and Shortland, Susan M. (2006), *Strategic International Human Resource Management: Choices and Consequences in Multinational People Management,* Kogan Page Publishers, London.

Peters, Rebecca Todd (2006), *In Search of the Good Life: The Ethics of Globalization,* Continuum International Publishing Group, New York.

Petrella, Ricardo (2001), *The Water Manifesto: Arguments for a World Water Contract*, Zed Books, London and New York.

Porta, Donatella Della and Diani, Mario (2006), *Social Movements: An Introduction,* Blackwell Publishing, Malden, USA.

Powell, Frederick W. (2007), *The Politics of Civil Society: Neoliberalism or Social Left?* The Policy Press, University of Bristol, Bristol.

Purdue, Derrick (2007), 'Dimensions of Civil Society', in Purdue, Derrick (ed.), *Civil Societies and Social Movements: Potentials and Problems,* Routledge, London and New York.

Putul, Alok Prakash (2009), *When Rivers are Sold for a Song*, available at, http://www.commodityonline.com/crops-weather, accessed on 2/2/09.

Putul, Alok Prakash (2007), *Sheonath Deal Slammed, No Action Yet*, Down to Earth, 31 May 2007, New Delhi.

Putul, Alok Prakash (2009), *Privatization unlimited: Rivers for Sale in Chhattisgarh,* available at, http://infochangeindia.org, accessed on 13/12/09.

Ray, Binayak (2008), *Water: The Looming Crisis in India,* Lexington Books (A division of Rowman and Littlefield),

Lanham.

Rigg, Jonathan (2007), *An Everyday Geography of the Global South*, Routledge, London and New York.

Rombouts, Heidy (2004), Victim Organizations and the Politics of Reparation: A Case-study on Rwanda, *Intersentia NV*, 2640 Mortsel (Antwerpen) Belgium.

Rootes, Christopher (1999), 'Environmental Movements: From the Local to the Global', in Rootes, Christopher, *Environmental Movements: Local, National, and Global*, Routledge, London and New York.

Roush, G. Jon (1991), 'Introduction', in Donald Snow, *Voices from the Environmental Movement: Perspectives for a New Era*, Island Press, Washington D.C.

Rupert, Mark (2000), *Ideologies of Globalization: Contending Visions of a New World Order*, Routledge, London and New York.

Sachs, Wolfgang (1999), *Planet Dialectics: Explorations in Environment and Development*, Zed Books, London.

Sajan, Thomas (2008), *The Clash of Domestic Economies: Micro credit and Household Economic Processes in the Migrant Settlements of Kerala, India*, M.Phil. Thesis, Department of Social Anthropology, University of Bergen, Bergen.

Salman and Lank Ford (2004), *The Human Right to Water*, World Bank, Washington D. C.

Sampath, Anitha et al. (2004), *Water Privatization and Implications in India*, Association for India's Development, University Station A 6220, SOC#108.Austin, TX, USA, available at, http//www.studentsorgs.utexas.edu, accessed on 14/5/07.

Sarvodaya Press Service Bulletin, 2 April 2003 and 18 May 2003, Raipur.

Schellnhuber, Hans-Joachim (2001), *World in Transition: Conservation and Sustainable use of the Biosphere*, Earthscan Publishers, London.

Sekhon, Joti (1999), 'Grassroots Social Action and

Empowerment in India: The Case of Action India Women's Program', in Jill M. Bystydzienski and Joti Sekhon, *Democratization and Women's Grassroots Movements,* Indiana University Press, Bloomington, Indiana.

Sethi, Aman (2006), *Private Water, Public Misery*, Frontline, 21 April 2006, Chennai.

Sharma, Sudhirendar (2003), 'Water Markets Exclude the Poor', in Smithu Kothari et al. (ed.), *The Value of Nature*, Rainbow, Noida.

Shellenberger, Michael and Nordhaus, Ted (2007), *Break Through: From the Death of Environmentalism to the Politics of Possibility,* Houghton Mifflin Company, New York.

Shiva, Vandana (1991), *Ecology and the Politics of Survival: Conflicts over Natural Resources in India,* Sage Publications, New Delhi.

Shiva, Vandana (1999), 'Ecological Balance in the Era of Globalization', in Nicholas Low, *Global Ethics and Environment,* Routledge, London and New York.

Shiva, Vandana (2006), *Earth Democracy: Justice, Sustainability, and Peace*, Zed Books, London.

Shiva, Vandana, (2002), *Water Wars; Privatization, Pollution and Profit,* India Research Press, New Delhi.

Singh, A. K. (2004), *Privatization of Rivers in India*, Vikas Adhayn Kendra, Mumbai.

Singh, A. K. (2004), *Privatization of Sheonath River*, Combat Law, June-July, Mumbai.

Singh, Arun Kumar (2004), *Privatization of Rivers in India,* Vikas Adhyan Kendra, Mumbai.

Singh, Bishwa Nath (2004), 'Economic Reforms and Environment: The Indian Evidence', in Singh, Jinithesh Kumar and Das, Debedra Kumar (ed), *Environmental Economics and Development*, Deep and Deep Publications, New Delhi.

Singh, Katar (1994), *Managing Common Pool Resources:*

Principles and Case Studies, Oxford University Press, New Delhi.

Singh, Raajen (2004), 'Water for All, Is Privatization the Only Solution'? *Combat Law*, June-July 2004, Mumbai.

Smith, Robert Leo (1972), *The Ecology of Man: An Ecosystem Approach,* Harper and Row Publishers, University of Wisconsin-Madison.

Srivastava, Amit (2010), 'Community Files Police Report Accusing Coca-Cola of Water Theft and Pollution', available at, http://www.indiaresource.org, accessed on 8/710.

Synott, John P. (2004), *Global and International Studies: Transdisciplinary Perspectives,* Thomson Learning, Nelson.

Szymanski, Ann-Marie E. (2003), *Pathways to Prohibition: Radicals, Moderates and Social Movement Outcomes,* Duke University Press, Durham.

Tarrow, Sidney (2002), 'From Lumping to Splitting: Specifying Globalization and Resistance', in Smith, Jackie G. and Hank Johnston (ed.), *Globalization and Resistance: Transnational Dimensions of Social Movements,* Rowman & Littlefield, Lanham.

Tarrow, Sidney G. (1998), *Power in Movement: Social Movements and Contentious Politics,* Cambridge University Press, Cambridge.

Tenth Five-Year Plan (2002-07) *Development Report, Perumatty Panchayat*, Palakkad.

Tharakan, Michael P.K. (2004), 'Historical Hurdles in the Course of the People's Campaign in Kerala, India', in John Harris et al (ed) *Politicizing Democracy: The new Local Politics of Democratization,* Palgrave Macmillan, New York.

Tyagi, Partosh C. (2009), 'Water Pollution and Contamination', Iyer, Ramaswamy R. (ed.), *Water and Laws in India,* Sage Publishers.

Upadhyay, Videh (2009), 'The Ownership of Water in Indian Laws', in Iyer, Ramaswamy R. (ed.), *Water and Laws in*

India, Sage Publishers.

V. Venkatesan (2000), *Chhattisgarh: Quiet Arrival*, Frontline, Volume 17, Issue 17, August 19-September 1, 2000, Chennai.

Vaidyanathan A. and Jairaj, Bharath (2009), *Legal aspects of Water, Resource Management in* Iyer, Ramaswamy R. (ed), *Water and Laws in India*, Sage Publishers.

VAK (2004): Report, Coca-Cola: Quit Plachimada: Quit India: The Story of Anti-Coca-Cola Struggle at Plachimada in Kerala, Vikas Adhyan Kendra, Mumbai.

Varkey, Shaji and Thomas, Sajan (2005), *Kerala Development Experience in a Technological Age*, in *ISDA Journal*, Vol. 15, Number 4, October-December 2005, Thiruvananthapuram.

Wagle, Subodh (2002), 'The Long March for Livelihoods: Struggle Against the Narmada Dam in India' in Byrne, John et al., *Environmental Justice: Discourses in International Political Economy*, Transaction Publishers, Edison, NJ.

Walters, Gregory J. (2002), *Human Rights in an Information Age: A Philosophical Analysis,* University of Toronto Press, Toronto.

Wilson, Richard A. (1997), *Human Rights, Culture and Context: Anthropological Perspectives,* Pluto Press, London.

Youngs, Gillian (2003), International Relations as we Enter the Twenty-first Century, in Kofman, Eleonore and Youngs, Gillian (ed), *Globalization: Theory and Practice,* Continuum, London.

Yuvajanavedi (2002), Report, The Environmental and Social Problems Raised by the Coca-Cola and Pepsi Companies in Palakkad District.

Zarsky, Lyuba (2002), 'Introduction: Conflicts, Ethics and Globalization', in Zarsky, Lyuba (ed.), *Human Rights and the Environment: Conflicts and Norms in a Globalizing World,* Earthscan Publishers, London.

Index

Index